European Perspectives on Transformation Theory

Ted Fleming • Alexis Kokkos
Fergal Finnegan
Editors

European Perspectives on Transformation Theory

palgrave
macmillan

Editors
Ted Fleming
Teachers College
Columbia University
New York, NY, USA

Alexis Kokkos
Hellenic Open University
Athens, Greece

Fergal Finnegan
The Department of Adult and Community
Education
Maynooth University
Maynooth, Kildare, Ireland

ISBN 978-3-030-19158-0   ISBN 978-3-030-19159-7   (eBook)
https://doi.org/10.1007/978-3-030-19159-7

© The Editor(s) (if applicable) and The Author(s) 2019
This work is subject to copyright. All rights are solely and exclusively licensed by the Publisher, whether the whole or part of the material is concerned, specifically the rights of translation, reprinting, reuse of illustrations, recitation, broadcasting, reproduction on microfilms or in any other physical way, and transmission or information storage and retrieval, electronic adaptation, computer software, or by similar or dissimilar methodology now known or hereafter developed.
The use of general descriptive names, registered names, trademarks, service marks, etc. in this publication does not imply, even in the absence of a specific statement, that such names are exempt from the relevant protective laws and regulations and therefore free for general use.
The publisher, the authors and the editors are safe to assume that the advice and information in this book are believed to be true and accurate at the date of publication. Neither the publisher nor the authors or the editors give a warranty, express or implied, with respect to the material contained herein or for any errors or omissions that may have been made. The publisher remains neutral with regard to jurisdictional claims in published maps and institutional affiliations.

This Palgrave Macmillan imprint is published by the registered company Springer Nature Switzerland AG
The registered company address is: Gewerbestrasse 11, 6330 Cham, Switzerland

Acknowledgements

The editors are grateful to so many people who have in many and quiet ways supported this project. The authors have generously written and without you there would be no project. We also look forward to future collaborations in ESREA and its networks.

The staff and editors at Palgrave have been patient and gently pushing the project forward always.

But in many ways the co-authors here are part of much larger communities of research and scholarship in and across Europe and America, and we acknowledge the enthusiasm, work and interests we share with all of them.

Contents

1 Introduction   1
Alexis Kokkos, Ted Fleming, and Fergal Finnegan

2 Context and Development of Transformation Theory in the European Field of Adult Education   7
Ted Fleming, Alexis Kokkos, and Fergal Finnegan

Part I   Reviewing and Expanding the Theory   27

3 Connected Knowing in Belenky and Honneth: Implications for Transformative Learning Theory   29
Ted Fleming

4 'Freedom Is a Very Fine Thing': Individual and Collective Forms of Emancipation in Transformative Learning   43
Fergal Finnegan

viii   Contents

5   Coming to Grips with Edge-Emotions: The Gateway to
Critical Reflection and Transformative Learning   59
Kaisu Mälkki

6   Theory Development Between Tradition and Innovation:
Exploring Systems Thinking Within and Beyond
Transformative Learning Theory   75
Saskia Eschenbacher

7   Time and the Rhythms of Transformative Learning   93
Michel Alhadeff-Jones

8   Communicative Practices in Work and Training Contexts:
Exercising Transformative Authority?   111
Jerome Eneau and Eric Bertrand

Part II   Connecting Theory with Educational Practice   127

9   Introducing the Method *Transformation Theory in
Educational Practice*   129
Alexis Kokkos

10   Disorienting Dilemmas and Irritations in Professional
Development: A Longitudinal Study of Swiss Teacher-
Students   145
Anna Laros and Julia Košinár

11   New Scenario for Transformation: How to Support
Critical Reflection on Assumptions Through the Theatre
of the Oppressed   161
Alessandra Romano

Contents   ix

12 Promoting Transformative Learning Through English as a
    lingua franca: An Empirical Study   177
    Nicos C. Sifakis and Stefania Kordia

13 The Theory and Practice of Evaluating Transformative
    Learning Processes   193
    Claudio Melacarne

14 Sustainability, Reflection, Transformation and Taking
    Back Our World   207
    Ian Jasper

Part III   Transformative Learning in Organizations   223

15 "Not Only a Man With a Drip": Cancer as a Shared Social
    Practice   225
    Loretta Fabbri and Elisabetta Di Benedetto

16 Reframing Professional Challenges Through Action
    Learning Conversations in Medical Organizations   241
    Maura Striano

17 Conclusions, Comparisons and Directions for Future
    Study   255
    Alexis Kokkos, Fergal Finnegan, and Ted Fleming

Index   261

Notes on Contributors

Michel Alhadeff-Jones is Adjunct Associate Professor in Adult Learning and Leadership at Teachers College, Columbia University, and the founder of the Sunkhronos Institute in Geneva, Switzerland.

Eric Bertrand is a research teacher in adult education at the University of Rennes (France) and a business consultant. His research and practices as a teacher and consultant focus on the plural dimensions of transformative learning (institution, organization, group, subject) in the context of work.

Elisabetta Di Benedetto graduated in Modern Languages and Literature, and is an employee of the University of Siena at the Department of Education, Human Sciences and Intercultural Communication. She is interested in research and development of a community of practice of oncologic patients.

Jerome Eneau PhD in Andragogy, is a full professor at the University of Rennes (France). His research focuses on the social dimensions of self-directed learning and adult learner autonomy.

xii   Notes on Contributors

Saskia Eschenbacher is a systemic therapist (IGST) and is Professor of Adult Education and Counselling at the Akkon University Berlin with a research focus on Transformative Learning Theory.

Loretta Fabbri is Director of the Department of Education, Humanities and Intercultural Communication at the University of Siena. She is Full Professor of Adult Education at the University of Siena and the co-director of the Italian Transformative Learning Network.

Fergal Finnegan is a lecturer at the Department of Adult and Community Education, Maynooth University (Ireland). He is one of the editors of the *Journal of Transformative Education* and is interested in critical realism, critical pedagogy, equality and democracy.

Ted Fleming is Adjunct Associate Professor of Adult Education at Teachers College, Columbia University. His interests are in critical theory and attachment theory. He is also external adviser to the UNESCO funded Learning City project in Larissa, Greece.

Ian Jasper is a senior lecturer at Canterbury Christ Church University. He directs a BA Education and Professional Training programme for mature students drawn mainly from vocational backgrounds.

Alexis Kokkos is Professor of Adult Education at Hellenic Open University, Chairman of the Hellenic Adult Education Association and co-convener of ESREA's European Network *Interrogating Transformative Processes in Learning and Education*. His interests are in critical reflection and aesthetic experience.

Stefania Kordia is a PhD candidate at the School of Humanities of the Hellenic Open University. Her research interests include teacher education, English as a lingua franca and transformative learning.

Julia Košinár is Professor of Professional Development and Practical School Training at University of Applied Sciences and Arts Northwestern Switzerland. Research focus: reconstruction of learning processes of (future) teachers from a longitudinal perspective using for example transformative learning theory.

Anna Laros is a research associate at the University of Applied Sciences and Arts, Northwestern Switzerland. Her research focuses are transformative learning and entrepreneurship; women studies; intercultural learning; transformative learning and professionalization and professional development.

Kaisu Mälkki is a senior lecturer and associate professor, Tampere University, Finland, and editor for Journal of Transformative Education. Interests: critical reflection, embodied basis of cognitive functions, building conceptual, practical and pedagogical tools for individual and community transformative learning.

Claudio Melacarne is Associate Professor of Social Pedagogy at University of Siena. He is interested in studying professional and organizational development processes in using transformative and collaborative research methodologies.

Alessandra Romano is Assistant Professor at University of Siena. Her interest of research is the study of experience-based methods for promoting transformative learning and professional community development.

Nicos C. Sifakis is Associate Professor in Applied Linguistics and TESOL at the Hellenic Open University. He has published extensively on teacher education and English as a lingua franca.

Maura Striano is Full Professor of Education at the University of Naples Federico II. Her main research focus is on educational reflective practices according to a Deweyan framework.

List of Figures

Chart 11.1	Comparative analysis of the three groups showing frequency of categories in percentages	167
Fig. 11.1	The model of critical transformative learning. How the process of change of meaning perspectives unfolds across the Theatre of the Oppressed steps	172
Chart 13.1	Characteristics of the tools for assessing transformations	201

1

Introduction

Alexis Kokkos, Ted Fleming, and Fergal Finnegan

The Aim of the Collection

Jack Mezirow's Transformation Theory, which he addressed to the community of adult educators beginning in 1978, had a catalytic role in creating the "transformative learning movement". Mezirow made an enormous contribution to adult education and learning theory and mobilized a highly active and diverse community of scholars concerned with transformative education and learning. Part of this contribution is that Mezirow's work was broad and rich enough to create common

A. Kokkos (✉)
Hellenic Open University, Athens, Greece

T. Fleming
Teachers College, Columbia University, New York, NY, USA
e-mail: ted.fleming@mu.ie

F. Finnegan
The Department of Adult and Community Education, Maynooth University, Maynooth, Ireland
e-mail: fergal.finnegan@mu.ie

© The Author(s) 2019
T. Fleming et al. (eds.), *European Perspectives on Transformation Theory*,
https://doi.org/10.1007/978-3-030-19159-7_1

2   A. Kokkos et al.

ground and lead to the reciprocal enrichment among varied views of transformative learning. Since then a large number of scholars developed parallel but related perspectives, that sometimes have similarities or affinities with Mezirow's view and sometimes in ways that are quite divergent from Mezirow's original conception. Through this process there has been a remarkable increase in research and publications concerning the entire field. However, this sometimes means the distinctions between Transformation Theory and other theoretical understandings of transformative learning[1] have been played down. Without careful theoretical scrutiny transformative learning as a body of evolving and somewhat conflicting ideas will wither and not achieve its potential to inform learning, education, research and policy formulation.

The objective of the book is to explore a "living theory" by paying careful and critical attention to how Mezirow's ideas have been received and interpreted in Europe. It offers practitioners, scholars and students a detailed overview of the development of the theory of transformative learning by European researchers and how it has built upon, critiqued, and enriched Mezirow's theory of transformative learning.

For a long period the development of the theory of transformative learning in Europe has lagged behind North American scholarship and research but as these ideas now move toward center stage in Europe this is an opportune moment to ask important questions. This collection asks primarily whether there is a European perspective on Mezirow's view of transformative learning that reflects this continent's traditions and contexts; what is the nature of that European perspective; and how it may be similar or different to that of our American colleagues.

To this end we have gathered a number of scholars from Finland, France, Germany, Greece, Ireland, Italy, Switzerland and the UK in a research project. The varied understandings in the book's texts are included under the heading of transformative learning that refers to this widening and sometimes diverging field with a special interest in exploring how they correlate with Mezirow's view. The book illustrates the unique European emphases on transformative learning theory; outlines new theoretical perspectives crucial for the future evolution of transformative learning's theoretical framework; explores theoretical perspectives in relation to practice across of range of settings (higher education, work-

1 Introduction 3

places, teacher training and health care training and development) and raises new questions and opportunities for future development of transformative learning.

The various ways transformative learning theory has been approached in Europe reflects the development of adult learning theory and indeed the field of adult education in Europe where national agendas, languages, educational histories and cultures play important roles. Individual approaches, whether the Workers' Education Association in the UK or Grundtvig inspired folk schools (*Volkshochschule*) in Austria, Hungary, Netherlands, Germany, Switzerland and the Scandinavian countries, as well as the movements of popular education in Greece and Italy, all contribute to this diversity and richness.

Since the establishment of the European Society for Research on the Education of Adults (ESREA) in 1992, there has been a more explicit, if not unified, European perspective on research (Nicoll, Biesta, & Morgan-Klein, 2014). Its *European Journal for Research on the Education and Learning of Adults*, established in 2010, plays a key role in supporting a European community of practice in the scholarship of adult learning. The ESREA network "Interrogating Transformative Processes in Learning and Education: An International Dialogue" reflects the growing interest in the theory and with conferences, seminars and collaborations supports a strong pan-European movement of transformative learning scholars, researchers and students.

This collection is not intended to mark any trans-Atlantic fault lines or divergences in approaches as cooperations and collaborations are rich and mutually beneficial. It is worth noting that the editors and the contributors actively participate in events and publications in North America and Europe. But we have also become aware of interesting and generative differences: We can trace orientations and certain lines of inquiry that point toward distinct theoretical priorities over the years. It is clear, for instance, that the soul work of Tisdell and of Dirkx along with the environmental orientation of O'Sullivan in Toronto give the American version of the theory a trajectory that Europeans do not have. The important influence of John Dewey on Mezirow's original work continues in America particularly in the scholarship associated with Teachers College. On the other hand, an interest in social theory and critical theory and the development of transformative learning theory, which we capture in this collection, give the European perspective its defining character. This is linked to differences across the adult education field as well as much wider experiences of politics and movements. It is remarkable how the work of a number of scholars in either Europe or America has been important in defining the approaches. Along with the early work of Illeris, we now add the work of an expanding number of scholars, some of whom collaborate in this present book.

Structure of the Collection and the Authors

The editors (Fleming, Kokkos and Finnegan) outline in Chap. 2 the context, contrasts and the European perspective on transformative learning theory as they find it in this collection. As emancipatory learning is central to Mezirow's work Finnegan (Ireland) takes up in a more explicitly differentiated conception of transformative learning which distinguishes between, and theorizes across, individual and collective forms of reflexive agency linked to emancipation and human flourishing. Kokkos (Greece) addresses the important pedagogical challenge of teaching through Transformation Theory particularly through the use of the arts as a prompt for reconsidering dysfunctional perspectives. Fleming (Ireland) addresses two critiques of Transformation Theory (as overly rational and individual in understanding adult learning) and maps a way forward utilizing the connected knowing of Belenky and the recognition theory of Honneth as allies.

Mälkki (Finland) suggests that our abilities to engage in transformative learning and critical reflection on our taken-for-granted assumptions may be significantly strengthened by gently yet critically harnessing "edge-emotions," which provide resistance to learning and change.

Eschenbacher (Germany) outlines how systems-thinking offers an in-depth perspective on processes of change and transformation involving above all the relational nature of those processes. She expands an understanding of Transformation Theory through systems theory.

Alhadeff-Jones (Switzerland) explores the role of temporality in the theory of transformative learning and outlines an exciting and novel proposal for putting "rhythmanalysis" at the heart of emancipatory education.

Jasper (UK) explores the idea of genuinely positive transformative education being bound up with the struggle against alienation in teaching on a bachelor of arts program for teachers working in non-university, post compulsory education and training in the UK. Overcoming alienation is a defining characteristic of transformative learning itself.

Sifakis and Kordia (Greece) discuss ways in which transformative learning could be fostered in teacher education that focuses on raising English language teachers' awareness of the implications of the current role of English as a lingua franca and the implications for Transformation Theory.

Eneau and Bertrand (France) discuss the notions of power and authority, as they are deployed in work and vocational training and present research that shows how they are at the heart of transformations.

Melacarne (Italy) aims at defining a framework for the most recent approaches and tools used to evaluate transformative learning process and its outcomes.

Laros and Košinár (Germany, Switzerland) research Swiss teacher training with the theory of transformative learning as theoretical lenses. The results suggest that an engagement with disorienting dilemmas already during practical training is an important setting for encouraging transformative learning processes.

Romano (Italy) discusses the ways in which Theatre of the Oppressed can support critiques of assumptions in degree programs in teacher education in Italy.

Fabbri and Di Benedetto (Italy), researching oncology patients in communities of practice can experience disorienting dilemmas in their interactions with staff facilitators. The transformative redefining of identities and organizational development is highlighted.

Striano (Italy) explores the complexity of the professional challenges faced by healthcare professionals within medical organizations and the opportunities for transformative knowledge and learning.

Note

1. It is interesting that Mezirow, in his later texts, uses alternatively the terms "Transformation Theory" and "transformative learning theory" in order to name his theory, while at the same time using the latter in order to refer to the broad transformative learning's theoretical framework (see Mezirow, 2006, 2009).

References

Mezirow, J. (2006). An overview on transformative learning. In P. Sutherland & J. Crowther (Eds.), *Lifelong learning: Concepts and contexts* (pp. 24–38). London: Routledge.

Mezirow, J. (2009). Transformative learning theory. In J. Mezirow, E. W. Taylor, & Associates (Eds.), *Transformative learning in practice. Insights from community, workplace and higher education* (pp. 18–32). San Francisco: Jossey-Bass.

Nicoll, K., Biesta, G., & Morgan-Klein, N. (2014). *(His)story of the European Society of Research on the Education of Adults (ESREA): A narrative history of intellectual evolution and transformation in the field of adult education in Europe.* Retrieved from http://www.esrea.org/wpcontent/uploads/2016/11/ESREA_HISTORY_REPORT_SUBMITTED.pdf

2

Context and Development of Transformation Theory in the European Field of Adult Education

Ted Fleming, Alexis Kokkos, and Fergal Finnegan

Key Formative Ideas of Transformation Theory

The theory of transformative learning is rooted in the 1970s concepts of social psychology and adult education. These include adult learning projects (Alan Tough), andragogy (Malcolm Knowles), personal constructs (George Kelly) and changing perspectives (Herbert Fingarette). These humanistic orientations along with the pragmatism of John Dewey (on critical reflection), and Mezirow's subsequent engagement with Roger Gould's work on adult development give the theory a very American

---

T. Fleming (✉)
Teachers College, Columbia University, New York, NY, USA
e-mail: ted.fleming@mu.ie

A. Kokkos
Hellenic Open University, Athens, Greece

F. Finnegan
The Department of Adult and Community Education, Maynooth University, Maynooth, Ireland
e-mail: fergal.finnegan@mu.ie

© The Author(s) 2019
T. Fleming et al. (eds.), *European Perspectives on Transformation Theory*,
https://doi.org/10.1007/978-3-030-19159-7_2

8   T. Fleming et al.

focus. At that time adult education had little in the line of a research-based indigenous adult learning theory that would have practical application, according to Mezirow (1970).

Mezirow's (1978) project was always about linking adult education with social justice and this is also the clear recollection of fellow researchers and students who worked with him in the 1970s—(Fleming, Marsick, Kasl, & Rose, 2016). In the intervening years the theory has often been interpreted as the testing of psychological assumptions but Mezirow's inclusion of Freire, Habermas and Marx gives the theory a critical and social justice orientation (Bloom & Gordon, 2015). Mezirow was not a radical, but like Freire, he supported challenging the dominant ideological assumptions of social and education policy.

Mezirow relied on John Dewey (1933) who defined reflection as a process of "assessing the grounds (justification) for one's beliefs" (Mezirow, 1990, p. 5) and as reflection on presuppositions. For Dewey (1933, p. 9) reflection was

> active, persistent and careful consideration of any belief or supposed form of knowledge in the light of the grounds that support it and the further conclusion to which it tends.

Reflection includes making unconscious assumptions explicit (Dewey, 1933, p. 281). This interest in Dewey is a defining characteristic of Mezirow's view.

Mezirow's Transformation Theory: What Is It?

Transformative learning is the "process by which learners become aware of and increasingly in control of habits of perception, inquiry, learning and growth that have become internalized" (Mezirow, 1981, p. 12). These habits emerge from a combination of individual life history and the collective set of ideas learned from society and culture. These meanings form a frame of reference, which provides tacit rules of thumb that guide action.

Frames of reference can be habits of mind or points of view (Mezirow, 1991, 1996). A habit of mind is a set of assumptions, broad generaliza-

2 Context and Development of Transformation Theory... 9

tions, predispositions that filter how we interpret the meaning of experience (Mezirow, 1991, 2000). There are different kinds of habits of mind, including: ideological and socio-linguistic; psychological (self-concept, personality trait); and epistemic (learning style). Mezirow (2000) expanded these to include philosophical (world view), aesthetic (tastes, values and judgments about what we mean by beauty) and moral ethical (moral or ethical norms) dimensions. Points of view allow habits of mind to be expressed. Being racist is a habit of mind with points of view that may involve being fearful or suspicious of others from different ethnic backgrounds (Mezirow, 1997).

According to Mezirow transformative learning is;

> the process of becoming critically aware of how and why the structure of our psychocultural assumptions has come to constrain the way in which we perceive our world, of reconstituting that structure in a way that allows us to be more inclusive and discriminating in our integrating of experience and to act on these new understandings. (Mezirow, 1985, p. 22)

Transformative learning requires critical reflection according to Mezirow (1996). Critical reflection is conducted through discussions in which every member is free to engage. Mezirow (1991) adopts the rules for discourse from Habermas and participants must have:

> full accurate and complete information; freedom from coercion and distorting self-deception; openness to alternative points of view: empathy and concern about how others think and feel; the ability to weigh evidence and assess arguments objectively; greater awareness of the context of ideas and, more critically, reflectiveness of assumptions, including their own; an equal opportunity to participate in the various roles of discourse; willingness to seek understanding and agreement and to accept a resulting best judgement as a test of validity until new perspectives, evidence or arguments are encountered and validated through discourse as yielding a better judgement. (Mezirow, 2000, pp. 13–14)

A new frame of reference is more inclusive than the previous problematic frame; more discriminating of experience; more open to change and emotionally capable of change in the future; more reflective so that it generates beliefs and opinions that will prove more true or justifiable as a guide for action (Mezirow, 1990).

The well-known steps of transformative learning are (Mezirow, 2000, p. 22):

A disorienting dilemma;
Self-examination with feelings of fear, anger, guilt or shame;
A critical assessment of assumptions;
Recognition that one's discontent and the process of transformation are shared;
Exploration of options for new roles, relationships and actions;
Planning a course of action;
Acquiring knowledge and skills for implementing one's plans;
Provisional trying new roles;
Building competence and self-confidence in new roles and relationships;
A reintegration into one's life on the basis of conditions dictated by one's new perspectives.

Mezirow builds the foundations for Transformation Theory on a number of key ideas from Habermas: The domains of learning (instrumental, interpersonal and emancipatory learning), critical reflection, and discourse. Mezirow attempted to locate Transformation Theory in the tradition of critical theory and indeed he proposes that Transformation Theory is a critical theory (Mezirow, 1981).

For Mezirow there are two kinds of learning—instrumental and communicative (Mezirow, 1991). Instrumental learning involves control over the physical environment and allows predictions about observable things or events that can be proved empirically correct or not. Communicative learning involves the ability to understand oneself, others and especially the meanings of communications.

Emancipatory learning (Mezirow, 1981) refers to the process of becoming liberated from assumptions that do not serve the pursuit of understanding or that have become problematic or redundant. Emancipatory learning applies to both instrumental and communicative learning. Emancipatory learning is a result of an interest in the ways in which one's history and biography find expression "in the way one sees one's self, one's roles and social expectations" (Mezirow, 1981, p. 5). Emancipation is from

> libidinal, institutional, or environmental forces which limit our options and rational control over our lives but have been taken for granted as beyond human control. These forces include the misunderstandings, ideologies, and psychological distortions in prior learning that produce or perpetuate unexamined relations of dependence. (Mezirow, 1991, p. 87)

Mezirow only reluctantly agreed to consider the possibility of other paths to transformation that would not involve critical reflection and the soul work of John Dirkx and the work of Elizabeth Tisdell on spirituality are good examples of empirical studies that point toward alternative routes to transformation that may not involve critical reflection. For Mezirow, without critical reflection there is no transformative learning.

A Transatlantic Journey

Since Mezirow presented his theory of transformative learning the theoretical field has grown exponentially. Taylor and Cranton (2013) argue that the publications which included transformative learning ideas have doubled every five years over the last fifteen years, primarily in North America. The majority of researchers who may be considered pioneers in this field live and work in the US and Canada. Most of the influential books on transformative learning have been published in the US (e.g., Cranton, 2006; Mezirow, 1991; Mezirow and Associates, 2000; Mezirow, Taylor, and Associates, 2009; Taylor, Cranton, and Associates, 2012). Twelve of the 13 International Conferences on transformative learning were held in North America.

This has changed somewhat in recent years. The interest in Mezirow in Europe started slowly with a number of scholars publishing in individual countries. Some of the earliest publications were in the 1980s (Fleming, 1984, 1986) followed by Mezirow's presentations in Ireland (Mezirow, 1996) and at the UK Standing Conference on University Teaching and Research in the Education of Adults (SCUTREA) at Birbeck College,

London (Armstrong, Miller, & Zukas, 1997). Knud Illleris developed these ideas in Denmark, eventually working toward a remarkable synthesis drawing on a wide variety of European thinkers, many of who are not well-known in the Anglophone world. Presentations by Mezirow in Greece (in 2007) contributed significantly to the further movement of these ideas throughout Europe. However, the presence of European scholars—at least in numerical terms—remained relatively weak within the field until the beginning of 2010s. A literature research (Kokkos & Koulaouzides, 2011) examining publications in 13 journals of adult education as well as the proceedings of transformative learning conferences and these of SCUTREA for the period 1991–2010 identified 26 papers by European authors. Among the 126 papers published from 2003 to 2009 in the *Journal of Transformative Education*, only 6 (4.8%) were written by European authors (Kokkos, 2012).

However, recently European scholars have become more involved in the field of transformative learning beginning at the 9th International Conference on Transformative Learning—held for the first time in Europe (in Athens in 2011). Adult educators and researchers in Austria, Bulgaria, Finland, France, Ireland, Italy, Germany, Greece, Poland, Serbia, Spain, UK, et cetera, have begun to research and develop transformative learning theory and practice. In 2013, a European Network titled "Interrogating Transformative Processes in Learning: An International Dialogue" was created under the auspices of the European Society for Research on the Education of Adults (ESREA). The network aims to create opportunities for dialogue on transformative learning between scholars from Europe and beyond. It also stresses that there is a number of issues, for example, the social dimension of transformative learning, which are associated with the European traditions of adult education and are welcomed within the debate. Its own literature states that

> there may be more of a European emphasis here, if not exclusively so, in which historic traditions of radical popular education, for instance, were rooted in ideas of collective struggle and social transformation.

This idea is also explicitly repeated in the *Call for Papers* of the 1st Conference of the Network—2014:

2 Context and Development of Transformation Theory... 13

Other scholars, located in Europe, for instance, but also in other continents, may share the purpose of Transformative Learning but offer alternative understanding of perspective transformation, using different conceptual frameworks, whether derived from critical theory, Bildung, Marxism, psychological studies, etc.

Moreover, the flyer shares the aforementioned concern regarding the fluid identity of transformative learning's theoretical framework: "There is an anxiety about the widespread use of the term 'transformative' and the danger being emptied of meaning, reduced, perhaps, to little more than a marketing slogan." Hoggan, Mälkki, and Finnegan (2017) fear that some of the ways in which the theory is utilized ignore the extent to which it has become a metatheory and identify any significant learning or change as transformational. Illeris (2014, p. 15) claims that the growing number of tendencies within the theory

> has involved discrepancies and sometimes also divisions which, as I see them, fundamentally have to do with a growing uncertainty about what today lies in the very concept of transformative learning and how it can be defined and practiced.

Furthermore, in 2013, the conference *Transformative Learning meets Bildung* aimed to explore the convergences between transformative learning and *Bildung*, a theory of learning for change that is developed in Germany and other European countries. A volume with the same title, edited by Laros, Fuhr, and Taylor (2017) was an outcome of this conference. In the following years, three International conferences were organized by the ESREA Network in Athens (2014, 2016) and Milan (2018), while the Greek and the Italian Associations of Transformative Learning were founded in 2016 and also organized international workshops.

Consequently, European research on transformative learning has been considerably increased and the International Conferences in Athens and Tacoma/US included 68 papers from European authors (83 papers were written by North Americans). Moreover, four collective books written mainly by Europeans appeared: *Jack Mezirow: La teoria dell'apprendimento trasformativo* [Jack Mezirow: The theory of transformative learning]

(2016), *Transformative Learning Meets Bildung* (Laros et al., 2017), *Expanding Transformation Theory: Connections between Jack Mezirow and Emancipatory Educationalists* (in press) and *Transformative Learning Theory and Praxis: New Perspectives and Possibilities* (in press). Finally, a special issue of the *Journal of Transformative Education* titled "Re-framing Transformative Learning: A North American/European Dialogue" was published in April 2014. The *Journal of Transformative Education* is currently co-edited by European and American academics but previously the editors were exclusively North American.

Situating Mezirow in the Field of Adult Education

We argue that we cannot make sense of Mezirow's work or the particular way his ideas have "traveled" and been adapted in different contexts, without situating him within adult education. Transformation theory is above all a theory produced for and about adult education.

The layered, complex and partly non-formal nature of adult education makes it hard to define in a schematic or simplistic way. It certainly cannot be understood as an educational "sector" or easily compared to institutions that form the compulsory education system. Building on Bourdieu (1984) we want to argue that adult education is usefully understood as a "field" of practice. Bourdieu (1984, 1996, 1998) makes the case that we can only understand a given field—that is a specialized area of human activity—through critical historical and sociological investigation. Specifically, a field is constituted by the organization of social powers structured by patterns in the accumulation and circulation of capitals and the ongoing classificatory struggles over the meaning and purpose of the field. In other words, the genesis and development of a particular field, such as adult education, depends on the incessant, often conflictual symbolic work of naming and orientating what the field does, and should do. Every field is defined by certain *practices, values, objectives, internal structures and dynamics*, which establish the boundaries of the field. In doing so a field responds, adapts and confronts the logic of social space as a whole. For reasons that become clear later, it is worth noting the field of adult education is a field of practice which has a very complex history in relation to the academy and scientific production of knowledge of, about and often for, the field.

When, using this theoretical lens, we examine the historical formation of adult education as a field (Finnegan, 2017, 2018; Rubenson, 2011) there are five things which are especially pertinent to understanding Mezirow's contribution and how he has been interpreted in Europe.

Firstly, something that is frequently noted but often misunderstood, is that adult education is composed of multiple settings and types of provision. Often policymakers, accustomed to the structures, values and rituals of compulsory education, find this "unclear" or even "messy." But within adult education this diversity and complexity of settings and purposes is taken as a given and even as a strength. The point of mentioning this here is that theoretical work on adult education, which wants to speak to and shape the field, has to be capable of being usefully deployed across diverse settings. Frequently, this has been done by making a general theory of learning and/or reflections on the ultimate goals of adult education. Mezirow's intervention reflects these conditions but is also far more than just a product of this field: Mezirow's theory is one of perhaps only three or four attempts in the past forty years that have played a truly significant formative role in adult education in naming the purpose of the field and identifying key lines of inquiry.

Secondly, as Kjell Rubenson (2011, p. 3) notes in his historical overview of the field:

> From its early beginnings, a defining character of the evolving field has been its strong international dimension built around shared values and aspirations. This has positioned adult education as an international movement promoting adult education as a way to combat inequalities, support democracy, and promote cultural and social, democratic development.

The orientation toward internationalism is worth noting, as is the relatively uneven influence of the nation-state on the field (e.g., high in some forms of vocational education and countries, for example Sweden or Singapore, but comparatively low in Latin America popular education).

This is very different to the formation of schooling which is far more tightly informed by the policies, directives and needs of nation states. Therefore, in many ways, it is useful to think of it as *a field which is both internationally and locally defined*. This means we should expect hybridity and the reworking of ideas and practices across time and spaces (Hake & Marriot, 1996). Think of how the idea of folk high schools migrated from Denmark to Tennessee (Horton, 2003), or the way andragogy has been redefined in the context of Yugoslavia and former Yugoslavia, or how Freirean ideas have rippled out and reconfigured themselves in different contexts. The interesting thing is not so much the "purity" of the idea, or its application, but tracing the specific way these practices get remade and why, and to explore the timing and mode of reception and development.

Thirdly, it is important to take note of the strong emancipatory tendencies of adult education that Rubenson also mentions. This reflects the strong connection adult education has had to social movements of all kinds—religious, nationalist et cetera.—but also the especially close bond there has been between radical and progressive movements and international adult education (Holst, 2002).

As a result of this, a cluster of linked ideas which form a type of democratic ethic have become a defining even constitutive ideal within the field. Regardless of specific political programmers and ideologies there is a widespread belief in adult education that the expansion of educational opportunities alongside the reform of pedagogy and curriculum in a responsive and appropriate way can build upon untapped human capacities and realize the promise of democracy. This has often been discussed in tandem with an analysis of the limits of traditional forms of educational provision. This is discernible in key works in the field (Freire, 1972; Knowles, 1980; Lindeman, 1926; Mezirow, 1991, etc.) but is also much more pervasive. We see it clearly articulated in the American and international handbooks of adult education, in a large portion of articles in all the key adult education journals, in practitioner and research bodies such as AAACE, ESREA, CONFINTEA and ICAE and even in some international policy directives. Practices such as learner-centredness, self-directed learning, dialogical methods and negotiated curriculum make little sense without reference to this democratic ideal. Mezirow's ideas *are one specific*

2 Context and Development of Transformation Theory... 17

iteration of this democratic and emancipatory tradition and that needs to be read as part of an ongoing conversation about equality, democracy and freedom in relation to the goals and processes of adult education.

Fourthly, and here we want to make a more explicitly Bourdieusian remark and point to the fact that boundaries of adult education as a field of practice are porous and loose. Adult education has typically been made of "marginal" institutions, often critical of mainstream education, in which low levels of dominant capital circulate and accrue. Entry to the field either as a student or a practitioner is typically very open but the status of the field is not high. This lends the field a distinctive and even peculiar doubleness: it is often poorly supported and "weak" in relation to other parts of the education system such as compulsory schooling: but this

> permeability also lent adult education a peculiar sensitivity to wider political currents in civil society, opened up space for innovation in pedagogy, fed a type of 'meta' critique of existing formal education, and meant it became a seedbed of new ideas and knowledge in education. (Finnegan, 2018, p. 6)

These various features of the field all have a bearing on grasping the importance of Mezirow's work.

This brings us to the fifth point—and this is of particular importance in thinking about how ideas circulate across the Atlantic—adult education in Europe and the US has followed highly varied, and somewhat divergent, paths of professionalization and institutionalization. The early professionalization of US adult education in the 1920s and the establishment of adult education programs, departments and doctorates is significant. This history, and the scale and wealth of the US as a society means that Mezirow's work can be characterized as an intervention in an established and stable academic environment. It was interdisciplinary, and borrowed heavily from European thought, but in a period in the US in which theory endogenous to the field itself was seen as credible and useful goal (Boyd & Apps, 1980), Mezirow aimed at deepening adult education theory *within* a field which was stable, practitioner orientated but more fragmented and less confident than other academic disciplines. To use

Gramsci's terms, it was an elaboration of the good sense of adult education in a more formal and academic direction.

But the professionalization and academicization of the European parts of the field has been much more fragmentary and occurred later (typically after the Second World War). In many iterations adult education as a whole remain connected to the ideas and values of radical social movements (for instance popular education in Scotland or Spain, community education in Ireland or Poland, Volksbildng in Austria et cetera, the folk highschools of Sweden). The fact that in many contexts the academic field is not well-defined or visible, and many adult education academics are initially trained in other disciplines, meant borrowing from and interdisciplinary work is very common (philosophy and sociology remain more influential than in the US).

The projects of transnational state building sponsored by the EU, in a Europe which was massively altered after the collapse of the Eastern bloc, meant that in various ways a European adult education identity has emerged within the same broad field. Nevertheless, we can also say within European scholarship there are powerful, very established core states— for example, Germany and France, which to a large extent remain endogenous and more peripheral smaller states—for example Ireland, Greece, Portugal—which we can speculate may be more likely to seek ideas and collaborations beyond the borders including across the Atlantic.

It is also important to note that the growing interest in Mezirow in Europe has happened in a period in which academic capitalism and globalization is speeding up certain forms of international exchange and in which the field itself may be weakening (Nylander & Fejes, 2019; Nylander, Österlund, & Fejes, 2018). Hybridity is being driven, in part, by a desire for branding and distinction and visibility as well as internationalism and scholarly exchange. Furthermore, the dominance of Anglophone journals in academia and adult education and the spread of English as the lingua franca of scholarship means many European scholars are forced to seek out outlets and partners in the English-speaking world.

In recent decades lifelong learning, at least in the EU, has provided a policy, a mantra, a set of goals and expectations (like them or not) for all EU education from pre-school to adult and higher education. The much younger US (if we leave unexplored the amazing native American Indian cultures) has a wonderful history and a more cohesive pattern of educational ideas, policies and practices. From the Great Awakenings to John Dewey, Horace Mann, the impact of Piaget more recently and Black schools and universities, No Child Left Behind, all give American education a history, and more so a coherence and unifying sense of purpose over decades. Lifelong learning was a well-established policy too in the US and Shulman (1975) gave the learning society a coherence matched by the Lifetime Learning Act (Mondale, 1975, p. S17747).

Today, Europe (especially the EU) is held together by the neoliberal market that has constructed and adopted lifelong learning. Yet, the antecedents are of reputable status and include the works of Yeaxlee in the UK, Faure in France, UNESCO, Gelpi, and Delors. All are associated with ideas and policies making an impact on and developing lifelong learning. Into this arrived perspective transformation that has now found a niche and rationale in Europe.

Convergence and Divergence Between North American and European Views

European scholars are actualizing their theoretical and practical potential within a social, cultural, and political context that is different from North America, and has its own historic background from which local paradigms concerning the phenomenon of learning emerge. Furthermore, some of the theoretical traditions that are shared by the Europeans are not widely expanded within the North American theoretical framework of transformative learning and vice versa.

A number of questions emerge: a) What are the meeting points and the divergences between the conceptions of North American and European scholars concerning the theory and practice of transformative learning? b) Is there a particular "European" perspective on transformative learning?

Undoubtedly, the common point is that transformative learning is conceived by European and North American scholars as a process that fundamentally challenges our ideas, values and behavior. A document produced by the European Network states: "Many (theorists and scholars) […] adopted the core purpose of this learning theory—the fundamental change in learners' dysfunctional frames of reference." Moreover, within the wider field of transformative learning and education is has been the work of Mezirow that has served as the main connecting tissue between the researchers in both continents. Indicatively, both North American and European scholars who presented papers in the International Conference on transformative learning in Athens and Tacoma/US (2016) include Mezirow's works (86% and 91% respectively). Also, both North American and European authors draw a great deal of ideas from other major transformative learning theorists, such as Taylor (51% and 31% respectively), Cranton (45% and 36%), Brookfield (28% and 27%), and Kegan (22% and 19%). In this sense, researchers from both continents share common reference points. As we have already noted, formal and informal collaborations and interactions between the American and European scholars and practitioners has increased in recent years.

Part of the excitement and richness of the collaborations involve the strengths that each partner brings to the explorations. In other words, difference and diversity is generative. But apart from national linguistic and cultural diversity are there other important divergences? It is probably true that Europeans (though not all) seem to be more excited than the Americans by an interest in philosophy and social theory, especially critical theory for the reasons outlined above. Authors who are located in Europe, in contrast with the attitude of the North Americans, have a good deal of references to European theorists, with whom they are obviously familiar, such as Habermas, Jarvis, Illeris, Bourdieu, Lefebvre, Foucault, Piaget, Honneth, et cetera).

This foregrounding of social theory and philosophical interest is also connected with a broader interest in radical social transformation and reflects the fact that socialism and the left have been much more powerful in Europe (Jarvis & Griffin, 2003). Europeans' references to the emancipatory approach of Freire are almost double that of the Americans' (29% and 16% respectively). This runs through this present collection and interestingly is used not only to address the perceived gap in transformative learning in relation to social change but is also used to highlight the

2 Context and Development of Transformation Theory... 21

embodied, emotional and relational nature of human existence and learning.

The American tradition has clearly a strong and sometimes to Europeans a surprising interest in the spiritual and a religious sensibility coloring transformative learning. One can be equally struck by the absence of this perspective across Europe. The North Americans seem to be more interested than the Europeans regarding theorists who deal with the extra-rational conceptions (for example Dirkx is referred with 35% and 14% respectively, Tisdell with 14% and 0%, as well as Lawrence with 10% and 0%). Finally, the organizational change is also an important and constant context in which transformative learning is discussed and researched in America—possibly because of the academic department in which this topic resides in Teachers College. In Europe the corresponding organizational interest is taken up mostly in health and hospital environments as well as in schools and particularly teacher training. This is reflected in this collection.

Though these comments are to some extent generalizations, they do not indicate, in our view, contradictions or conflicts but how transatlantic collaborations are hugely productive and important. Friendships, exchanges, conferences and teacher exchanges continue to be the interpersonal dynamic that enhances the potential to weave a richer tapestry. This is possible without losing the diversities but enhancing the ways in which each is better grounded and most importantly a critical mass of global researchers and teachers achieve a critical mass of scholarship and practice.

However, these findings, regarding the divergences, though they offer just vague and only quantitative indications regarding the authors' attitudes, may lead to some provisional interpretative attempts. The European authors are familiar with the intellectual heritage that was developed in Europe and is rooted in the ideas of humanism, socialism, and critical social tradition (Jarvis & Griffin, 2003). Adult learning was supposed to be associated with social movements, the struggles of trade unions, popular and community education, women's movement, et cetera. This may explain why European scholars tend to involve in their frame of reference—more than their American colleagues—the Freirian and Habermasian conceptions of social emancipatory learning, while, on the contrary, they are not so open to alternative versions of transformative learning that deal with individual emancipation.

References

Armstrong, P., Miller, N., & Zukas, M. (1997). *Crossing borders, breaking boundaries: Research in the education of adults – Proceedings of the 27th annual SCUTREA conference*. London: Birbeck College, University of London.

Bloom, N. (Producer), & Gordon, J. (Director). (2015). *Jack Mezirow on transformative learning: Conversations at home with Jack Mezirow* [Video]. United States: Timeframe Digital Communications. Retrieved December 1, 2017, from https://www.youtube.com/watch?v=iEuctPHsre4

Bourdieu, P. (1984). *Distinction: A social critique of the judgement of taste*. London: Routledge and Kegan Paul.

Bourdieu, P. (1996). *The rules of art: Genesis and structure of the literary field*. Cambridge: Polity.

Bourdieu, P. (1998). *The state nobility: Elite schools in the field of power*. Oxford: Polity.

Boyd, R. D., & Apps, J. W. (Eds.). (1980). *Redefining the discipline of adult education*. San Francisco: Jossey-Bass.

Cranton, P. (2006). *Understanding and promoting transformative learning*. San Francisco: Jossey-Bass.

Dewey, J. (1933). *How we think*. Chicago: Regnery.

Finnegan, F. (2017). Under the sovereign's baleful gaze: Policy, practice and the making of Irish FET. In M. Daley, K. Orr, & J. Petrie (Eds.), *The principal: Power and professionalism in further education*. London: Institute of Education Press.

Finnegan, F. (2018). The degeneration and possible renewal of democratic adult education in Ireland. Paper read at *Adult education and struggles for democracy in precarious times* ESREA Research Network on Active Democratic Citizenship and Adult Learning conference, 20th October 2018 Linköping University.

Fleming, T. (1984). Adult education in the technological age. *The Mount Oliver Review, 1*, 22–41.

Fleming, T. (1986). A theoretical foundation for adult education. In T. Inglis (Ed.), *Priority areas in adult education* (pp. 31–38). Dublin: Aontas.

Fleming, T., Marsick, V., Kasl, E., & Rose, A. (2016). Dancing at the crossroads: Recollections and reflections on Jack Mezirow's early work. In A. Nicolaides & D. Holt (Eds.), *Engaging at the intersections: Symposium paper* (pp. 87–99). Proceedings of the XII International Transformative Learning Conference: Tacoma, WA: Pacific Lutheran University. http://transformativelearning.ning.com/page/pastconferences

Freire, P. (1972). *Pedagogy of the oppressed*. London: Penguin.

Hake, B. J., & Marriot, S. (1996). Adult education between cultures: Encounters and identities in European adult education since 1890. *Leeds Studies in Continuing Education: Cross-Cultural Studies in the Education of Adults, 2*, 1–10.

Hoggan, C., Mälkki, K., & Finnegan, F. (2017). Developing the theory of perspective transformation: Continuity, intersubjectivity and emancipatory praxis. *Adult Education Quarterly, 67*(1), 48–64.

Holst, J. (2002). *Social movements, civil society, and radical adult education. Critical studies in education and culture series*. Westport, CT: Bergin and Garvey.

Horton, M. (2003). *The Myles Horton reader: Education for social change*. Knoxville: Tennessee University Press.

Illeris, K. (2014). *Transformative learning and identity*. London and New York: Routledge.

Jarvis, P., & Griffin, C. (Eds.). (2003). *Adult and continuing education: Major themes in education*. London, UK: Routledge.

Knowles, M. S. (1980). *The modern practice of adult education: Andragogy versus pedagogy*. New York: Association Press.

Kokkos, A. (2012). Transformative learning in Europe: An overview of the theoretical perspectives. In E. W. Taylor & P. Cranton (Eds.), *The handbook of transformative learning: Theory, research, and practice* (pp. 289–303). San Francisco: Jossey-Bass.

Kokkos, A., & Koulaouzides, G. (2011). Divergence and convergence in transformative learning: Insights from the "Old Continent" and the "New World". In M. Alhadeff-Jones & A. Kokkos (Eds.), *Proceedings of the 9th international transformative learning conference*. New York and Athens, Greece: Teachers College, Columbia University and Hellenic Adult Education Association.

Laros, A., Fuhr, T., & Taylor, E. W. (2017). *Transformative learning meets Bildung*. Rotterdam: Sense.

Lindeman, E. (1926). *The meaning of adult education*. New York: New Republic.

Mezirow, J. (1970). Toward a theory of practice in education with particular reference to the education of adults. Paper presented at the Adult Education Research Conference Minneapolis, MN (Feb. 26–27, 1970). (ERIC 036 755).

Mezirow, J. (1978). Perspective transformation. *Adult Education, 28*, 100–110.

Mezirow, J. (1981). A critical theory of adult learning and education. *Adult Education Quarterly, 32*(1), 3–24.

Mezirow, J. (1985). A critical theory of self-directed learning. In S. Brookfield (Ed.), *Selfdirected learning from theory to practice* (pp. 17–30). San Francisco: Jossey-Bass.

Mezirow, J. (1990). How critical reflection triggers transformative learning. In J. Mezirow & Associates (Eds.), *Fostering critical reflection in adulthood: A guide to transformative and emancipatory learning* (pp. 1–20). San Francisco: Jossey-Bass.

Mezirow, J. (1991). *Transformative dimensions of adult learning.* San Francisco: Jossey-Bass.

Mezirow, J. (1996). Adult education and empowerment for individual and community development. In T. Fleming, D. McCormack, B. Connolly & Ryan (Eds.), Radical learning for liberation (pp. 5–14). Maynooth: MACE.

Mezirow, J. (1997). Transformative Learning: Theory to Practice. In P. Cranton (Ed.), *Transformative Learning in Action: Insights from Practice* (pp. 5–12). New Directions for Adult and Continuing Education, No. 74. San Francisco: Jossey-Bass.

Mezirow, J. (2000). Learning to think like an adult: Core concepts of transformation theory. In J. Mezirow & Associates (Eds.), *Learning as transformation: Critical perspectives on a theory in progress* (pp. 3–34). San Francisco: Jossey-Bass.

Mezirow, J., & Associates (Eds.). (2000). *Learning as transformation: Critical perspectives on a theory in progress.* San Francisco: Jossey-Bass.

Mezirow, J., Taylor, E. W., & Associates (Eds.). (2009). *Transformative learning in practice: Insights from community, workplace and higher education.* San Francisco: Jossey-Bass.

Mondale, W. (1975, October 8). *Congressional record, 121*, S 17747–S 17749.

Nylander, E., & Fejes, A. (2019). *Mapping out the research field of adult education and learning.* Basel, Switzerland: Springer.

Nylander, E., Österlund, L., & Fejes, A. (2018). Exploring the adult learning research field by analysing who cites whom. *Vocations and Learning, 11*, 113–131.

Rubenson, K. (2011). The field of adult education: An overview. In K. Rubenson (Ed.), *Adult learning and education* (pp. 3–14). Oxford: Academic Press/Elsevier.

Shulman, C. H. (1975). *Premises and programs for a learning society*. Washington, DC: American Association for Higher Education.

Taylor, E. W., & Cranton, P. (2013). A theory in progress? Issues in transformative learning theory. *European Journal for Research on the Education and Learning of Adults, 4*(1), 33–47.

Taylor, E. W., Cranton, P., & Associates (Eds.). (2012). *The handbook of transformative learning: Theory, research and practice*. San Francisco: Jossey-Bass.

Part I

Reviewing and Expanding the Theory

3

Connected Knowing in Belenky and Honneth: Implications for Transformative Learning Theory

Ted Fleming

Introduction

Mezirow's theory of transformative learning (Mezirow, 1978) is now widely accepted as informing our understanding of adult learning. It has also been critiqued and identified as having weaknesses (Taylor & Cranton, 2013) or as some call it, a certain "stuckness" (Hoggan, Mälkki, & Finnegan, 2017). Two examples of these critiques form the subject matter of this chapter. One critique refers to the overly individual nature of learning as understood by Mezirow in contrast to a more socially aware understanding of learning required by the adult education tradition that addresses social topics and social justice. Critiques have always argued that transformation theory has an inadequate understanding of the social (Clarke & Wilson, 1991; Collard & Law, 1989) and this is a continuing issue (Cranton & Taylor, 2012). The second critique refers to the perception that critical reflection is overly rational to the detriment of more

T. Fleming (✉)
Teachers College, Columbia University, New York, NY, USA
e-mail: ted.fleming@mu.ie

© The Author(s) 2019
T. Fleming et al. (eds.), *European Perspectives on Transformation Theory*,
https://doi.org/10.1007/978-3-030-19159-7_3

30   T. Fleming

emotionally aware ways of making meaning. Attempts have been made to address some of these issues (Fleming, 2002, 2016, 2018) and a more unified theoretical understanding of transformative learning sees learners engaged in both individual and social transformations that complement each other (Cranton & Taylor, 2012). Critical reflection is indeed a challenging process and in this chapter, I argue for a more collaborative and connected way of knowing critically that is not clear in the highly abstract and rational version in Mezirow. Critical theory (Habermas) and feminist epistemology are strong allies in this study.

Few scholars propose solutions to these enduring critiques (Arends, 2014). Mezirow's colleagues at the XII International Transformative Learning Conference agreed that his thinking did not ignore social learning (Fleming, Marsick, Kasl, & Rose, 2016). For instance, the stages of perspective transformation always included identifying one's own problem as part of broader social issues (Mezirow, 1998) and took seriously the shared culturally assimilated nature of one's unquestioned assumptions. The discourse that Mezirow borrowed from Habermas and that defined the learning processes of transformative learning included not only full and equal participation for all but asserted that discourse required empathy (Mezirow, 1998). The remedies, however, remain incomplete and the way forward will be plotted in two ways.

First by referring to the work Mary Belenky and her colleagues that Mezirow identified as important (Belenky, Clinchy, Goldberger, & Tarule, 1986), we identify an important source of ideas that highlights and addresses the critique that transformation theory is overly abstract and rational (Belenky, Bond, & Weinstock, 1997). This proposal comes from within the community of transformative learning scholars. Second, we extend Mezirow's theory by referring to what is possible if we go beyond Habermas and incorporate the work of Axel Honneth to address these questions.

Mary Belenky and *Women's Ways of Knowing*

Belenky and Staunton (1998) presented their work at the First National Transformative Learning Conference and their work remains highly regarded in adult education (Merriam, Caffarella, & Baumgartner, 2007).

3 Connected Knowing in Belenky and Honneth: Implications... 31

In their study, careful attention is paid to the voice of learners. Voice is the capacity to formulate thoughts and ideas, to express (voice) them and feel heard. Interestingly, the conversations among the women they researched were about worlds of conflict and dispute, including the Gulf War, which was a political issue at the time. The voices were categorized as silent, received, subjective, procedural and constructed knowers. Procedural knowledge has two modes (separate and connected) that were integrated into constructed knowledge (Belenky et al., 1986).

Silent knowledge involves not trusting one's own voice, having a voice that may be passive and an identity defined by others.

Received knowledge is where people's ideas are received uncritically often from other more powerful people. This knowledge is literal, concrete and thinks in polarized ways as in good or bad.

Subjective knowledge is located within oneself, it is not received from others, people are their own ideas and vouch for the truth of their own subjective experience and knowledge. Subjective knowledge is personal, private and resists critical reflection.

Procedural knowledge involves two forms—separate and connected knowing. The former is the knowing of rational, logical argument, discussion and critical reflection. Connected knowing involves discussions with others so that the more the participants disagree the more they try to see things from the perspective of others in empathy, support and solidarity—rather than through investigative rationality. This caring and feminist discourse of Belenky in which women draw each other out (Belenky et al., 1997; Belenky & Staunton, 2000) supports the development of each other through connected knowing.

Constructed knowledge integrates both procedural ways of knowing and becomes critical reflection with empathetic understanding and care. The individual is capable of understanding that there are systems of thought to be examined. This knowledge is contextual. In a summary, Stanton makes this statement about one of the women participants and affirmed that these words also represent her understanding of Mezirow's theory;

> It all comes down to getting people to feel like they can say what they feel and not be punished for it. You have to have enough time to let your

32   T. Fleming

conversation go full circle,….You have to let the debate carry through until everybody has come to some sort of understanding. It doesn't mean that everybody has to agree at the end, but everybody has to have some sort of greater understanding of what the problem is. (Staunton quoted in Belenky & Staunton, 1998, p. 12)

Belenky and Staunton (1998) use the concept of "full circle conversations" in which people do not necessarily agree, but they talk with one another until they come to a place of new understanding and this is central to creating environments that support the possibility of transformative experiences. There is a close relationship between the ideal conditions of discourse (in Habermas) and what Belenky et al. (1986, pp. 143–146) refers to as "really talking" that involves active listening; the absence of domination; the exercise of reciprocity and cooperation; where judgment is withheld until one empathetically understands another's point of view. Mezirow (2000, p. 14), quoting Belenky states;

Compared to other positions, there is a capacity at the position of constructed knowledge to attend to another person and to feel related to that person in spite of what may be enormous differences…Empathy is a central feature in the development of connected procedures for knowing… attentive caring is important in understanding not only people but also the written word, ideas, even impersonal objects.

Belenky acknowledges the importance of transformative learning but highlights the absence in transformation theory of an understanding of how to encourage and support learners whose starting position may be silent knowing or received knowing and move them toward more critical and contextualized engagements with the world. The discourse of Mezirow requires maturity and this contrasts with silent knowers who may sometimes be more typical of where learners in community education start their journeys. Adult educators grapple with this, Mezirow does not. Though Mezirow (2000) explicitly shared Belenky's view, it could be argued he did not realize its full implications for his concept of critical reflection.

I suggest that Mezirow saw transformations as paradigm shifts in meaning schemes or meaning structures where people moved from silent

3 Connected Knowing in Belenky and Honneth: Implications... 33

or received positions to separated/connected positions and on to constructed knowers. He reasoned that the task he faced was to firmly ground transformation theory not only in philosophically accepted concepts and theories (Habermas) but also in empirically based developmental psychology constructs like Belenky's work. This was a successful project and allowed an interdisciplinary cohort of academics and practitioners accept it as a theory and practice of adult education. But transformation theory did not take on board the full implications of Belenky's work—in particular her concept of connected knowing. A more feminist perspective by Mezirow might have led to a more satisfactory integration.

Belenky sees women as active constructors of knowledge who learn how to create spaces where they can feel at home, a safe space for full circle conversations (Belenky & Staunton, 2000) which in their openness and participatory nature parallel Mezirow's women's groups. But Belenky and her colleagues went further. They described the close interpersonal bonding of their conversations, the ability to forge links and connections so that discussions allowed participants to mirror and see themselves in a new light including as reflected by others. It is not the power of the most rational argument that wins the day but the ability of women to discuss and collaborate within relationships and friendships so that, as far as that is possible, they wait for each other to connect and know their situations in connected knowledge.

Belenky's constructed knowing is in contrast to the separated knowing of rational discourse with its logic, analysis and interest in identifying the weaknesses of another's point of view or "playing the doubting game" (Belenky & Staunton, 2000, p. 86). Connected knowing involves perspective taking, identifying and building on strengths, empathy, imagination, storytelling and learning through nurturing and caring. This involves transcending the dualisms of thinking/feeling, public/private—that create hierarchies (Belenky & Staunton, 2000). This involves drawing people out, so to speak (Belenky et al., 1997) and supporting the transformation of others through connected knowing. The more people try to understand each other, they enter into the perspective of others and through perspective taking and empathy knowledge is enhanced.

Loughlin (1993) added further empirical confirmation of Belenky's work. In his preface to Loughlin's work, Mezirow welcomes "attempts to integrate the cognitive, conative and emotional holistic dimensions of significant learning experiences" (Mezirow in Loughlin, 1993, p. xi). In addressing what Mezirow calls the "primary goal" of adult education, he asks whether we develop change agents for social reconstruction by educating for personal development or for social action itself. This issue, he correctly asserts, has bedeviled the field of adult education from its beginnings and Loughlin, he states, has shown how and why transformative learning as personal development within a community of knowers, effects social commitment and results in decisive social action by women in communications, politics and education (Mezirow in Loughlin, 1993). In fact, Mezirow explicitly shared Belenky's views (Mezirow, 2000). These connected and constructive conversations help reveal that "there are hidden agendas of power in the way societies define and validate and ultimately genderize knowledge" (Goldberger, Tarule, Clinchy, & Belenky, 1996, p. 7). This study of material within the ambit of transformation theory utilizes feminist epistemology to address an enduring critique that the theory is lacking a feminist perspective and its discourse is overly rational.

Honneth and Transformative Learning

Mezirow borrowed a number of ideas from Habermas. He relied on him for the three domains of learning (instrumental, hermeneutic and emancipatory) as well as an understanding of the concepts of discourse and critical reflection. More recently, Axel Honneth (a colleague and former student of Habermas at the Frankfurt School) sets out to refocus critical theory by reframing the distorted communication of Habermas as disrespect (Honneth, 1995). Denials of recognition that result in indignations, guilt and shame drive social struggles for recognition and social freedom (Honneth, 2014). The living conditions of

> Modern capitalist societies produce social practices, attitudes, or personality structures that result in a pathological distortion of our capacities for reason...They always aim at exploring the social causes of a pathology of human rationality. (Honneth, 2009, p. vii)

He foregrounds a theory of intersubjectivity and the "struggle for recognition" as the new direction for critical theory.

According to Honneth, quoting Mead (1934), only by taking the perspective of others toward oneself can one begin to construct a sense of self (Patete, 2016). The perspectives of others are shaped by culture, life history and by internalizing these, individuals grow and develop. Honneth argues that the struggle for recognition, based on the need for self-esteem and the experience of disrespect, also explains *social* development.

> It is by the way of the morally motivated struggles of social groups—their collective attempt to establish, institutionally and culturally, expanded forms of recognition—that the normatively directional change of societies proceeds. (Honneth, 1995, p. 92)

Social change is driven by inadequate forms of recognition and internal (psychic) conflict leads to social change. The social and personal are connected. Honneth sees taking the perspectives of others as moments of recognition;

> …for it is his taking of the attitude of the others that guarantees to him the recognition of his own rights. To be a 'me' under these circumstances is an important thing. It gives him his position, gives him the dignity of being a member in the community. (Mead in Honneth, 1995, p. 79)

This moves the debate about emancipation away from the perceived highly cognitive and rational discourse of Habermas toward an alternative theory of intersubjectivity. This has the potential to resolve the problem in transformation theory as to whether learning is an individual or social phenomenon. Transformative learning and communicative action are always more than the following of linguistic rules of discourse (Habermas, 1987) and involve mutuality and intersubjectivity (Honneth, 1995). The antidote to being too individualistic lies in critical theory as articulated by Habermas and Honneth.

Honneth argues that there are three distinct modes of recognition. The first he calls <u>self-confidence</u> that is established and developed in relationships of friendship and love. If one experiences love an ability to love one's self and others is developed and one is then capable of forging an identity. This can only be achieved through being recognized by others. The second mode is self-respect, when a person in a community of rights is given recognition as a morally and legally mature person (Honneth, 1995). The third kind of recognition is called self-esteem and is provided through work and whether the community will honor one's contribution through work. In relationships of solidarity with others in work and other collaborative social activities, one is recognized as having something to contribute to the community (Honneth, 1997). This recognition enhances self-esteem.

If people are denied rights, their self-respect may suffer (Honneth, 1995). In this way, Honneth brings private matters to the center of sociological attention and internal conflicts lead to social change. Inadequate forms of recognition drive social change. The theory of recognition establishes a link between the social causes of experiences of injustice and the motivation for emancipatory movements (Fraser & Honneth, 2003). We begin to see how the social and personal are connected. On the other hand, one's private relationships of love and attachment are a precondition for participation in public life and political will-formation. It implies that not only is the personal political but the political is personal. Transformative learning becomes both personal and social (Fleming, 2014).

This recognition turn has implications for transformative learning. Mutuality according to Habermas (1987) means that we strive toward mutual understanding as long as we follow rules of discourse. These have shaped transformation theory. The antidote to being too individualistic lies in these critical theory foundations of transformation theory.

Honneth tries to make social issues such as poverty, unemployment, injustices, globalization and abuses of power open to being understood in terms of recognition. Unemployment is experienced as misrecognition—and this is a way of emphasizing that Honneth's theory is not merely a psychology of internal processes but a thorough social psychology with the key critical theory intent of understanding and changing the material conditions of society. The more recent work of Honneth (2014) is testament to his ability to reframe his work in response to sustained critique (Fraser & Honneth, 2003) and continue to understand the inextricable link between the personal and political.

Implications for Transformation Theory

Transformative education has a clear mandate to work in the seams and at the boundaries of systems to humanize and transform them so that they operate in the interests of all. Mezirow believed that effective learners in an emancipatory, participative, democratic society—a learning society—become a community of cultural critics and social activists (Mezirow, 1995) and the dichotomy of individual and society is transcended by an epistemology of intersubjectivity. Transformation theory now asserts that the dichotomy between individual and social development is a spurious one for educators.

The full incorporation and integration of these ideas from Habermas and Honneth into transformation theory leads to the conclusion that transformation theory is grounded in and infused with a sense of the social. These ideas point to a dual agenda for transformative education. This "recognition turn" suggests that the high rationality required by Mezirow's transformative learning is "softened" by this understanding of the interpersonal recognition that underpins democratic discourses in learning environments. Struggles for recognition are a motivation for learning. Without altering the importance of communicative action or of critical reflection for transformative learning there is now the possibility of reframing the theory of transformative learning so that rational discourse is seen as based on an interpersonal process of support and recognition that builds self-confidence, self-respect and self-esteem. Mezirow (and Habermas) see democratic participation as an important means of self-development that produces individuals who are more tolerant of difference, sensitive to reciprocity and better able to engage in discourse (Mezirow, 2003). This recognition turn is a precondition for rational discourse, without losing rigor or the ambition to remain connected to the emancipatory agenda of critical theory and transformative learning. Belenky might well concur, again.

The idea that transformative learning is individual or social can now be reframed as a fundamentally intersubjective process of mutual recognition. This implies that transformative learning is best supported by interactions that are not only respectful but that explicitly recognize the individual worth of each individual along with the aspirations, dreams and desires that prompt their struggles for recognition. Transformative learning may in this way escape the charge of being overly individual or rational.

It is now clear that personal problems are intimately and necessarily connected to broader social issues. This is a philosophically important and essential step in interpreting the world that cannot be understood properly without both personal and political perspectives being taken into account. The personal is indeed political but the political is also personal and transformative learning necessarily involves making these connections. At an obvious level, transformative learning requires the ability to perceive the world in this way—the personal and social are connected.

Transformative learning theory as understood by Mezirow has followed the communicative turn of Habermas (Mezirow, 1991). I suggest that this learning theory might now follow the recognition turn of fellow critical theorist Honneth. Transformative learning is critical of presuppositions; aims to create discursive spaces in which the force of the better argument is the only force and in which all have full and equal rights to participate freely in democratic will-formation. Transformative learning requires critical reflection and now recognition becomes central to the learning process.

In order to engage in the critical discourse associated with transformative learning, we now assert that the formation of democratic discussions requires three forms of self-relating. We need caring and loving individuals (teachers), and these are produced through and by those with self-confidence. It requires recognition of the reciprocal nature of legal rights and, as one might anticipate, a person who possesses self-respect (the capacity to know one's own rights) is better able to recognize the rights of others. And thirdly, a democratic discursive society (as well as an adult learning group) requires the reciprocal recognition provided by work and solidarity. A person with self-esteem can better recognize the contributions of others—connected, and critical and procedural.

Without altering the importance of communicative action or of critical reflection for transformative learning, there is now the possibility of reframing transformation theory so that rational discourse is seen as based on an interpersonal process of support and recognition that builds self-confidence, self-respect and self-esteem. This allows a bridge between critical reflection, recognition and connected knowing—a linking of Habermas, Honneth and Belenky.

The emphasis on whether learning is individual or social (Cranton & Taylor, 2012) can be reconfigured similar to the way Freire (1970) reconfigured the dualisms of subject/object, teacher/learner, best expressed in his concept of *praxis*. The previously referred to individualism of Mezirow's theory can now be reframed as a fundamentally intersubjective process of mutual respect and recognition and connection. These relations of mutuality are preconditions for self-realization, critical reflection and transformative learning. Recognition and emancipation are connected; recognition becomes the foundation on which communicative action, emancipatory learning and social change are based. This implies that transformative learning is best supported by interactions that are not only respectful but that explicitly recognize the individual worth of each individual along with the aspirations and dreams that prompt their struggle for recognition and connection.

One of the stages of the transformative process involves making connections between one's own individual problem (that may have prompted learning) and broader social issues. It is now clear from this study of Honneth that personal problems are intimately connected to broader social issues. The connection is not just an empirically grounded finding in transformative learning but is a philosophically important and essential step in interpreting the world. The personal is indeed political but now the political is personal and the transformative learning process necessarily involves the making of this connection. At an obvious level transformative learning requires the ability to perceive the world in this way—as personal and political and social. One does not understand the world correctly or in a transformative way without both personal and social insights.

Epilogue

Most recently, Honneth explores the concept of freedom that is also important for Mezirow who borrowed it from Freire and Habermas. Honneth (2014, 2017) reimagines freedom in terms of social coopera-

40 T. Fleming

tion and mutual recognition in the spheres of the economy, interpersonal relationships and politics (Jay, 2017). Freedom in one of these spheres presupposes freedom in the others. This suggests that there is another chapter of the living theory of transformative learning to be written that takes into account the idea that emancipation (and democracy) involve not only the political spheres but emancipated families and a socialized market. As Honneth (reinterpreting Hegel) asserts, these spheres "mutually influence each other, because the properties of one cannot be realized without the other two" (Honneth, 2014, p. 345). The interconnectedness of these spheres suggests that the project of this chapter is further enhanced by the most recent work of Honneth. It suggests that learning (and teaching) for the development of the "we" of democratic discourse may be a vital and necessary task for transformative education. Everything is connected.

References

Arends, J. (2014). The role of rationality in transformative education. *Journal of Transformative Education, 12*(4), 356–367.

Belenky, M. F., Bond, L. A., & Weinstock, J. S. (1997). *A tradition that has no name: Nurturing the development of people, families and communities.* New York: Basic Books.

Belenky, M. F., Clinchy, B. M., Goldberger, N. R., & Tarule, J. M. (1986). *Women's ways of knowing: The development of self, voice and mind.* New York: Basic Books.

Belenky, M. F., & Staunton, A. (1998). Women and transformative learning: Connected ways of knowing and developing public voice. In J. Mezirow, V. Marsick, C. A. Smyth, & C. Wiessner (Eds.), *Changing adult frames of reference: Proceedings of First National Transformative Learning Conference* (pp. 9–15). New York: Teachers College.

Belenky, M. F., & Staunton, A. V. (2000). Inequality, development and connected knowing. In J. Mezirow & Associates (Eds.), *Learning as transformation: Critical perspectives on a theory in progress* (pp. 71–102). San Francisco: Jossey-Bass.

Clarke, M. C., & Wilson, A. (1991). Context and rationality in Mezirow's theory of transformational learning. *Adult Education Quarterly, 41*(2), 75–91.

Collard, S., & Law, M. (1989). The limits of perspective transformation: A critique of Mezirow's theory. *Adult Education Quarterly, 39*(2), 99–107.

Cranton, P., & Taylor, E. W. (2012). Transformative learning theory: Seeking a more unified theory. In E. W. Taylor, P. Cranton, & Associates (Eds.), *The handbook of transformative learning: Theory, research and practice* (pp. 3–20). San Francisco: Jossey-Bass.

Fleming, T. (2002). Habermas on civil society, lifeworld and system: Unearthing the social in transformation theory. *Teachers College Record On-line*, 1–17. Retrieved from http://www.tcrecord.org. ID Number: 10877.

Fleming, T. (2014). Axel Honneth and the struggle for recognition: Implications for transformative learning. In A. Nicolaides & D. Holt (Eds.), *Spaces of transformation and transformation of space. Proceedings of the 11th International Transformative Learning Conference* (pp. 318–324). New York: Teachers College.

Fleming, T. (2016). Reclaiming the emancipatory potential of adult education: Honneth's critical theory and the struggle for recognition. *European Journal for Research on the Education and Learning of Adults, 7*(1), 13–24.

Fleming, T. (2018). Critical theory and transformative learning: Rethinking the radical intent of Mezirow's theory. *International Journal of Adult Vocational Education and Technology, 9*(3), 1–13.

Fleming, T., Marsick, V. J., Kasl, E., & Rose, A. D. (2016). Dancing at the crossroads: Recollections and reflections on Jack Mezirow's early work. In A. Nicolaides & D. Holt (Eds.), *Engaging at the intersections: Proceedings of the XII International Transformative Learning Conference* (pp. 87–99). Tacoma, WA: Pacific Lutheran University.

Fraser, N., & Honneth, A. (2003). *Redistribution or recognition? A political-philosophical exchange*. London: Verso.

Freire, P. (1970). *Pedagogy of the oppressed*. New York: Seabury.

Goldberger, N. R., Tarule, J. M., Clinchy, B. M., & Belenky, M. F. (Eds.). (1996). *Knowledge, difference and power*. New York: Basic Books.

Habermas, J. (1987). *The theory of communicative action, Vol 2: The critique of functionalist reason*. Boston: Beacon.

Hoggan, C., Mälkki, K., & Finnegan, F. (2017). Developing the theory of perspective transformation: Continuity, intersubjectivity and emancipatory praxis. *Adult Education Quarterly, 67*(1), 48–64.

Honneth, A. (1995). *The struggle for recognition: The moral grammar of social conflicts*. Cambridge, MA: MIT Press.

Honneth, A. (1997). Recognition and moral obligation. *Social Theory, 64*(1), 16–35.

Honneth, A. (2009). *Pathologies of reason: On the legacy of critical theory*. New York: Columbia University Press.

Honneth, A. (2014). *Freedom's right: The social foundations of democratic life*. Cambridge: Polity.

Honneth, A. (2017). *The idea of socialism*. Cambridge: Polity.

Jay, M. (2017). Positive freedom. *The Nation*. Retrieved from https://www.the-nation.com/article/socialisms-past-and-future/

Loughlin, K. A. (1993). *Women's perception of transformative learning experiences within consciousness raising*. San Francisco: Mellen Research University Press.

Mead, G. H. (1934). *Mind, self and society*. Chicago: University of Chicago Press.

Merriam, S. B., Caffarella, R. S., & Baumgartner, L. M. (2007). *Learning in adulthood: A comprehensive guide* (3rd ed.). San Francisco: Jossey-Bass.

Mezirow, J. (1978). Perspective transformation. *Adult Education, 28*, 100–110.

Mezirow, J. (1991). *Transformative dimensions of adult learning*. San Francisco: Jossey-Bass.

Mezirow, J. (1995). Transformation theory of adult learning. In M. Welton (Ed.), *In defense of the lifeworld* (pp. 39–70). New York: SUNY Press.

Mezirow, J. (1998). Transformation theory of adult learning: Core propositions. In J. Mezirow, V. Marsick, C. A. Smyth, & C. Wiessner (Eds.), *Changing adult frames of reference: Proceedings of First National Transformative Learning Conference* (pp. 59–67). New York: Teachers College.

Mezirow, J. (2000). Learning to think like an adult: Core concepts of transformation theory. In J. Mezirow & Associates (Eds.), *Learning as transformation: Critical perspectives on a theory in progress* (pp. 3–34). San Francisco: Jossey-Bass.

Mezirow, J. (2003). Transformative learning as discourse. *Journal of Transformative Education, 1*(1), 58–63.

Patete, N. (2016). *Interazione e riconoscimento*. Rome: Aracne Editrice.

Taylor, E. W., & Cranton, P. (2013). A theory in progress? Issues in transformative learning theory. *European Journal for Research on the Education and Learning of Adults, 4*(1), 33–47.

4

'Freedom Is a Very Fine Thing': Individual and Collective Forms of Emancipation in Transformative Learning

Fergal Finnegan

It is a foundational assumption of Mezirow's work that adult education which is democratic in aim and form has enormous emancipatory potential. This chapter will critically explore exactly how emancipation is envisaged by Mezirow and the strengths and lacunae of his theory in this regard. The first section of the chapter will consist of a detailed review of how Mezirow conceptualises freedom and autonomy. As noted in the second chapter of this book Mezirow's work is best understood as a theory which elaborates and develops ideas about emancipatory learning which have helped to define adult education as a whole. In order to situate and work through Mezirow's ideas, and in particular to think about emancipation on different 'levels'—namely the individual and the collective—I want to explore Mezirow and Freire's conceptions of emancipatory education alongside each other. This will be the focus of the second section of the chapter.

F. Finnegan (✉)
The Department of Adult and Community Education, Maynooth University, Maynooth, Ireland
e-mail: fergal.finnegan@mu.ie

© The Author(s) 2019
T. Fleming et al. (eds.), *European Perspectives on Transformation Theory*,
https://doi.org/10.1007/978-3-030-19159-7_4

I want to take a different tack from the two most common ways of working through these two philosophies of critical adult education though. Probably the most widespread approach—and certainly one that predominates in the Transformative Learning Conference proceedings over the past twenty years—is to assume that the 'family' resemblances between Mezirow and Freire's ideas are so strong that they can be treated as more or less complementary theories. I am not persuaded this is the case and I am convinced that this approach also skates over conceptual problems which need to work through for the development transformative learning theory. On the other hand, there is a well-established line of critique that takes Mezirow to task for not properly addressing issues of social emancipation (e.g., Cunningham, 1998; Hart, 1990; Inglis, 1997; Newman, 2012 inter alia). Although these critiques are rich interventions, they have rarely been built upon to reconstruct transformative learning theory (for an example of an exception, see especially the work of Fleming 2016). This 'stuckness' (Hoggan, Mällki, & Finnegan, 2017) reflects, amongst other things, just how deeply entrenched dichotomous ways of thinking of individual and collective emancipation are in adult education and further afield. Thus the overall purpose of the chapter, which is outlined in the last section, is to sketch out how these two traditions of emancipatory thought might begin to be usefully integrated together without conflating or overlooking important differences. This requires, I believe, conceptual bridging and to do this I will also draw on the British philosopher Roy Bhaskar's (1979) critical realist analysis of the meaning of emancipation alongside the work of Castoriadis (1987) on autonomy. In doing so, the chapter makes a case for working towards a more explicitly differentiated conception of transformative learning which distinguishes between, and theorises across, individual and collective forms of emancipation.

Mezirow's Conception of Emancipation

Mezirow's (1981, 1990, 1991, 2007) theory of transformative learning was developed over several decades and went through considerable elaboration and change (Cranton & Taylor, 2012; Hoggan, 2016) but the core

4 'Freedom Is a Very Fine Thing': Individual and Collective...

proposition—the beating heart of the theory—which is directly related to his conception of emancipation has not changed. Put simply, it is this: deep critical reflection can lead to new forms of thinking and action which foster individual and social emancipation. Before I explore how exactly Mezirow understands emancipation, I think it is important in the context of this discussion to pause and note something about the overall of characteristics of Mezirow's theory. It is probably best described as a critical synthesis of radical, humanist and pragmatist educational ideas underpinned by the insights of developmental psychology which serves as a comprehensive theoretical framework for adult education within a North American context. I will argue below that the synthetic quality and the ambition to offer a comprehensive account of adult learning in this particular context are directly pertinent to the strengths and weaknesses of his understanding of emancipation.

Mezirow puts *meaning making and praxis* right at the centre of his learning theory and indeed human life more generally. Knowing and doing are viewed as contingent processes which need to be understood in relation to a given socio-historical context. The nature of modern society is such—fluid and complex—that to flourish we need to develop our capacities to make meaning, critically reflect and act in a flexible and open way (2007). This also means being able to critically handle the various forms of knowledge produced in society. Mezirow (1991), *pace* Habermas, identifies two different 'domains' of learning—the instrumental and communicative—which have different logics of use and modes of validation. Thus, according to Mezirow (1991, 2007), we need to develop forms of adult education which can adequately respond to these historical conditions and to deal with the variety, complexity, and in this virtual age, the volume of knowledge and information available to us. But—and this is both a challenge and opportunity for adult education—our capacity for critical learning is often 'stunted' (Mezirow, 1990, p. 359) through primary socialisation, (mis)education and ideological distortions.

Only through critical reflection, according to Mezirow, can we fully exploit the immanent potential of the knowledge and information at our disposal in an empowering and even emancipatory way. Specifically, Mezirow (1981, 1990, 1991, 2007)) maintains that it is through critical

46   F. Finnegan

reflection that we can begin to think more rationally and systematically about our own circumstances and self to grasp the reasons and causes behind things. This defence of critical rationality, of realism and shared procedures of validation as the basis of emancipatory knowledge is worth underlining—and defending—in a period in which 'alternative facts' have become acceptable and widely traded currency in public discourse. Mezirow (1991), p. 104 and all of Chap. 4) makes a further important distinction and argues that critical reflection can be carried out with varying degrees of intensity and depth and distinguishes between reflection on content, processes or fundamental premises.

Learning is truly transformative, and potentially emancipatory, when previously taken for granted assumptions and norms and roles are reflected upon and modified. This involves rethinking deeply held, and often distorted beliefs, about who we are and our lifeworld. Mezirow (1991, pp. 167–174) maintains this process of 'subjective reframing' follows identifiable phases in which the learner moves from a disorienting dilemma through to self-examination based on collaborative dialogue to a major rethinking of one's assumptions. If successful Mezirow (1991, p. 155) indicates that this can lead:

> toward a more inclusive, differentiated, permeable, and integrated perspective and that, insofar as it is possible, we all naturally move toward such an orientation […] It should be clear that a strong case can be made for calling perspective transformation the central process of adult development.

Tapping into this successfully also reconfigures relationships and results in novel courses of action (1991, p. 167).

Perspective transformation also makes us more capable of acting in a way that enhances personal and collective freedom. Freedom—as a value and a practice—is understood by Mezirow primarily, but not exclusively it should be said, as freedom *from* constraints on thought and action:

> Emancipation from libidinal, linguistic, epistemic, institutional, or environmental forces that limit our options and our rational control over our lives but have been taken for granted or seen beyond human control. (Mezirow, 1991, p. 87)

Emancipation comes from breaking free of the shackles of prejudice, the dead weight of tradition and unaccountable authority. By becoming more self-aware in pursuit of rational individual and social interests. Thus, fostering 'liberating conditions for making more autonomous and informed choices and developing a sense of self-empowerment is the cardinal goal of adult education' (Mezirow, 2000, p. 26).

This way of thinking about emancipation as the removal of constraints which enhance an *individual's capacity for autonomy* has a long history in Western philosophy which links Mezirow to the liberal tradition (especially Mill). This also reflects the debt Mezirow owes to psychological theories of development and learning—a discipline which remains, for the most part, very firmly bound to methodological individualism. Tellingly, if you examine carefully how learning and change is envisaged by Mezirow (1991, esp. Chap. 6) the pivot point, for analytical and practical purposes, is the individual's assumptive world. His explication of transformative learning, including the diagrams, directs the reader to focus on how individuals' 'meaning schemes' made up of specific beliefs, knowledge, value judgements and feelings are embedded in broader sets of socially constructed 'meaning perspectives' change (see 1991 esp. pp. 5–6 and pp. 154–156). The critically reflective and agentic individual is the wellspring of freedom, and this is reflected in the weight, care and attention given to topic in Mezirow's work. There is a real density, in the positive sense, in Mezirow's (1991) discussion of these issues.

It is important to note—despite what some critics of Mezirow have argued—that while his theory focuses on the individual, it is not irredeemably individualistic. The context for learning and the process of meaning making are very clearly depicted by Mezirow (1990, 1991, 2000, 2007, et cetera) as socialised processes and he repeatedly stresses the centrality of dialogue to transformative learning alongside the fundamentally intersubjective nature of critical reflection. The socio-cultural and sociological dimensions of learning *are* in view—Mezirow could not be clearer that he is interested in supporting democratic movements and progressive social change—but they are not foregrounded in a systematic way. Mezirow mainly uses his sociological imagination to frame the contours of his theory of learning—offering a type of bird's eye view of society—which the individual confronts and works within but it is the inner mental world that is held in close view, and explored precisely and from multiple angles.

Furthermore, although Mezirow is concerned with advancing social emancipation it is usually described as one possible *subset* of transformative learning (1990, 1991, 2000). Transformative learning is always empowering (in the sense of strengthening individuals and communities' capacity to think and act rationally and justly) but it is not necessarily socially emancipatory in the way this has typically been described in radical adult education (i.e., resulting in social action which seeks to change social structures in an egalitarian way). We benefit by reshaping our assumptions through rational democratic deliberation but the precise relationship to broader social change is described as contingent on circumstances and needs of learners. Unreflective activism and political manipulation is strongly criticised (Mezirow, 1991, p. 204). Acting for social emancipation depends on individual free choice and Mezirow (1990) is at pains to stress that dogma, regardless of political hue, is the enemy of transformative learning and genuine autonomy. Consequently, the site of change—as well as agency—is envisaged primarily in terms of the transformation of the inner mental landscape of an individual learner which may, or may not, have broader social consequences.

Deep critical reflection is thus presented as the 'germ cell' of transformative learning. Mezirow explicitly presents this as the 'common ground' (1990, p. 363) of adult education, and social change adult education is described as one particular, albeit highly valued, branch of much larger field. As a basic empirical observation this is true and non-trivial but as a theoretical presentation of learning and emancipation is ambiguous and even problematic as it offers no clear evaluative framework from which to assess emancipatory claims. To return to a point made earlier, this reflects Mezirow's desire to offer comprehensive synthesis for North American adult education: it transcends andragogy, dovetails with progressive thought, and can be accepted by liberals as well as embraced by radicals.

Mezirow made an enormous contribution to adult education by developing a highly detailed, careful account of how deep critical reflection serves emancipatory ends. As a psychologically orientated conception of freedom which is especially alert to the undoing of constraints on the individual it is valuable, even necessary but it offers no clear basis for understanding why collective activity is so important for advancing freedom.

Freire's Conception of Emancipation

Mezirow (1990, 1991) frequently acknowledged that Freire's understanding of learning and democratic praxis was a key influence on his work especially Freire's notion of conscientisation (see below). But a key argument of this chapter is that although they are certainly not incompatible perspectives, they are very distinct. As we have seen, Mezirow views freedom as a principle which is activated through critical reflection and realised through the exercise of autonomy. In various ways, directly and indirectly, reflective autonomy contributes to the vitality of democracy. But for Freire (1972, 1998) freedom is treated as something far more *ontologically basic* than this. Drawing on Erich Fromm's notion of biophilia—a love of life and living akin to a basic drive in the Freudian sense—Freire sees the need for freedom and the desire for autonomy as fundamental to human flourishing. Making sense of the world, deep curiosity and hopefulness are inextricably linked to this biophiliac desire by Freire. The practice of freedom is thus viewed as integral to rich learning, useful knowledge, psychic health and ultimately a humane society. Freire's (1972, p. 66) condemnation of banking education, oppression and domination—the dulling or blocking of the 'vocation to be human' are also rooted in this conception of human freedom. To be unfree is to be cut away from the power to explore, name and act in the world, locked into a 'culture of silence' (p. 116), resigned to pre-given fate and even to fear of freedom. While this might be overstated, or at least needs qualification and amendment, this is a very rich and suggestive proposal.

Freire (1972) is, like Mezirow, a humanist but his immersion in activism and his debt to Marxism and Fanon's postcolonial thinking means his conception of *freedom is relational, entirely social and largely collective.* Freedom and unfreedom may be ontologically basic but acts of freedom—even on the scale of an uttered word or a single gesture of an individual—are always framed by Freire within a wider power analysis of

50   F. Finnegan

social relations, institutions and history (Freire, 1970, 1972; Freire & Macedo, 1987; Freire & Shor, 1987; Freire, Giroux, & Macedo, 1985). Stark inequalities in ownership of, and access to, cultural and economic resources create a line of power between the oppressed and oppressors in which biophiliac and necrophilic tendencies can be discerned operating at societal and institutional levels as well in everyday encounters. Real freedom depends on the oppressed obtaining power and resources that have been withheld or denied to them in the current order. Expanding freedom requires breaking with—mentally and organisationally—oppressive and alienating social practices in a way that confronts dominant power and creates 'counter-power'. Thus, Freire offers a layered conception of freedom as a basic human capacity and need and as a historical practice based on collective solidarity. Notably, it is assumed that individual freedom is served through finding common cause with others. Emancipation is the recovery of inalienable human powers which leads to the *emergence* of new practices, ideas and values. In this respect there is a stronger emphasis on freedom 'to' than Mezirow and this is articulated explicitly within a radical conception of what it means to make history from 'below' (Freire, 1972; Freire & Macedo, 1987; Freire et al., 1985).

For readers unfamiliar with the history of left-wing movements and cosmologies, the vision underpinning these arguments may not yet be entirely clear. It can be concretised by turning to Freire's notion of *conscientisation*. This—the process of becoming critically aware and more agentic—according to Freire (1972), begins with dialogue and the exploration of shared problems and 'limit situations', that inhibit and block freedom and human flourishing. Such inquiry can lead to seek the reasons behind things—to make an epistemic break with the 'givenness' of the world—and to reconstruct our experience and assumptions in order to overcome limits and act for freedom. The similarities to Mezirow's conception of transformative are deep and not at all accidental. But Freire is explicit that the most important barrier to development is the way society is organised. We internalise social structures, according to Freire (1970, 1972) but external social relations are conceived as prior and distinct from reflexive agency. It follows that conscientisation depends on: 1) developing adequate socio-historical explanations of the genesis and reproduction of power structures; 2) identifying how limits on freedom

4 'Freedom Is a Very Fine Thing': Individual and Collective... 51

and equality lead to unnecessary suffering; 3) discovering immanent sources of collective agency with; 4) the explicit aim of the transforming structures. Consequently, Freire is far more concerned than Mezirow with the mediating value of political knowledge in 'naming our world' inside and outside adult education. Ultimately, *freedom depends on the work of emancipatory social movements* for the elaboration of analyses, stories, symbols, events and modes of action—organisational repertoires of resistance—to create and support political cultures which valorise certain ways of feeling, being and acting as emancipatory.

Freire sees freedom as ontologically basic, always social, primarily collective and advanced through social movements. These various foci lead Freire to a stronger concern with the emergence of new social practices which allow us to name, imagine, and act in emancipatory ways.

Beyond an 'Either/or' Approach to Emancipation

Reading Mezirow through Freire, we can see clear limitations in the way emancipation is understood in relation to how social structures enable and constrain various forms of autonomy. For example, one could mention Mezirow's discussion of issues of employment in *Transformative dimensions of adult learning* (Mezirow, 1991) or the way he approaches ethnocentrism (Mezirow, 2007) which he treats as questions of experience and belief with very little analysis of social structures. Freire's stress on the centrality of mass creativity and movements in advancing freedom also makes it clear what is missing from Mezirow's account and just how truncated and linear Mezirow's 'line of emancipation' is as well as shedding light on the problem with 'decoupling' questions of individual and collective emancipation.

On the other hand, when we read Mezirow against Freire we see other problems. Freire subsumes, and to a large extent disregards, distinct and important aspects of individual autonomy and biographical change in his theory. Along with this is a consistent exaggeration of the political and collective dimensions of freedom. There are innumerable phenomena—

vital to adult education and a flourishing life—which require deep critical reflection, which are in some respects political but are poorly grasped if treated primarily in terms of social power. For example, if we think about grief and bereavement or coping with serious illness of oneself or a loved one or the effect of living in a new country these experiences are often deeply transformative but served badly if placed on the grand stage of history. Can we say all these efforts to live in a more emancipatory way are marginal? I think not and my research (Finnegan, Merrill, & Thunborg, 2014; Fleming, Loxley, & Finnegan, 2017), mainly with non-traditional students in higher education, indicates that something akin to 'subjective reframing', often linked to major life transitions, leading to more integrated and inclusive ways of thinking and acting is a major phenomenon for which we need concepts and theories to effectively understand and foster.

Mezirow and Freire sensitise us to different forms of emancipation but for empirical and theoretical reason, I believe we need to build bridges between them. I think this requires an inclusive conception of freedom which builds on the distinct insights of Mezirow of Freire but also offers a clear normative and analytical framework for thinking *across* these approaches.

In some ways developing a conception of freedom drawing on Mezirow and Freire should be relatively straightforward. After all there are shared 'stem cell' ideas at the very heart of their work: both see emancipatory learning as emerging through egalitarian dialogue about limits and dilemmas encountered through lived experience and through enhancing reflexive agency. So why is this done so infrequently in a way that also acknowledges the very real differences between them? This is, I think and was mentioned earlier, because dichotomous ways of thinking about the individual and society are so deeply embedded in science, politics and everyday life. To address this fully we need to look beyond Freire and Mezirow and draw on theoretical resources 'external' to adult education which explicitly seek to address this problem of 'either/or' thinking. I want to turn to Roy Bhaskar's (1979, 2011) careful work on emancipatory knowledge and the Greek philosopher Cornelius Castoriadis' work on autonomy (Castoriadis, 1987, 1991) who both seek to theorise emancipation in a less 'one-sided' way.

This is not the place to offer an overview of each of these thinkers. Rather, I want to selectively draw on specific concepts in order to redescribe emancipatory transformative learning in a way that we can 'hold'

4 'Freedom Is a Very Fine Thing': Individual and Collective... 53

the insights of Freire and Mezirow together and also addresses some of the gaps identified in the critical review of their ideas. First, we can say with Bhaskar (2011) that emancipation is the movement from *unwanted to wanted determinations* in support of a flourishing life. This formulation overcomes the simplifying and flattening effect of a theory of freedom which stresses overcoming constraint over the importance of emergence, and vice versa. Second, and here we are not going beyond Mezirow and Freire at all in saying this, emancipation is a learning process in which we, as individual subjects, organisations or movements, become more *reflexively agentic*. The practice of critical reflexivity, vested in and towards freedom, entails a commitment to rational inquiry (Castoriadis, 1987) which leads to 'a stronger sense of being free, namely as knowing and possessing the power and disposition to act in or towards one's real interests' (Bhaskar, 2011, p. 178). Third, this allows one to elaborate *projects of autonomy*, which allow one to 'escape from the servitude of repetition, to reflect about oneself, about the reasons of one's thoughts and the motives of one's actions, guided by the intention of truth and the elucidation of one's desire' (Castoriadis, 1991, p. 165). Crucially, projects of autonomy are multiple in scale and direction and we should not, argues Castoriadis (1991, p. 165), dichotomise between the lucid and self-aware collective work needed to build a truly participatory society—a reflexive democracy—or the 'radical imagination of the singular human being as source of creation and alteration and allows this being to attain an effective freedom'.

In developing this sketch a little further, I want to turn to the intriguing proposal of Gregory Bateson (2000) who maintained that the most useful ways of differentiating between types of learning is the degree and extent to which a given type of learning is reflexive. If we approach Bateson's proposal historically and sociologically, the question becomes how reflexive learning and projects of autonomy maintain and/or transform human culture in emancipatory ways (Engeström, 1987). Logically this entails differentiating and evaluating learning processes according to and the extent to which various modes of reflexive activity enhance autonomy and allow us to reorganise social practices in an emancipatory way. More precisely, we need to look at: (1) scope and intensity of varied modes of reflexive agency; (2) the depth of the social structures that reflexive agency seeks to act upon; (3) the extent to which this activity supports the creation of practices and institutions which are emancipatory and that can endure over time.

Within this framework, Mezirow's theory offers a way of thinking about how adult education can enhance reflexivity in a way that connects very directly with everyday challenges and transitions. It responds to the imperative to act and make sense of the world on a biographical level. It is 'narrow' in scope but effectively describes and supports deep personal change which is capable of altering the terms under which a person acts and interprets social relations. It also—through Mezirow's account of the layered and complex nature of knowledge domains—alerts us to how everyday collaboration and communication at work, via social media and in the family creates possibilities for emancipatory reflexive agency. This type of activity is crucial for developing a reflexive democracy (Honneth, 2011). Freire envisages reflexive agency in a collective and historical way— so he is concerned with broader scope and activity of varying intensities— and aims to transforms social structures and create new institutions. Without this explicitly political and movement orientated notion of emancipation, efforts to create a reflexive democracy will inevitably falter and fail. Contributing to, and linking with, emancipatory movements, to misquote Sartre, remains an 'unsurpassable horizon' for transformative educators and while we should certainly not seek to subordinate biographical exploration to political projects of autonomy we obviously cannot decouple questions of emancipation from questions of political power and participation and the issues of social recognition and redistribution.

From this perspective one of the main tasks of critical, educational research is to trace how collective forms of emancipatory activity are dialectically related to, or disconnected from, individuals' experiences of autonomy and freedom, including on a 'everyday' non-political level, and how this informs, or should inform learning and education (see also Alhadeff-Jones, 2017). This cannot be explored if we cleave to dualistic either/or thinking about individuals and society. Emancipation cannot, and should not, be traced in one direction as both Mezirow and Freire claim from different perspectives: the pulse of freedom can move from the questioning individual through to groups, movements and institutions; it can also be generated within movements and alternative institutions as spaces of transformative learning in which freedom is expanded but which individuals often pass through without experiencing transformative learning as individuals. It can be supported through large-scale existing institutions which have learnt, in small and large matters, to be reflexive and democratic; and it can be elaborated in quite temporary ways in brief shared situations which leave only small but important residues. As is more commonly pointed out, and experienced on a daily basis there are also obvious conflicts and contradictions between projects of collective and individual autonomy. To make sense of this complexity is a matter of empirical research and practical experiment. The challenge, I think, is to develop a theory and practice of adult education, which is sensitive to the diversity and range of projects of autonomy but which remains strongly cognisant of the socio-political conditions for advancing freedom.

References

Alhadeff-Jones, M. (2017). *Time and the rhythms of emancipatory education: Rethinking the temporal complexity of self and society.* London: Routledge.

Bateson, G. (2000). *Steps to an ecology of mind.* Chicago: University of Chicago Press.

Bhaskar, R. (1979). *The possibility of naturalism: A philosophical critique of the contemporary human sciences.* Atlantic Highlands, NJ: Humanities Press.

Bhaskar, R. (2011). *Reclaiming reality: A critical introduction to contemporary philosophy.* London: Routledge.

Castoriadis, C. (1987). *The imaginary institution of society.* Cambridge, MA: MIT Press.

Castoriadis, C. (1991). *Philosophy, politics, autonomy.* Oxford: Oxford University Press.

Cranton, P., & Taylor, E. (2012). Transformative learning theory: Seeking a more unified theory. In E. W. Taylor & P. Cranton (Eds.), *The handbook of transformative learning: Theory, research, and practice* (pp. 3–20). San Francisco, CA: Jossey-Bass.

Cunningham, P. M. (1998). The social dimension of transformative learning. *PAACE Journal of Lifelong Learning, 7,* 15–12.

Engeström, Y. (1987). *Learning by expanding: An activity-theoretical approach to developmental research*. Orienta-Konsultit: Helsinki.

Fleming, T. (2016). Reclaiming the emancipatory potential of adult education: Honneth's critical theory and the struggle for recognition. *European Journal for Research on the Education and Learning of Adults, 7*(1), 13–24.

Fleming, T., Loxley, A., & Finnegan, F. (2017). *Access and participation in Irish Higher Education*. London: Palgrave Macmillan.

Freire, P. (1970). *Cultural action for freedom*. Cambridge, MA: Harvard Educational Review.

Freire, P. (1972). *Pedagogy of the oppressed*. Harmondsworth: Penguin.

Freire, P. (1998). *Pedagogy of freedom: Ethics, democracy, and civic courage*. Lanham: Rowman and Littlefield.

Freire, P., Giroux, H. A., & Macedo, D. P. (1985). *The politics of education: Culture, power, and liberation*. New York: Bergin and Garvey.

Freire, P., & Macedo, D. P. (1987). *Literacy: Reading the word and the world*. London: Routledge and Kegan Paul.

Freire, P., & Shor, I. (1987). *A pedagogy for liberation: Dialogues on transforming education*. Westport, CT: Bergin and Garvey.

Hart, M. (1990). Critical theory and beyond: Further perspectives on emancipatory education. *Adult Education Quarterly, 40*, 125–138.

Hoggan, C. (2016). Transformative learning as a metatheory: Definition, criteria, and typology. *Adult Education Quarterly, 66*, 57–75.

Finnegan, F., Merrill, B., & Thunborg, C. (Eds.). (2014). *Student voices on inequalities in European higher education: Challenges for policy and practice in a time of change*. London: Routledge.

Honneth, A. (2011). *Freedom's right: The social foundations of democratic life*. Cambridge: Polity Press.

Hoggan, C., Mällki, K., & Finnegan, F. (2017). Developing the theory of perspective transformation: Continuity, intersubjectivity, and emancipatory praxis. *Adult Education Quarterly, 67*, 48–64.

Inglis, T. (1997). Empowerment and emancipation. *Adult Education Quarterly, 48*, 1–15.

Mezirow, J. (1981). A critical theory of adult learning and education. *Adult Education Quarterly, 32*, 3–24.

Mezirow, J. (1990). Toward transformative learning and emancipatory education. In J. Mezirow & Associates (Eds.), *Fostering critical reflection in adulthood* (pp. 354–375). San Francisco: Jossey-Bass.

Mezirow, J. (1991). *Transformative dimensions of adult learning*. San Francisco: Jossey-Bass.

Mezirow, J. (2000). Learning to think like an adult. In J. Mezirow & Associates (Eds.), *Learning as transformation: Critical perspectives on a theory in Progress* (pp. 3–33). San Francisco: Jossey-Bass.

Mezirow, J. (2007). Adult education and empowerment for individual and community development. In B. Connolly, T. Fleming, D. McCormack, & A. Ryan (Eds.), *Radical Learning for Liberation 2* (pp. 10–17). Maynooth: MACE.

Newman, M. (2012). Calling transformative learning into question: Some mutinous thoughts. *Adult Education Quarterly, 62*, 36–55.

5

Coming to Grips with Edge-Emotions: The Gateway to Critical Reflection and Transformative Learning

Kaisu Mälkki

Introduction

Critical reflection—becoming aware of and critically assessing taken-for-granted assumptions—lies at the heart of Mezirow's (1981, 1991, 2000, 2009) transformative learning theory that aims to foster the development of adequate and reliable knowledge in a world of continuous change. While decades have passed since Mezirow's original publications, the theory has not lost its relevance. Quite the contrary, during times of turbulence, disinformation, challenges to democracy and continuous changes in societal structures, critical reflection is vital. Furthermore, the complexity of societal and individual problems brings new kinds of pressure to continuously learn, broaden our meaning perspectives, solve complex problems and tolerate and live with ambiguity and contradictory information (see Hämäläinen, 2014; Raami, 2019).

In the twenty-first century, this theory needs to involve a conceptual understanding of the process of critical reflection and its actualities,

K. Mälkki (✉)
Tampere University, Tampere, Finland
e-mail: kaisu.malkki@uta.fi

© The Author(s) 2019
T. Fleming et al. (eds.), *European Perspectives on Transformation Theory*,
https://doi.org/10.1007/978-3-030-19159-7_5

prerequisites, challenges and how to deal with these (see also Illeris, 2007; Mälkki, 2010, 2011). The theory of edge-emotions can offer such a perspective. It was originally developed as a response to the question of what would make reflection difficult and how we could better foster reflection, both in our personal efforts and as practitioners aiming to foster critical reflection in education (Mälkki, 2010, 2011; Mälkki & Green, 2016).

The theory is based on both theoretical and empirical analyses of what I call edge-emotions (see Mälkki, 2011), those unpleasant emotions that arise when our assumptions are being challenged. Its theoretical roots lie in Mezirow's (e.g., 1981, 1991, 2000) theory of transformative learning and Damasio's (1999, 2010) theory of consciousness and emotions (see Mälkki, 2010, 2011). In short, the theory of edge-emotions depicts the resistance to reflection as deeply rooted in the biology of emotions and cognitive functions acting together in favour of self-preservation. When our assumptions are challenged, the coherence-producing mechanism of our cognitive functions is threatened, in turn arousing unpleasant emotions, such as fear, anxiety or anger. These emotions also prime us for action to restore our sense of comfort and security. This mechanism is manifested in our orientation towards staying within our comfort zones, for example, by interpreting the situation in a way that no longer appears threatening, blaming others, rationalising it or withdrawing from the interaction. There are multiple avoidant reactions to being confronted with the realisation of our invalid assumptions. To overcome this biologically rooted and culturally supported inhibition regarding the transformation of our mindsets, I argue that we need to learn to embrace edge-emotions, consciously elaborate on them and even harness them to develop our meaning perspectives.

In this chapter, I focus on how to harness edge-emotions in support of critical reflection. Edge-emotions form critical thresholds for developing our ability to critically reflect. First, I situate the theory of edge-emotions in relation to Mezirow's transformative learning theory and the research field more generally. Second, I elaborate the theory by illustrating the challenges in recognising them and how to overcome these challenges. Finally, I consider how we can train ourselves in practice to harness edge-emotions in developing critical reflection.

Situating Edge-Emotions in Relation to Transformative Learning Theory and Beyond

Mezirow's work has offered us concepts to think about and to understand adult learning processes, in terms of how we may learn to critically reflect on 'the lenses we use to filter, engage and interpret the world' (Belenky & Stanton, 2000, p. 71) in the quest for more valid knowledge in changing circumstances (Mezirow, 2000).

Mezirow's theory conceptualises critical reflection from the rational and cognitive perspective, within a frame of a broader adult education theory. As noted by scholars (Clark & Wilson, 1991; Illeris, 2004; Jokikokko, 2009; Mezirow, 2009; Newman, 2012; Yorks & Kasl, 2002), this focus has limitations. In the scholarly discussion on Mezirow's theory, the role of emotions has been explored through empirical research (see, Mälkki, 2012; Taylor, 2007; Walker & Palacios, 2016). However, relatively little work has led to theoretical development regarding the emotional dimension (see Dirkx, 2008; Jordi, 2011; Mälkki, 2010; Taylor, 2007; Yorks & Kasl, 2002). Mezirow's depiction of the rational aspects of the critical reflection process can be considered useful in increasing our understanding of the ideal process. Furthermore, Mezirow's theory describes the basic elements of the process that allows us to recognise it *when* it occurs. To foster reflection also where it does not easily occur, whether in our personal or educational practices, we need to understand the dynamics that make reflection challenging in the first place (see Illeris, 2007; Mälkki, 2010). This is where the theory of edge-emotions becomes relevant and indicates how the integration between cognition and emotion, proposed by neurobiologists (e.g., Damasio, 1999), occurs in transformative learning processes.

To understand the nature of the theory of edge-emotions, it is useful to delineate its interfaces with other constructs from different research paradigms. First, edge-emotions may be viewed as situating the praxis of critical reflection between the practices of mindfulness and critical thinking, involving a particular balance between non-judgemental and judgemental processes. Bringing together these two processes is also an aspect of critical contemplative pedagogy (see Kaufman, 2017). The theory of edge-emotions focuses on biological and emotional perspectives on what makes these processes challenging to acquire and how to acquire them.

Siegel's (e.g., Siegel, 2010, 2012) concept of the 'window of tolerance' is similar to the comfort zone concept that I use in the theory of edge-emotions. Siegel considers the biological survival mechanisms and the ways of using different strategies to broaden our window of tolerance and return to or remain in the comfort zone where our nervous system's arousal level is neither too high nor too low. In contrast with Siegel's work, the theory of edge-emotions is not primarily concerned with the context of trauma but with the micro-traumas of everyday life. In this case, being drawn out of the comfort zone not only poses a challenge to human functioning but is also (when dealt with delicately) a vital resource for learning, development and transformation of social practices.

Damasio has developed educational applications based on his neurobiological research (Immordino-Yang & Damasio, 2007). This work brings an understanding of the interrelation between cognition and emotions regarding educational processes, such as memory, decision making, creativity and rational thinking. The theory of edge-emotions is based on Damasio's (1999, 2010) understanding of the intertwined nature of emotion and cognition and the role of emotions in assuring basic functioning and survival. Additionally, the theory focuses on *everyday threats to the functions of our meaning perspectives* and how we can learn to transform these challenges into learning events. Furthermore, Festinger's (1957) theory of cognitive dissonance bears many similarities to the theory of edge-emotions.

Dynamics of Edge-Emotions

Edge-emotions indicate how our thinking processes are naturally inhibited by the dynamics of our basic psychological needs and biologically based emotions (Mälkki, 2010, 2011). When our meaning perspectives

5 Coming to Grips with Edge-Emotions: The Gateway to Critical... 63

are questioned (e.g., something or someone questions our assumptions or sense of being accepted), unpleasant edge-emotions arise. These emotions are rooted in the biology of emotions, functioning in favour of survival. They orient us back towards our comfort zones where we can avoid the threat to our meaning perspectives. When our assumptions are questioned, our immediate return to our comfort zones is possible by interpreting the situation in a way that no longer appears threatening (i.e., emotions orient our cognitive functions). This protective/defensive reaction can produce serious obstacles to learning, development and critical reflection or responding pedagogically, in the case of teaching. To overcome this natural inhibition regarding the transformation of our mindsets, we can learn to embrace, be with and disentangle our edge-emotions. Indeed, edge-emotions can be perceived as forming a gateway to developing our meaning perspectives.

Our assumptions are formed in social interactions in specific cultural settings (Mezirow, 1991). We tend to feel accepted and validated by those who share our assumptions. Thus, when we intervene with our assumptions, we also intervene with our social acceptance and face the risk of cultural suicide (Brookfield, 1994). Questioning conventional assumptions poses the risk of exclusion from the culture that has defined and sustained us until that point. I argue that collective comfort zones (Mälkki, 2011; Mälkki & Green, 2016) support the maintenance of shared assumptions and social structures. A supportive and critically reflective social group may offer significant support for our personal reflections. In an unreflective social group, our personal reflections may face extra challenges, along with the risk of cultural suicide.

In the following sections, I focus on the individual dimensions of critical reflection. Even though individual meaning perspectives and individual practices of reflection are constructed in social and cultural contexts. These social origins of assumptions bring the entanglement of individual and social dimensions into the heart of critical reflection (Mezirow, 1981).

Transient Nature of Edge-Emotions

Edge-emotions offer both a tool to transform our meaning perspectives and a gateway to the knowledge that is inaccessible from our current meaning perspectives. However, it is often challenging to recognise and utilise edge-emotions because they are transient by nature. Usually, we can automatically get rid of experiencing edge-emotions before even noticing that we have experienced them. This is due to the biological function of emotions (as the backdrop of everyday living) that takes care of our survival. Now I describe the survival mechanism of emotions regarding physical activity.

Since emotions function to keep us alive (Damasio, 1999, 2010), they are oriented towards informing us of danger or safety and guiding our actions in the direction of self-preservation. On the bodily level, we automatically gather information through our senses, whether the environment is dangerous or safe. If something alarming appears, our bodies register it, and we start feeling uncomfortable. If we perceive a direct threat, our emotions immediately mobilise us for action, without conscious awareness or deliberation. If we have an intuition about a harmful indirect or a more indirect hunch of things not being right, we start feeling uncomfortable, and our attention is directed to inquire further about the phenomenon—whether a smell, a sound or a feeling of something risky. This delicate mechanism monitors our safety even when we are concentrating on other matters (Damasio, 1999).

When our meaning perspectives are questioned, the coherence-producing mechanism of our minds is interrupted. We are no longer able to interpret the situation based on our previous experiences. Instead of just one set of assumptions being questioned, this case brings us the *experience* that our basic sense of control (i.e., our ability to survive and manage) is being questioned. Similarly, a person traumatised by being bitten by a dog may be excessively scared of any dog or place that reminds one of the original overwhelming experience. Our minds tend to overreact when facing threats to our mental functions. When we have not acquired a more delicate vocabulary to understand our bodily signals, our bodies need to inform us in clumsy terms. Let us examine these dynamics more closely.

5 Coming to Grips with Edge-Emotions: The Gateway to Critical... 65

Our ability to make judgements concerning our safety may be viewed as developing along with practical experience; our environment provides concrete feedback about our ability to make adequate judgements. For example, an experienced hiker may have a more developed sense of the threats in a forest, whereas an inexperienced hiker may easily overreact to unexpected noise or risk one's life without knowing it. We practise our ability to distinguish *between the experience of a threat and the actual nature and seriousness of the threat.*

Similarly, we can learn to develop our ability to distinguish between our *experience* and the *nature* of a threat *to our meaning perspectives.* An added complexity stems from the issue that the mind's functions are the objects of the threat; at the same time, they should work critically and creatively on the dilemma. Specifically, edge-emotions automatically orient our cognitive functions, for example, by skewing our perception or interpretation (Mälkki, 2010, 2011). *Thus, we may get rid of the experience of a threat and return to our comfort zones before even having the time to consciously notice the threat's existence.*

Automatically returning to our comfort zones allows us to feel secure again but we may not gain an understanding of the nature of the threat. We do not recognise *what* has been challenged, precluding any critical reflection on our assumptions as well. We then resort to our habitual cognitive tools at hand, allowing us to return to our comfort zones. In other words, we may rationalise, blame others or ourselves, avoid the situation or even meditate—whatever has become part of our implicit toolkit.

When automatically returning to our comfort zones, we do not develop skills to discern between mild, constructive threats and severe, overwhelming ones. Without such skills, we tend to react to any kind of threat as if our existence or the integrity of our minds is at stake, or questioning our assumptions that bind us to like-minded people would signify that we are being abandoned. Thus, we tend to avoid dealing with the issue, rationalise it or one-sidedly blame others (or ourselves) so as to preserve our sense of coherence (Mälkki, 2010, 2011).

Urge to Act as an Indicator of Edge-Emotions

Edge-emotions offer us *signals of threats* to the functions of our meaning perspectives. Consequently, the surfacing of edge-emotions could point to the assumptions that are being questioned. However, as described, we may not always be aware of these emotions.

Edge-emotions mobilise us for action because they *feel* unpleasant as part of our survival instinct (see Damasio, 1999) and push us back to our comfort zones. This push can be experienced not merely as a quickly emerging readiness for action but also an *urge to act*.

Imagine yourself receiving an email with a mistaken interpretation of your earlier constructive response; what is your experience? Do you calmly read the text and peacefully think that the sender has misunderstood your message and is now considering you indiscreet, without any real basis? Alternatively, are you immediately filled with energy, experiencing an accelerated heart rate, shallow breathing and flushed cheeks, as if you need to defend yourself at this moment? These cases indicate how our cognitive functions are entangled with the mechanisms of self-preservation. Our cognitive 'actions' become our tools to return to our comfort zones when our meaning perspectives are challenged (see Mälkki, 2011). We are filled with an urge to act concretely, verbally or mentally. We feel forced to define and resolve the situation or change our perception. We no longer ponder on alternatives; instead, matters appear certain or self-evident, as if there is no need or space for considering them anymore. *Although the situation is not carefully considered, we feel as if it were.* In these cases, we often end up with habitual responses, provided by our previous experiences and customary, taken-for-granted assumptions.

The urge to act turns our focus to solving a situation in readily available ways. The unpleasant experience becomes the background, self-evidently present, forming the jump-off point, but not the focus of our attention. We primarily want to *resolve* the issue by returning to our comfort zones, rather than making the effort to understand the nature of the threat. Returning to our comfort zones is often taken as *the solution* to the original problem or challenging situation, merely because it relieves the distress involving edge-emotions. Thus, the ideal or intention of starting to critically reassess our premises in order to form a deeper understanding of both the situation and our assumptions (that turn out to be limited) appears to be set aside as the function of self-preservation kicks in. To exaggerate, if we feel ourselves airborne, we understandably look for a safe place to land, rather than wondering what caused us to fly. We can learn to deal with these urges and intentions in a way that makes critical reflection possible. Our understanding of the nature of edge-emotions and how they tend to steer our cognitive functions, as described, may be quite helpful. The more we understand the nature of these processes, the less confined we may be by them; we may find ways to work with them and even purposefully utilise them in our learning, which is discussed next.

Training in the Anaerobic Threshold of the Mind

So far, I have portrayed the ability to come to grips with edge-emotions as a skill that we can practise. I have earlier suggested that in the Western culture, we do not usually learn to discern between the nature and the experience of the threat, as we may be able to do with some physical threats. Such limitation leaves us susceptible to either overreacting or underreacting, without the ability to develop our skills to discern the nature of the threat, along with increasing experience. Compared with physical exercise, an example of overreacting would be quitting all activity as soon as we feel any sensation in our muscles or our heart rate accelerates. On the other hand, we could be entirely inattentive to any physical pain and push forward too far by injuring our muscles and tissues. Between these two extremes lies an intermediate phase where training may be efficient in the context of sensitivity. Sensitive awareness of different sensations, while some may be unpleasant, is a vital tool for an athlete. Edge-emotions impose a similar requirement to tolerate some discomfort, while keeping up our sensitivity to what we can bear and utilise and what the discomfort signals to us.

When we start practising to recognise and deal with edge-emotions, it is often easiest to first explore a situation where upon reviewing the incident, we can easily distinguish that our reaction might have been induced by edge-emotions. We locate a situation where we thought that most of the alternatives had been depleted, with just one or two left that felt pressing at the time. From these instances, with the help of our conceptual understanding of the dynamics of edge-emotions, we may practise to disentangle the emotional aspect, the urge to act, and the orientation towards staying in our comfort zones. As we perform this kind of analysis of the previous situation with the frame of the theoretical understanding of edge-emotions, the analysis becomes more natural to us. Thus, we may learn to conduct this kind of analysis *while* in our comfort zones, aided by newly emerging habitual ways of thinking.

As it becomes more familiar and normal for us to approach situations and our reactions, the more it is possible to transfer this type of approach to situations where edge-emotions occur. First, we may practise with situations where, we can anticipate that something challenging may emerge for us, and we may locate the directions from which the potential 'threat' may arise. After this kind of practice becomes easier for us, it may be easier to practise having the perception of edge-emotions turned on as a natural part of our everyday or professional practice. The understanding of edge-emotions can become part of our everyday emotional vocabulary. Thereby, we could open up a gateway to learn more about the situation in which we find ourselves (where our meaning perspectives are challenged), in terms of both the assumptions that brought us there and the experiences that were impossible to make sense of from the perspective of these assumptions.

Approaches to Edge-Emotions

To sum up, there are roughly four ways that we may respond to a case where edge-emotions have emerged. These are all necessary and useful parts of the range of our human responses, but it is useful to distinguish among them and thereby be more aware about using them in different situations.

First, we may let our focus shift towards finding solutions so that we may return to our comfort zones. Thus, we tend to try to resolve the issue

5 Coming to Grips with Edge-Emotions: The Gateway to Critical...

at hand in ways that we commonly attempt to settle similar ones, for example, by blaming others, avoiding dealing with the issue, simplifying it and so on.

Second, we may use the discomfort of edge-emotions only as a mechanical signal of the direction where we could extend our comfort zones. In other words, we may forcefully push *against* our unpleasant feelings and internal resistance, without maintaining the connection to feeling the emotion. In this way, we risk overruling our emotions, thus losing their information potential. We may be able to act in novel ways or even push ourselves into landscapes of meaning where we have not been before. However, it does not necessarily allow integrating our new understanding with our existing knowledge (see Mezirow, 2000). Furthermore, it may not strengthen our ability to comfortably and sensitively navigate the edges of our comfort zones later on. Rather, it can be viewed as pushing us towards an increased disconnection from our emotions, as if propelling us to induce trauma (see, e.g., Greenberg & Paivio, 2003; Grossman, 2004). However, it is useful to understand the possibility or the risk of this kind of artificial shortcut, since it may feel easier to mechanically push directly against the feeling of unpleasantness, as if bulldozing it away, rather than try to *be relaxed with, feel oneself having the urge to act* (without acting according to it).

The third approach to edge-emotions is that of mindfulness. This would allow us to perceive and attend to our emotions, fostering our connection to them and grounding us to a more relaxed bodily state, out of the state of alarm (see Bengtsson, 2013; Ergas, 2015). However, without the intent to discern them and engage in critical reflection, we can neither increase our awareness of the questioned assumptions nor relate our revision processes to our environment. Thus, the actual obstacles or skewed structures may not become visible to us; consequently, our ability to take action based on our learning remains limited.

The fourth way to respond to edge-emotions entails embracing them as signals. Specifically, they offer us access to knowledge that we could not perceive from our existing meaning perspectives. As described earlier, this approach involves discerning edge-emotions and exploring our taken-for-granted assumptions by first noticing our emotional experience in the situation. *An important aspect here is to recognise and linger on the urge to act, which allows us to gently reframe and let go of these urges while attending to the questioned issues.* Although edge-emotions may appear in the situation as a redundant nuisance, embracing them offers us the gateway to critically reflect on our assumptions.

Conclusions

In this paper, I have offered an understanding of the dynamics of edge-emotions and suggested ways in which we can learn to harness edge-emotions. The ability to consciously elaborate on edge-emotions may be perceived as a prerequisite for optimal functioning in our complex environments. Our 'human animal'[1] is equipped with an ability to function optimally in its environment. This ability entails refreshing and updating the accuracy of our meaning frameworks while fostering deepening awareness and understanding of ourselves in relation to our contexts. Without conscious elaboration of edge-emotions, the validity of our critical reflection is diminished.

From the perspective of edge-emotions, unpleasantness as such may not add value to our learning or thinking processes. Rather, the essential issue is to find ways to obtain information from those unpleasant emotions. As I have suggested, recognising and lingering on the urge to act may be significantly helpful in addressing the challenged assumptions.

Edge-emotions tend to escape our awareness. For this reason, we cannot connect to them by pushing; rather, we need to give them space to emerge into our awareness. Our abilities to engage in transformative learning and critical reflection on our taken-for-granted assumptions may be significantly strengthened by gently yet critically harnessing edge-emotions as our guiding friends in our intellectual and psychological development processes.

Note

1. Shayna Hornstein used this term in the workshop that she and Jude Walker conducted at the *Interrogating Transformative Processes in Learning, ESREA Network Conference*, Milan, Italy, June 2018.

References

Belenky, M. F., & Stanton, A. V. (2000). Inequality, development, and connected knowing. In J. Mezirow & Associates (Eds.), *Learning as transformation: Critical perspectives on a theory in progress* (pp. 71–102). San Francisco: Jossey-Bass.

Bengtsson, J. (2013). Embodied experience in educational practice and research. *Studies in Philosophy and Education, 32*(1), 39–53.

Brookfield, S. D. (1994). Tales from the dark side: A phenomenography of adult critical reflection. *International Journal of Lifelong Education, 13*(3), 203–216.

Clark, M. C., & Wilson, A. L. (1991). Context and rationality in Mezirow's theory of transformational learning. *Adult Education Quarterly, 41*(2), 75–91.

Damasio, A. R. (1999). *The feeling of what happens: The body and emotion in the making of consciousness.* New York: Hart Court Brace.

Damasio, A. R. (2010). *Self comes to mind. Constructing the conscious brain.* New York: Pantheon Books.

Dirkx, J. (2008). The meaning and role of emotions in adult learning. *New Directions for Adult and Continuing Education, 120*, 7–18.

Ergas, O. (2015). The deeper teachings of mindfulness-based curricular interventions as a reconstruction of "education". *Journal of Philosophy of Education, 49*(2), 204–220.

Festinger, L. (1957). *A theory of cognitive dissonance.* Stanford, CA: Stanford University Press.

Greenberg, L. S., & Paivio, S. (2003). *Working with emotions in psychotherapy.* New York: The Guilford Press.

Grossman, D. (2004). *On combat: The psychology and physiology of deadly conflict in war and in peace.* Millstadt: Warrior Science Publications.

Hämäläinen, T. J. (2014). In search of coherence: Sketching a theory of sustainable well-being. In T. J. Hämäläinen & J. Michaelson (Eds.), *Well-being and beyond – Broadening the public and policy discourse.* Cheltenham: Edward Elgar Publishing.

Illeris, K. (2004). Transformative learning in the perspective of a comprehensive learning theory. *Journal of Transformative Education, 2*, 79–89.

Illeris, K. (2007). *How we learn: Learning and non-learning in school and beyond.* London: Routledge.

Immordino-Yang, M. H., & Damasio, A. (2007). We feel, therefore we learn. The relevance of affective and social neuroscience to education. *Mind, Brain and Education, 1*(1), 3–10.

Jokikokko, K. (2009). The role of significant others in the intercultural learning of teachers. *Journal of Research in International Education, 8*(2), 143–164.

Jordi, R. (2011). Reframing the concept of reflection: Consciousness, experiential learning, and reflective learning practices. *Adult Education Quarterly, 61*(2), 181–197.

Kaufman, P. (2017). Critical contemplative pedagogy. *Radical Pedagogy, 14*(1), 1–20.

Mälkki, K. (2010). Building on Mezirow's theory of transformative learning: Theorizing the challenges to reflection. *Journal of Transformative Education, 8*(1), 42–62.

Mälkki, K. (2011). *Theorizing the nature of reflection.* Doctoral dissertation, University of Helsinki, Institute of Behavioural Sciences. Studies in Educational Sciences, 238.

Mälkki, K. (2012). Rethinking disorienting dilemmas within real-life crises: The role of reflection in negotiating emotionally chaotic experiences. *Adult Education Quarterly, 62*, 207–229.

Mälkki, K., & Green, L. (2016). Ground, warmth, and light: Facilitating conditions for reflection and transformative dialogue. *Journal of Educational Issues, 2*(2), 169–183.

Mezirow, J. (1981). A critical theory of adult learning and education. *Adult Education, 32*, 3–24.

Mezirow, J. (1991). *Transformative dimensions of adult learning.* San Francisco: Jossey-Bass.

Mezirow, J. (2000). Learning to think like an adult: Core concepts of transformation theory. In J. Mezirow & Associates (Eds.), *Learning as transformation: Critical perspectives on a theory in progress* (pp. 3–33). San Francisco: Jossey-Bass.

Mezirow, J. (2009). An overview on transformative learning. In K. Illeris (Ed.), *Contemporary theories of learning: Learning theorists in their own words* (pp. 90–105). London: Routledge.

Newman, M. (2012). Calling transformative learning into question: Some mutinous thoughts. *Adult Education Quarterly, 62*, 36–55.

Raami, A. (2019). Toward solving the impossible problems. In J. W. Cook (Ed.), *Sustainability, human well-being and the future of education* (pp. 201–233). London: Palgrave Macmillan.

Siegel, D. J. (2010). *Mindsight: The new science of personal transformation.* New York: Bantam Books.

Siegel, D. J. (2012). *Pocket guide to interpersonal neurobiology: An integrative handbook of the mind.* New York: W. W. Norton.

Taylor, E. W. (2007). An update of transformative learning theory: A critical review of the empirical research (1999–2005). *International Journal of Lifelong Education, 26,* 173–191.

Walker, J., & Palacios, C. (2016). A pedagogy of emotion in teaching about social movement learning. *Teaching in Higher Education, 21*(2), 175–190.

Yorks, L., & Kasl, E. (2002). Toward a theory and practice for whole-person learning: Reconceptualizing experience and the role of affect. *Adult Education Quarterly, 25*(3), 176–192.

6

Theory Development Between Tradition and Innovation: Exploring Systems Thinking Within and Beyond Transformative Learning Theory

Saskia Eschenbacher

Introduction

Transformative Learning Theory develops its self-conception as a *theory in progress* (Mezirow and Associates, 2000). As such it is in need of constant critical reflection about its own premises. Considering this essential feature, it is surprising that the debate on Transformative Learning Theory's premises is partly deficient. Taylor and Cranton identified a "stagnation and lack of theoretical development" (Taylor & Cranton, 2013, p. 35) within Transformative Learning Theory. Following them, "despite the intense interest in this theory, much of the research is redundant, (…) while overlooking the need for more in-depth theoretical analysis" (Cranton & Taylor, 2012, pp. 12–13), an evaluation with which I agree. This dilemma goes along with unresolved issues that derive from the use of various scientific theories and different philosophical underpinnings upon which Transformative Learning Theory is built (humanism, constructivism and critical theory) (e.g., Mezirow, 1991). Constructivist assumptions are shared with systems thinking, a theory

S. Eschenbacher (✉)
Akkon-University of Applied Human Sciences, Berlin, Germany

© The Author(s) 2019
T. Fleming et al. (eds.), *European Perspectives on Transformation Theory*,
https://doi.org/10.1007/978-3-030-19159-7_6

76 S. Eschenbacher

that is inherently tied to the dynamics of change. This chapter is concerned with both, revealing the tradition of systems thinking within Transformative Learning Theory that is barely made explicit by Mezirow (though other scholars have been more reflective about its connectedness to systems thinking) and exploring systems thinking beyond its current embeddedness within the theory in order to foster, what Taylor and Cranton (2013) demand: a more in-depth theoretical analysis of Transformative Learning Theory. In that sense, the innovative character of this chapter is traditional in so far as it aims to go back to the very notion of Mezirow's Transformative Learning Theory and its self-conception as a *theory in progress* (Mezirow and Associates, 2000). Therefore, the chapter explores (1) the embeddedness of systems thinking within Transformative Learning Theory; (2) outlines core concepts of systems thinking regarding the question of how to comprehend and conceptualize change and transformation; and (3) fosters theory development between tradition and innovation, by expanding Transformative Learning Theory through systems thinking.

Systems Thinking Within Transformative Learning Theory

The perspective of systems thinking crystallizes within Transformative Learning Theory in various ways. Daloz reflects one of the benefits of systems thinking for transformative learning regarding the attitude of an adult educator: "A systems perspective provides a valuable inoculation against the illusions of omnipotence endemic to our trade" (Daloz, 1999, p. 183). Instead of solely reflecting on the adult educator he values the *relational* aspect of systems thinking in regard to transformative learning:

> Systems theory thus allows us to see not only how individuals behave but how individuals and environments interact. It reminds us that we must look to complex sets of contingencies that variously affect the developing person. (Daloz, 1999, p. 182)

6 Theory Development Between Tradition and Innovation... 77

Systems thinking aims at making a difference. Daloz translates this core assumption of systems theory in the context of adult education: "How we engage with difference makes all the difference" (Daloz, 2000, p. 112).

Systems thinking is prominent within but not limited to the works of Daloz. Various scholars (Alhadeff-Jones, 2012; Tisdell, 2012; see Swartz & Sprow, 2010, for an overview) refer to complexity science or locate transformative learning explicitly within the context of systems theory (Alhadeff-Jones, 2012). Others work with core concepts of systems thinking: the relational aspect (Lange, 2012), the concept of self-organization (Lange, 2012; Tisdell, 2012) or the theory of *autopoiesis* (Lange, 2012). Lange refers to the transformative dimension of reorganizing or restructuring in comparison to processes of change: "The fundamental deep structure of the organism is changed, not just the surface appearance and not just a developmental evolution of certain elements" (Lange, 2012, p. 202). Lange rethinks the process of perspective transformation regarding the question of change and insistence, which have to be placed on equal footing according to her

> Yet living systems are fluid and responsive, continuously oscillating between habitual and novel patterns. Living systems require stability, and thus patterns of repetition are maintained within a state of dynamic balance. (Lange, 2012, p. 202)

At the same time we learn from Lange, "that at the point of greatest instability lies the greatest potential" (Lange, 2012, p. 203) for deep change and transformation and confirms a disorienting dilemma as a starting point for adult education (Lange, 2012, p. 203).

Tyler and Swartz (2012) locate their narrative approach within the context of systems thinking based on the shared notion of the dynamic of change: "This perspective is chosen because it is inherently tied to the dynamics of change, and transformative learning is about change" (Tyler & Swartz, 2012, p. 455). In a more concrete way, they connect the process of story-telling to basic ideas of systems thinking: "When the system instability forces the old linear narrative to fall apart, the story can re-story itself into a more complex form" (Tyler & Swartz, 2012, p. 465). Tyler and Swartz trace concepts and ideas from the perspective of systems thinking within Transformative Learning Theory or more precisely within Mezirow's Transformation Theory, referring to the impact of cybernetics or the work of Bateson (1972) on his work. The analysis of Swartz and Sprow (2010) shows that between 30 and 40 percent of all submissions for the International Transformative Learning Conference between 1998 and 2009 are related to systems thinking or complexity science. Transformative Learning Theory (Cranton & Taylor, 2012, p. 5) and systems thinking (Simon, Clement, & Stierlin, 2004, p. 185f.) are both based on constructivist assumptions and share several core concepts.

Systems Thinking: Comprehending and Conceptualizing Change and Transformation

The term *system* derives from the Greek word *systema*, describing an entity that consists of several parts or elements. Following older approaches of systems theory, the differentiation between an element or part of the system and the entity itself is crucial. The main focus of attention is on the way the interaction between those different elements is organized. Newer approaches to systems theory follow the differentiation of the system itself and its environment. Their shared interest is in the processes that lead to the distinction between systems and their environments (Simon et al., 2004, p. 324). These systems are described as *autopoietic* (see Maturana & Varela, 1980, 1987), a process through which a living system reproduces itself in differing from its surroundings. These processes are organized in a self-referential way; the components or elements of a living system fashion themselves through a network of processes that is produced by the components of this same living system (Simon et al., 2004, p. 38f.). The inner side of a system is characterized by its complexity reducing mode, which is highly selective: very little information is processed from the outside. Due to the self-referential character of living systems these informations are being processed within the current structure of the system. According to Bateson (1972), an *information* is a difference that makes a difference. It is an event or an experience that makes

6 Theory Development Between Tradition and Innovation...   79

a difference as it leads to a structural reorganization of the system itself, in the sense that it affects change (Simon et al., 2004). Self-referential systems are characterized by the dilemmas of disintegration and continuation. Considering the self-referential character of living systems, the main focus of any context that is associated with the idea of promoting change and or transformation is to gain a more in-depth understanding of what could be considered as an information in the sense of its ability to make a difference. Besides the question of how adult education as a context could contribute to processes of change within individuals (and on a societal level as well), there is a need to translate these ideas in the context of an individual (the adult learner and the adult educator).

Luhmann (2002) suggests differentiating between the organism, the psyche, and the patterns of communication as three autonomous systems that are separate from each other and that constitute environments for each other, regarding individuals (Simon et al., 2004, p. 325). Each system is determined through its inner structures and processes; they are characterized by their *operational closure*—any experience or event is being processed within the existing structure—while surrounding environments limit the freedom of each system. In that sense, an *information* can be described as a phenomenon that is the result of a *perturbation* caused by an environmental incident. If we assume that adult education could or should be an environment that makes a difference for the individual learner, then we have to ask what and how processes of change and transformation can be induced in the best possible way. Regarding Luhmann's differentiation between biological, psychological and communication systems we need to figure out what system we are trying to address as adult educators. Following the assumption that systems are characterized by *operational closure*, the idea of *instructive interaction* or communication becomes obsolete. One of the guiding assumptions of this chapter is that our main business as adult educators is concerned with communication.

The question, therefore, has to be how we as adult educators are able to challenge the intrapersonal communication through interpersonal communication. Changes in one of the systems, in this case the communication system, affect the other two systems, acting as their environments. In that sense, systems theory, or more precisely Luhmann's conceptual model, paves the way for a holistic approach, as not only the psychological dimension is addressed but it is also on equal footing with biological processes (bringing the body back into the process of change and transformation) while our main business as adult educators is the communicative dimension.

Pursuing that line of thought, systems thinking could be helpful if it offers us an opportunity to gain a deeper understanding of how interpersonal communicative processes can challenge intrapersonal communicative patterns. This question can then be translated into the context of adult education by asking how we as adult educators can create reasonable, more advantageous environments for communicative processes that increase the space for exploring alternative options. This thought can be attached to the question of what the interaction between an individual (learner) and an environment (adult education) should look like, if we aim at increasing the likelihood of change and transformation.

Systems theory offers a *relational* way of thinking. It is concerned with the *organization* of the relationships between the different elements that constitute a system, and its *function* in terms of the effect it has. In addition to that, it offers a more in-depth understanding of the *structure*, the whole as a sum of its parts and the relationship between its parts. Systems theory is also concerned with the *process* that describes the changes that the entire system or parts of it go through, their structures and functions over time (Simon et al., 2004, p. 247). Those structures are iterative processes that lead to a stable result. As long as a certain worldview is being confirmed, there is no need for a structural reorganization. This provides us with a deeper understanding of the dynamics that lead to the continuity or transformation of systems over time. In addition to that, we would be able to differentiate between processes of change and processes of transformation. Systems thinking operates from the distinction between first- and second-order change: A system can change or transform itself in two ways: (1) A first-order change can be described as a constant change of single parameters while the structure of the system itself does not change. (2) Second-order change involves the change of the system itself in a discontinuous and qualitative way. The latter is caused by a shift of the system's frame of reference or by an internal reorganization (Simon et al., 2004, p. 348f.). Systems thinking provides an in-depth understanding of the differentiation between change (first-order change) and transformation (second-order change). In addition to that, it offers an explanatory concept of why some systems change while others do not.

Theory Development Between Tradition and Innovation: Expanding Transformative Learning Theory Through Systems Thinking

Transformative learning can be defined as "an approach to teaching based on promoting change", following Mezirow and Taylor ", where educators challenge learners to critically question and assess the integrity of their deeply held assumptions about how they relate to the world around them" (Mezirow & Taylor, 2009, p. xi).

As such, it aims to foster what Mezirow calls a transformation in meaning perspectives:

> Perspective transformation is the process of becoming critically aware of how and why our assumptions have come to constrain the way we perceive, understand, and feel about our world; changing these structures of habitual expectation to make possible a more inclusive, discriminating, and integrative perspective; and, finally making choices or otherwise acting upon these new understandings. (Mezirow, 1991, p. 167)

In order to foster transformation in meaning perspectives one has to gain a deeper understanding of the relations between one's assumptions and one's way of being in the world. In addition to that, Mezirow stresses the importance of becoming critically aware of *how* our assumptions have come to constrain our being in the world. Instead of simply reflecting on the content of one's assumptions, Mezirow suggests reflecting on the aforementioned relationship. He aims at changing the *structures* of one's meaning perspective or *belief system* toward a more inclusive, discriminating and integrative perspective. "He eventually named this process perspective transformation to reflect change within the core or central meaning structures (meaning perspectives) through which we make sense of the day-to-dayness of our experiences" (Dirkx, 1998, p. 4). The structure of the system itself has to undergo a process of change. This transformation or second-order change can be attained by what he describes as a premise reflection: "Premise reflection is the dynamic by which our belief systems—meaning perspectives—become transformed" (Mezirow, 1991, p. 111). The inside *structure* of those belief systems is considered to be more inclusive, discriminating, permeable, and integrative of experience than before (Mezirow, 1991, p. 111).

While Mezirow is very explicit regarding the outcome of a perspective transformation, he is less precise in how to achieve this outcome. He stresses the relational aspect regarding the reasons and consequences that are related to one's habits of judgment (Mezirow, 1991, p. 105). Instead of focusing on how to best solve a problem, he is more concerned with the question of problem posing, which can only be understood by relational means. According to Mezirow, a set of assumptions constitutes a frame of reference or meaning perspective, which reveals the systemic, relational characteristic of Mezirow's notion of Transformative Learning Theory, without referring explicitly to it. Following him, a meaning perspective is constituted by several meaning schemes. A "[p]erspective transformation can occur either through an accretion of transformed meaning schemes resulting from a series of dilemmas or in response to an externally imposed epochal dilemma" (Mezirow, 1991, p. 168). In that sense, systems thinking provides not only an explanatory construct regarding the very idea of a belief system or meaning perspective but offers us an idea of how to change these systems. In order to attain a structural reorganization of the system itself, it is necessary to reflect on the very structure of it, and one needs to externalize this structure first. The idea is to

> *look* at what before it could only *look through*. In other words, our way of knowing becomes more complex when we create a bigger system that incorporates and expands on our previous system. (Kegan & Lahey, 2009, p. 51)

Kegan and Lahey suggest that "to alter our mindset so that a way of knowing or making meaning becomes a kind of 'tool' that *we have* (and can control or use) rather than something that *has us* (and therefore

6 Theory Development Between Tradition and Innovation... 83

controls and uses us)" (Kegan & Lahey, 2009, p. 51). The perspective of systems thinking might expand Transformative Learning Theory by providing a deeper understanding of the circular relation between oneself and one's problem and how to change that structure. Critical reflection on assumptions and critical self-reflection on assumptions, as two central concepts of Transformative Learning Theory (Mezirow, 1990b), both require an idea of the form, the relation between oneself and one's assumptions. In order to achieve a structural reorganization, there needs to be an idea of what the current structure looks like and how it preserves itself in a self-referential way before it can be reformed.

The *autopoietic* character of a meaning perspective or belief system becomes apparent in how Mezirow conceptualizes a belief system, meaning perspective or frame of reference which act as environments for one's being in the world:

> What we perceive and fail to perceive, and what we think and fail to think are powerfully influenced by habits of expectation that constitute our frame of reference, that is, a set of assumptions that structure the way we interpret our experiences. (Mezirow, 1990b, p. 1)

Mezirow describes the process of learning in adulthood from an interactional, relational perspective:

> Learning is a dialectical process of interpretation in which we interact with objects and events, guided by an old set of expectations. Normally, when we learn something, we attribute an old meaning to a new perspective. (…) In transformative learning, however, we reinterpret an old experience (or a new one) from a new set of expectations, thus giving a new meaning and perspective to the old experience. (Mezirow, 1991, p. 11)

Furthermore, he describes how one's old experiences shape and delimit one's being in the world. The concept of *homeostasis* that describes the process by which living systems obtain their structure, which is central to systems thinking, provides an idea of how a belief system is being maintained. Only if a currently employed belief system is no longer able to handle anomalies in a new situation, can a transformation in meaning

84   S. Eschenbacher

perspectives emerge. A process that can be described as a first-order change would not suffice to deal with the current situation: "Adding knowledge, skills, or increasing competencies within the present perspective is no longer functional; creative integration of new experience into one's frame of reference no longer resolves the conflict" (Mezirow, 1978, p. 104). In that case, a structural reorganization is the answer to the question of how to resolve the conflict, by a second-order change or transformation. What systems thinking describes as a structural reorganization or classifies as second-order change is consistent with Brookfield's definition of transformative learning:

> an act of learning can be called transformative only if it involves a fundamental questioning and reordering of how one thinks or acts. If something is transformed, it is different from what it was before at a very basic level. (Brookfield, 2000, p. 139)

This transformation of the internal structure of a system can be seen as a "shift in the tectonic plates of one's assumptive clusters" (Brookfield, 2000, p. 139).

In order to accomplish the task of transforming one's meaning perspective or belief system, the adult learner needs to participate in rational discourse, according to Mezirow, who locates transformative learning within the discourse. He draws on the work of Habermas and his conception of an ideal speech situation, which is "theoretically based, with little support from empirical research" (Taylor, 1997, p. 54). Regarding the fact that Habermas himself says that "[t]he expression 'ideal speech situation' is delusive, insofar as it suggests a concrete form of life" (Habermas, 1985, p. 161), it appears appropriate to search for alternative ways of how to promote transformative learning: "[T]here needs to be continued exploration into the practice of fostering transformative learning, recognizing the limits of promoting ideal practice" (Taylor, 1997, p. 55). One of those alternative ways is offered by systems thinking in providing an idea of how to challenge intrapersonal through interpersonal communication (Eschenbacher, 2017). Staying with this line of thought and the tradition of Transformative Learning Theory at the same time, we can

6 Theory Development Between Tradition and Innovation... 85

focus on how the individual and the (learning) environment interact. As stated in the beginning,

> [s]ystems theory thus allows us to see not only how individuals behave but how individuals and environments interact. It reminds us that we must look to complex sets of contingencies that variously affect the developing person. (Daloz, 1999, p. 182)

Regarding the question what kind of *environment* adult educators should create, we can turn back to the transformative learning literature. Mezirow characterizes adult educators as "social environmentalists and empathic provocateurs" (Mezirow, 1995, p. 60, 1998, p. 60). They should "create protected learning environments" (Mezirow, 2000, p. 31) that are "both supportive and challenging" (Dirkx, 1998, p. 10). Keeping in mind Luhmann's differentiation regarding all three systems, the biological, the psychological, and the one that is concerned with communication and their circular relationship with one and another, it "involves creating a learning environment conducive to whole-person learning; [and, S. E.] working with learners within that environment" (Yorks & Kasl, 2006, p. 51).

The idea of making a difference is not solely located on a metatheoretical level, but is a central theme within transformative learning. According to Mezirow, adult learning is about becoming aware of "how we are caught in our own history and are reliving it" (Mezirow, 1978, p. 101). This raises the question of how this (critical) awareness can be achieved and how a transformation in meaning perspectives or belief systems can be fostered against this background.

> However, learning aimed at changes not only in *what* we know but changes in *how* we know has an almost opposite rhythm about it and comes closer to the etymological meaning of education ('leading out'). 'Informative' learning involves a kind of leading in, or filling of the form .... Trans-*form*-ative learning puts the form itself at risk of change (and not just change but increased capacity). (Kegan, 2000, p. 49)

86   S. Eschenbacher

This idea is tied up with the differentiation between first- and second-order change (Simon et al., 2004, p. 348f.) that is a core theme within systems thinking, and as such it is able to inform and extend Transformative Learning Theory as a theory in general. Furthermore, it allows us to draw a distinction between processes of change and processes of transformation which is clearly needed: Kegan states that the notion of "[t]ransformation begins to refer to any kind of change or process at all" (Kegan, 2000, p. 47). He argues that there is a need to distinguish transformative learning more precisely and clearly from other ways of learning (Kegan, 2000, p. 47). Following Kegan, "[t]ransformation should not refer to just any kind of change, even to any kind of dramatic, consequential change" (Kegan, 2000, p. 49). Brookfield (2000, p. 139) criticizes the "misuse of the word *transformative* to refer to any instance in which reflection leads to a deeper, more nuanced understanding of assumptions".

In addition to the need for being able to distinguish transformative learning more clearly from other forms of learning, we need to broaden our current understanding of transformative learning and the phenomenon of non-learning. Transformative learning or critical thinking is, according to Brookfield, in that respect "not a continuously joyful exercise in creative self-actualization. It is psychologically and politically dangerous, involving risks to one's livelihood, social networks, and psychological stability" (Brookfield, 1990, p. 179). Mezirow is aware of the fact that "one may find transformative learning threatening, exhilarating, and empowering" (Mezirow, 1990a, p. xiii). At the same time, there is a theoretical void regarding the phenomenon of non-learning. The question of how adults learn, develop and change is at the heart of Transformative Learning Theory.

However, there is a need to add another dimension in order to understand processes of change and transformation. This dimension involves the question of the phenomenon of how adults manage not to learn or change, for an illustrating example see "The story of Gladys who refused to grow" (Daloz, 1988). The phenomenon of resistance or even an *immunity to change* (Kegan & Lahey, 2009) is central to our understanding of change and transformation and requires explanation. How can we preserve resistance and stability in an ever changing world? How do people manage not to change over time? How can we learn not to learn,[1] in order

6 Theory Development Between Tradition and Innovation... 87

to preserve those values that are valuable to us? And how can we change these mechanisms when we need to learn and change? According to Mezirow (1991), learning can be either confirmative or transformative. As adult educators our task is to assist learners in gaining curiosity in critically questioning their existing perspectives and paradigms for understanding themselves and the world. We need to develop ways of inviting learners to "leave the mental homes [we] have furnished and made familiar" (Kegan, 1994, p. 272) when adding new knowledge no longer resolves the conflict and processes of change and transformation become necessary. Systems thinking provides a deeper understanding of why some systems change and others do not, regarding their *autopoietic* character and the concept of *homeostasis*. From Lange, we have learned that "living systems are fluid and responsive, continuously oscillating between habitual and novel patterns. Living systems require stability, and thus patterns of repetition are maintained within a state of dynamic balance" (Lange, 2012, p. 202). This perspective broadens our current understanding of transformative learning and the phenomenon of non-learning and offers us an explanatory construct to understand why some adult learners undergo processes of transformation while others do not.

Final Thoughts

Exploring systems thinking within and beyond Mezirow's notion of Transformative Learning Theory is interesting in various ways. As a thought system, Transformative Learning Theory could be considered as a system itself that differentiates from other forms of learning by the way it is tied to deep processes of structural reorganization and transformation. As such, it oscillates between habitual and novel patterns, in this case the embeddedness of systems thinking within Transformative Learning Theory. Exploring the former in the context of the latter corresponds with the theory's self-conception as a *theory in progress* (Mezirow and Associates, 2000). Keeping a living system or theory in a state of dynamic balance, to some extent a state of *homeostasis*, and taking seriously its self-conception (as a *theory in progress*), there is a need to reflect on its premises. In this specific case, exploring systems thinking as a way to comprehend and conceptualize change and transformation, by identifying core concepts that are relevant for Transformative Learning Theory, and searching for ways to expand our current understanding of the theory itself, pay justice to the theory's self-conception. As a theory, transformative learning focuses on freedom, that we are not trapped by one way of looking at the world. Its goal is to create an awareness that there is always another possibility to be explored instead, and thus our way of looking at the world is subject to change. The same also applies to the question of how to promote transformative learning. We are not trapped by fostering transformative learning processes only through rational discourse; instead we can increase the amount of alternative ways to develop transformative learning by further investigating how to challenge intrapersonal communication through interpersonal communication. A new (additional) approach can be added to the theory. Existing structures (or traditions) can be strengthened and new, innovative perspectives can emerge and restructure the theory itself if need be. The distinctive character of transformative dimensions of adult learning can be sharpened by exploring systems thinking within and beyond the theory, while at the same time new phenomena like non-learning can be explored.

Note

1. Fleming (2009, p. 118) refers to Habermas saying we have "an automatic inability not to learn" (Habermas, 1975, p. 15) and states that "[w]e are condemned to learn".

References

Alhadeff-Jones, M. (2012). Transformative learning and the challenges of complexity. In E. W. Taylor & P. Cranton (Eds.), *The handbook of transformative learning: Theory, research, and practice* (pp. 178–194). San Francisco: Jossey-Bass.

Bateson, G. (1972). *Steps to an ecology of mind*. Chicago: University of Chicago Press.

Brookfield, S. D. (1990). Using critical incidents to explore learners' assumptions. In J. Mezirow & Associates (Eds.), *Fostering critical reflection in adulthood: A guide to transformative and emancipatory learning* (pp. 177–193). San Francisco: Jossey-Bass.

Brookfield, S. D. (2000). Transformative learning as ideology critique. In J. Mezirow & Associates (Eds.), *Learning as transformation: Critical perspectives on a theory in progress* (pp. 125–148). San Francisco: Jossey-Bass.

Cranton, P., & Taylor, E. W. (2012). Transformative learning theory. Seeking a more unified theory. In E. W. Taylor & P. Cranton (Eds.), *The handbook of transformative learning: Theory, research, and practice* (pp. 3–20). San Francisco: Jossey-Bass.

Daloz, L. A. P. (1988). The story of Gladys who refused to grow: A morality tale for mentors. *Lifelong Learning, 11*(4), 4–7.

Daloz, L. A. P. (1999). *Mentor: Guiding the journey of adult learners*. San Francisco: Jossey-Bass.

Daloz, L. A. P. (2000). Transformative learning for the common good. In J. Mezirow & Associates (Eds.), *Learning as transformation: Critical perspectives on a theory in progress* (pp. 103–123). San Francisco: Jossey-Bass.

Dirkx, J. M. (1998). Transformative learning theory in the practice of adult education. An overview. *PAACE Journal of Lifelong Learning, 7*, 1–14.

Eschenbacher, S. (2017). Transformative learning theory and systems thinking: Enabling transformation through communication. In A. Laros, T. Fuhr, & E. W. Taylor (Eds.), *Transformative learning meets Bildung: An international exchange* (pp. 141–152). Rotterdam: Sense Publishers.

Fleming, T. (2009). Condemned to learn: Habermas, university and the learning society. In M. Murphy & T. Fleming (Eds.), *Habermas, critical theory and education* (pp. 111–124). New York: Routledge.

Habermas, J. (1975). *Legitimation crisis*. Boston: Beacon Press.

Habermas, J. (1985). *Die neue Unübersichtlichkeit*. Frankfurt am Main: Suhrkamp.

Kegan, R. (1994). *In over our heads: The mental demands of modern life*. Cambridge: Harvard University Press.

Kegan, R. (2000). What "form" transforms? A constructive-developmental approach to transformative learning. In J. Mezirow & Associates (Eds.), *Learning as transformation: Critical perspectives on a theory in progress* (pp. 35–69). San Francisco: Jossey-Bass.

Kegan, R., & Lahey, L. L. (2009). *Immunity to change: How to overcome it and unlock the potential in yourself and your organization*. Boston: Harvard Business Press.

90 S. Eschenbacher

Lange, E. A. (2012). Transforming transformative learning through sustainability and the new science. In E. W. Taylor & P. Cranton (Eds.), *The handbook of transformative learning: Theory, research, and practice* (pp. 195–211). San Francisco: Jossey-Bass.

Luhmann, N. (2002). *Einführung in die Systemtheorie*. Heidelberg: Carl-Auer Systeme Verlag.

Maturana, H., & Varela, F. (1980). *Autopoiesis and cognition*. Boston: Reidel.

Maturana, H., & Varela, F. (1987). *Der Baum der Erkenntnis*. Berlin: Scherz.

Mezirow, J. (1978). Perspective transformation. *Adult Education Quarterly, 28*(2), 100–110.

Mezirow, J. (1990a). Preface. In J. Mezirow & Associates (Eds.), *Fostering critical reflection in adulthood: A guide to transformative and emancipatory learning* (pp. XIII–XXXI). San Francisco: Jossey-Bass.

Mezirow, J. (1990b). How critical reflection triggers transformative learning. In J. Mezirow & Associates (Eds.), *Fostering critical reflection in adulthood: A guide to transformative and emancipatory learning* (pp. 1–20). San Francisco: Jossey-Bass.

Mezirow, J. (1991). *Transformative dimensions of adult learning*. San Francisco: Jossey-Bass.

Mezirow, J. (1995). Transformation theory in adult education. In M. R. Welton (Ed.), *In defense of the lifeworld: Critical perspectives on adult learning* (pp. 39–70). Albany: SUNY.

Mezirow, J. (1998). On critical reflection. *Adult Education Quarterly, 48*(3), 185–198.

Mezirow, J. (2000). Learning to think like an adult: Core concepts of transformation theory. In J. Mezirow & Associates (Eds.), *Learning as transformation: Critical perspectives on a theory in progress* (pp. 3–33). San Francisco: Jossey-Bass.

Mezirow, J., & Associates (Eds.). (2000). *Learning as transformation: Critical perspectives on a theory in progress*. San Francisco: Jossey-Bass.

Mezirow, J., & Taylor, E. W. (2009). Preface. In J. Mezirow & E. W. Taylor (Eds.), *Transformative learning in practice: Insights from community, workplace, and higher education* (pp. XI–XIV). San Francisco: Jossey-Bass.

Simon, F. B., Clement, U., & Stierlin, H. (2004). *Die Sprache der Familientherapie. Ein Vokabular*. Stuttgart: Klett-Cotta.

Swartz, A. L., & Sprow, K. (2010). Is complexity science embedded in transformative learning? In P. Gandy, S. Tieszen, C. Taylor-Hunt, D. Flowers, &

V. Sheared (Eds.), *Proceedings of the 51st adult education research conference* (pp. 461–467). Sacramento: California State University.

Taylor, E. W. (1997). Building upon the theoretical debate. A critical review of the empirical studies of Mezirow's transformative learning theory. *Adult Education Quarterly, 48*(1), 34–59.

Taylor, E. W., & Cranton, P. (2013). A theory in progress? Issues in transformative learning theory. *European Journal for Research on the Education and Learning of Adults, 4*(1), 33–47.

Tisdell, E. J. (2012). Themes and variations of transformative learning. Interdisciplinary perspectives on forms that transform. In E. W. Taylor & P. Cranton (Eds.), *The handbook of transformative learning: Theory, research, and practice* (pp. 21–36). San Francisco: Jossey-Bass.

Tyler, J. A., & Swartz, A. L. (2012). Storytelling and transformative learning. In E. W. Taylor & P. Cranton (Eds.), *The handbook of transformative learning: Theory, research, and practice* (pp. 455–470). Hoboken: John Wiley and Sons.

Yorks, L., & Kasl, E. (2006). I know more than I can say: A taxonomy for using expressive ways of knowing to foster transformative learning. *Journal of Transformative Education, 4*(1), 43–64.

7

Time and the Rhythms of Transformative Learning

Michel Alhadeff-Jones

Conceiving Transformative Processes Between Continuity and Discontinuity

As we are reminded by Slattery (1995) most educators and researchers still envision the everyday life as linear, paced by the regular succession of seconds, minutes, hours, days, months and years. In formal education, learning is thus conceived as "proportional" to the time "invested" in classroom activity. Educational "effectiveness" appears as a matter of time measurement, and time is therefore conceived as an independent variable to be manipulated in order to improve educational outcomes. The social imaginary of time remains captive to Newtonian assumptions (Ardoino, 2000; Slattery, 1995): time is traditionally conceived as "invariant, infinitely divisible into space-like units, measurable in length and expressible as number" (Adam, 1994, p. 50). Such a conception also privileges the idea of reversibility (Alhadeff-Jones, 2017, p. 21) suggesting that any

M. Alhadeff-Jones (✉)
Teachers College, Columbia University, New York, NY, USA
e-mail: maj@sunkhronos.org

© The Author(s) 2019
T. Fleming et al. (eds.), *European Perspectives on Transformation Theory*,
https://doi.org/10.1007/978-3-030-19159-7_7

changes of position, independently of when they occur, could be reversed without leaving net effects, like the swing of a frictionless pendulum.

Education, learning, transformation or development do not, however, constitute linear and frictionless processes. They exhibit temporal features much closer to the phenomena studied by thermodynamics (e.g., energy dissipation). The evolution of a complex system—a person, a collectivity—cannot be simply "rewound"; it involves directionality. Like ink dropped into water constitutes an action that cannot be simply undone, there is a necessity to recognize and integrate the irreversibility of educational time. Furthermore, as exemplified by the "butterfly effect", the emergence of a transformation is not necessarily proportional to the efforts that triggered it; not every instant is experienced with the same intensity and value. Such a complex phenomenon defeats linear temporal representations and simple explanations (Alhadeff-Jones, 2017, p. 23). Conceiving the temporalities of transformative processes, therefore, requires one to take into consideration their regularity and constancy, as well as their irregularity and inconstancy.

Since Antiquity, the philosophical study of time has been animated by considerations on the continuous and discontinuous nature of time (Gonord, 2001). This duality appears as a relevant entry point to interpret further the temporalities involved in transformative processes. Envisioning transformative learning (Mezirow, 1991) from a temporal perspective requires one to conceive the articulation between its continuous and discontinuous aspects. In practice and in research, it is not unusual to analyze those two features as distinct and separate from each other: transformation is often assimilated with crucial events that constitute discontinuities (e.g., life crisis, disorienting dilemma); it is also traditionally conceived as requiring and based upon on-going processes whose continuity remains critical (e.g., dialogue, critical self-reflection). Such a distinction remains, however, problematic. The aim of this chapter is to propose a conceptual framework in order to elaborate more thoroughly the dialogical relationship that exists between the continuities and discontinuities shaping transformative processes, in order to rethink transformative learning, not only as a phenomenon inscribed in time, but more radically as a process characterized by its own "rhythmicity" (this term will be explained below). Doing so, this reflection constitutes also an attempt to pursue the project initiated 30 years ago by pioneers of adult education such as Pineau (2000), who started envisioning the importance of focussing on the temporalities of human existence and *éducation permanente*, as well as the formative relevance of a dedicated praxis, informed by the study of rhythms (e.g., Bachelard, 1931, 1950; Lefebvre, 1992/2004).

The Discontinuities of Transformative Learning

If transformative learning had to be reduced to one feature, it would probably be the shift triggered by the experience of a "disorienting dilemma" (Mezirow, 1991). Thus, it is not unusual—even if misleading—to assimilate transformation to the situation that encapsulates how such a change is initiated. It typically involves an event disrupting what would have been otherwise experienced as an on-going, more or less ordered, sequence of actions.

The use of the concept of epiphany (from the Greek word *epiphainesthai* meaning to appear or to come into view) tends to stress the psychological dimensions associated with the experience of discontinuity. The term generally refers to an experience of great revelation and a catalyst for personal growth (McDonald, 2005, p. 11). In human sciences, Denzin (1989, 1990, as quoted in McDonald, 2005) has defined epiphanies as interactional moments that leave a mark on people's lives and have the potential to create transformational experiences for the person. They are related to existential crises, whose effects may be both positive and/or negative. Epiphanies reveal someone's character and alter the fundamental meaning structures in a person's life. They also affect one's own sense of identity. Frequently used in social theory, the concept of *épreuve* (ordeal) refers to critical events that test and reveal the values and qualities of the subjects involved in a situation, whose outcome remains fundamentally uncertain. For Boltanski and Thévenot (1991/2006), an *épreuve* refers to a situation of conflict that disrupts the normal course of events and everyday routines, and reveals the socially constructed assumptions according to which such a dispute is evaluated and judged. For Martuccelli (2006), the succession of a series of *épreuves* (e.g., passing one's final exams in school, having to lay off a co-worker, experiencing a divorce, et cetera) is what constitutes the subjective experience and the singularity of someone's life. They cannot be separated from the history of the subject (Ricoeur, 1990) and, at the same time, they display some kind of test through which the individual's resources are evaluated within a socially and historically determined situation. *Epreuves* articulate the social and contextual order that defines for instance an institution (education, work, family) at a specific time in its history, with the singular trajectory of a person (Baudouin, 2010).

Epiphanies and *épreuves* provide one with opportunities to question and challenge taken for granted assumptions and realities, and to reveal hidden characteristics of the self and implicit social standards. They may be experienced as disorienting and potentially transformative, because of the relative novelty, singularity and uncertainty, each occurrence involves. It remains that such disrupting events rarely appear as totally disconnected from previous or further experiences: they are usually intertwined with situations, places, relationships, feelings, norms, institutions or meanings that are already present in one's life, and that display a relative permanence beyond the experience of discontinuity. Moreover, despite being unique, epiphanies and *épreuves* reoccur through the life course, even if they are different each time. To some extent, their repetition—even if never self-similar—is constitutive of how people narrate and interpret the life course (Ricoeur, 1990). As periods punctuate the sentences of a text, epiphanies and *épreuves* introduce ruptures within the continuum of a life story. As a form of discontinuity, they also keep recurring. As soon as they start being reflected or shared through a narrative, such disruptive events appear intertwined into a larger movement that integrates them into the fabric of experiences that constitute the continuity of one's life.

The Continuities of Transformative Learning

If transformative learning is often reduced to the disorienting dilemma that triggers a significant change in someone's life, the processes it involves typically refer to phenomena whose continuity is usually taken for granted. First, if transformative learning is envisioned as a disruption or as an emergence within a continuum, then continuity refers to the very phenomena that appear as disrupted. In Mezirow's theory, meaning schemes and meaning perspectives constitute the main entities whose stability is challenged by the experience of disruptive events. Their permanence throughout the life course is what provides the self with a sense of identity, coherence, stability and predictability. For Mezirow (2000, p. 16), a meaning perspective refers to "[t]he structure of assumptions and expectations through which we filter sense impressions...It selectively shapes and delimits perception, cognition, feelings and dissipation by predisposing our intentions, expectations, and purposes ....". Such frames of reference are thus made of "habits of mind" and "points of view" that mobilized "meaning schemes", consciously or not, on an everyday basis. Once a transformation occurred, it leads to the stabilization of new ways of being, that will display some form of continuity and serve as a new base for the self to continue evolving in a more autonomous manner.

Second, transformative learning refers to on-going psychological and social processes through which such meaning schemes and perspectives are reconstructed in order to be more inclusive (Mezirow, 1991). Processes such as critical self-reflection or dialogue require some duration in order to unfold and produce significant effects. Once appropriated through the acquisition of language, the exercise of introspection and the experience of socialization, such processes also display a form of continuity. They provide the learners with the on-going possibility to challenge, deconstruct, explore and rebuild the ways they interpret their own actions and the world around them, in order to reshape their meaning perspectives and their sense of identity.

A third aspect of transformative learning theory that expresses some form of continuity can be found through the "phase model" it relies on. Although differences and divergences remain in the literature (Nohl, 2015), contributions to transformative learning theory often assume—explicitly or not—a developmental framework that transcends contexts. Thus, for Mezirow (2000, p. 22), transformative learning is organized around an established sequence of actions including successively: disorienting dilemma, self-examination, critical assessment of assumptions, recognition that one's discontent and transformation are shared, exploration of new options, planning action, acquisition of knowledge and skills, trying new roles, building self-confidence, reintegration of the new perspective. Such a structure is ultimately what provides practitioners with a sense of coherence for the work they do. They can refer to it to position their contribution within a continuum that defines their purpose and the way they implement their educational strategy.

If meaning schemes, meaning perspectives, critical self-reflection, dialogue or the phases through which adults may transform themselves are all conceived through the relative stability of their features, it is nevertheless misleading to assume their permanence. Indeed, none of those phenomena displays a strict continuity. They are not mobilized every instant of one's life. They incrementally evolve through time, and they depend on situations which are never self-similar. As suggested by Mezirow himself—even if he does not develop the theoretical implications of such an assumption—transformative learning is based on the repetition of patterns of activity (e.g., experiencing a dilemma, interpreting, questioning, dialoguing) that produce a feeling of continuity.

Toward a Rhythmic Conception of Transformation in Adult Education

Bachelard's Assumptions Around the Rhythmic Nature of Existence

In the early twentieth century, the contribution of Bachelard (1931) has explored the relevance of considering the dialogical relationship between continuity and discontinuity, focusing on the rhythmic attributes of living phenomena. Bachelard's (1950) view grounded the concept of rhythm against the concept of substance. Like a photon or a chemical substance, he conceived the self as temporal being that "vibrates", locating the experience of discontinuity at its core (e.g., the divided time of one's action, or the fragmented time of one's consciousness). The evolution of the self was, therefore, conceived as "undulatory" (Bachelard, 1950, p. 142), as a fabric made of tensions and alternating states. Among such tensions, one may for instance consider the fluctuations between autonomy and dependence, feeling empowered and disempowered, experiencing high and low levels of self-confidence or competency, et cetera. Bachelard suggested to conceive such tensions as "patterns of duality" (*motifs de dualité*) that could be balanced (Bachelard, 1950, p. 141). Thus, on the one hand, the life course could appear as fundamentally divided between successive states, feelings or actions that keep fluctuating. On the other hand, such discontinuities may also appear as organized through time and express rhythmic patterns that could be organized.

Bachelard's philosophy was orientated toward an ethic of care, expressing his concern for the development of a capacity to regulate one's own evolution in order to maintain a sense of continuity. His contribution privileged, therefore, a mode of analysis based on the study of rhythms to provide individuals with a resource to develop balance and coherence (Bachelard, 1950). Such an approach led him to conceive the basic idea of a rhythmanalytical method; a project that was later reinterpreted from a philosophical and sociological perspective by Lefebvre (1992/2004. Because it focuses on the rhythmic aspects of the everyday life, and of the lifespan as a whole, rhythmanalysis provides us with stimulating assumptions to critically reinterpret the aims and the praxis of adult education (Alhadeff-Jones, 2017). As discussed by Pineau (2000) and Lesourd (2001), it opens a relevant path toward a renewed conception of adult learning and development, more sensitive to the temporalities and the rhythms it involves. Such contributions demonstrate the value inherent to educational efforts focusing on the rhythmicity of one's own self-development (*auto-formation*). They appear as an invitation to envision the development of a field of practice, characterized by the careful, reflexive and rhythmically informed interpretation of life experiences, characterized by their fluctuations, to increase autonomy and promote emancipation. From an educational perspective, it remains that the features and the conceptual base required to develop such an approach have to be elaborated and consolidated.

Rhythms and Temporal Complexity

The reflection conducted in this chapter assumes that shifting the point of view from a "temporal" to a "rhythmic" perspective constitutes a strategic move, for at least three reasons. First, the experience of a rhythm constitutes a privileged way to access, describe and questions one's experience of time, both from an existential perspective and a more mundane and daily one. Second, the adoption of a rhythmic approach appears particularly congruent with an epistemology which values the complexity of human experience. The concept of rhythm appears particularly appropriate in order to describe the temporal organization that characterizes complex living phenomena, involving aspects of one's existence that are both ordered and disordered. Rhythm constitutes also a fundamental property of any phenomena shaped by antagonistic forces or drives (whether physical, biological, psychological, cultural or social). Thus, whenever patterns of duality are found in the course of one's life, revealing for instance fluctuating moods, ambivalent psychological states, or opposite actions, rhythms may be identified. Thus, a third benefit associated with the use of this concept is that it brings one to conceive the complementarities and antagonisms that characterize some of the tensions inherent to learning, transformation and educational dynamics (Alhadeff-Jones, 2017, pp. 63–64).

Rhythms and the Experience of Time

If time and rhythm appear as closely related, it remains nevertheless important to clarify how they are linked to each other. The perception of time refers to the capacity to relate changes that display some form of organization. If one can perceive such changes, time itself cannot be observed (Pomian, 1984). It becomes perceptible through specific experiences; among those, one has to consider rhythmic ones. As suggested by Sauvanet (2000a), rhythms make humans sensitive to the qualities and the passage of time; they express the "sense of time". Because rhythm always reveals a differential of durations that can be discriminated (e.g., alternance between strong and weak beat, high and low intensity of change), it is through rhythm that we can perceive time. Second, rhythm gives time a direction, expressing both, repetition and irreversibility (e.g., difference): seasons reappear through the same cycle, but every year's weather features remain unique. Third, in terms of meaning, rhythm provides one with significations in order to interpret the experience of time. For instance, when adults write their own autobiography, the way they describe the chronology of their life expresses specific rhythms. Thus, the choices made to "slow down" and describe in detail some specific events, or to "fast forward" and skip the descriptions of entire years of one's life, inform the meanings and the value given to the events or periods considered (Baudouin, 2010). Rhythm does not provide us with an abstract measure of time; it gives it a concrete and oriented reality. In order to fully grasp the relationship between time and rhythm, one must also consider the interval itself (e.g., nothingness, blank, silence, emptiness), quantitatively as a near-zero intensity, but qualitatively as a significant element of the temporal experience. According to Sauvanet (2000a), such an interval is not only what allows one to perceive rhythm, but also to partially access time.

Three Criteria to Theorize the Rhythms of Transformation

As their evolution displays both continuity and discontinuity, transformative processes may be conceived through the rhythmic dimensions they display. To define their features, it appears particularly relevant to consider three criteria identified as nodal by Sauvanet (2000a, 2000b). Accordingly, a rhythmic phenomenon may be defined by the pattern, the periodicity and the movement that characterize it.

Pattern

Pattern is the first criterion used by Sauvanet (2000a, p. 168) to define a rhythm. It stresses the idea of construction, layout (*agencement*), composition or imbrication. Its meaning highlights an interdependency between each element, structurally constitutive of a whole. A pattern configures a rhythmic phenomenon with a principle of unity and organization (Sauvanet, 2000a, p. 168.) What distinguishes a pattern is the fact that it designates an ephemeral configuration or setting (*disposition*) rather than the form constitutive of the essence or existence of a being (Sauvanet, 2000a, p. 168) For instance, the ways people relate with each other through time display patterns of interactions that are more or less structured, depending on formal and informal planning, scripts or routines experienced. Rhythmic patterns can also be observed in discourses (e.g., ways of thinking or speaking) and embodied activity (e.g., biological and physiological rhythms, feelings, ways of moving) (Michon, 2005). Thus, most of human activities reveal organized patterns that fluctuate through time. When considering transformative learning theory, meaning schemes, meaning perspectives, dialogical situations, the exercise of critical self-reflection, or the phases through which a transformation may unfold, all those phenomena are characterized by specific patterns of activity. They are recognizable because they are organized, even if such an organization remains fluctuating.

Periodicity

Periodicity (from the Greek *periodos*, which designates a circuit or a circular march) is the second criteria identified by Sauvanet (2000a, p. 177) to define rhythmic phenomena. Periodicity covers all the rhythms that are perceived or conceived as cycles, returns, alternances, repetitions, cadences and so on. Rhythms that are considered as influential always involve periodicities. Thus, rhythmic patterns such as those suggested above should be considered through the periodic features associated with them. At the level of the institution, the equilibrium of a system is sustained through the repetition of the patterns that defines its temporal organization: sequences of actions, cycles of activity, and so on. Repetitions also characterize actions at a smaller scale: routines and rituals that shape the everyday life within formal settings (e.g., classrooms) or throughout informal activities (e.g., taking care of oneself). From the point of view of the individual, repetitions characterize every aspect of one's own

7 Time and the Rhythms of Transformative Learning 103

experience, including biorhythms (e.g., the frequency of sleep, digestion or sexual activity), cognitive functions (e.g., reproduction of meaning schemes), emotions, movements and behaviors (e.g., cadences of gestures, frequency of interactions). At every level, learning and transformation are shaped not only by the period that characterizes the repetition of a pattern (time spent between two occurrences), but also by its frequency (how many times a pattern is repeated) and its tempo (how does the rate of repetition evolve through time). As a second criterion, periodicity provides us with another entry point from which to conceptualize the rhythmicity of transformative processes and determine more specifically their value. To be sustained, a transformation requires indeed the reproduction through time of the features and patterns that characterize an emerging mode of organization (e.g., a way of thinking or living).

Movement

Sauvanet's (2000a, p. 188) introduced the term "movement", as a third criterion to define a rhythmic phenomenon. Based on its etymology (from the Greek *metabolè*), Sauvanet (2000a, p. 189) stresses the "transformational" connotation of a movement, including the ideas of inconsistency, inconstancy, renewal or exchange. Conceiving rhythms through their movement highlights the assumption according to which a rhythm goes beyond mere repetition and remains fundamentally shaped through the indeterminacy of an irregular configuration. At their core, transformative processes involve some form of ruptures that disturb living, psychological, social or symbolic orders. As discussed in the previous section, they are usually conceived in relation to an event (e.g., epiphany, ordeal, disorienting dilemma) or a series of distinct events introducing discontinuities. One way to explore further the relationship among rhythm, movement and transformation is to explore what Sauvanet (2000b, p. 114) groups under the term "syncope"; a notion that evokes a suspended time that recalls a rhythm. A syncope is found whenever an interval, a crisis, a break or a leap is lived. Such phenomena may have freeing effects because they momentarily liberate from, and eventually renew, the pattern and the strict repetition that characterize a rhythmic experience.

For instance, reentering into a formal cursus of education may introduce a pause in between two periods of professional activity and, by doing so, may instill a new rhythm in someone's life. The experience of a syncope is not transformative per se. It may, however, contribute to a transformative process, whenever the discontinuity it introduces is perceived as irreversible, as it is for instance the case when one gets out of a habit, obtains a diploma, gives birth or after an accident.

Conceiving the Rhythmic Tensions That Shape Transformative Learning

We can now turn to a central argument of the chapter if we explore transformative processes as rhythmic phenomena it provides us with an original framework to grasp the tensions that shape them from a temporal perspective.

The Rhythmic Patterns of a Transformation

Rhythmic patterns define what is affected by a transformation (e.g., a way of thinking, a routine), as much as they organize transformative processes through time (e.g., the temporal organization of an educational reform). They can be for instance conceived from the perspectives of sociality (e.g., how people interact with each other), discourse (e.g., what people think, say or write) or corporeality (e.g., what people experience or express through their body) (Michon, 2005). Thus, the experience of change is shaped by rhythmic configurations that are constantly evolving (e.g., educational programs, organizational planning, routines, dialogical situations, narratives). Those patterns do not define a transformative process per se, although they provide—at a given time—a configuration that determines its expression at the micro level of individual activity and social interactions, at the meso level of the life course, and at the macro level of organizations and institutions. To grasp the functions played by rhythmic patterns in transformative processes, it seems critical to consider the way they evolve through time: what is their level of rigidity or fluidity?

7 Time and the Rhythms of Transformative Learning   105

Whenever rhythmic patterns appear as too rigid or too fluid, transformative processes may be difficult to sustain: either changes are not integrated into new patterns, or they do not lead to the emergence of a stable configuration. Additional questions may be considered: Do rhythmic patterns fluctuate at a specific time or in a specific context? Who has the capacity and what are the resources required to influence or impose such configurations? What justifies the rigidity of rhythmic patterns or, at the opposite, the absence of a rhythmic structure organizing one's experience?

Repetitions and Transformation

The experience of repetitions represents a locus of transformation (e.g., the changes of routines, rituals or habits), as much as reoccurrence is required to sustain transformative processes through time. Thus, emerging social, discursive and corporeal configurations (e.g., ways of interacting with others, meaning perspectives, ways of feeling or moving one's body) have to be reproduced in order to be integrated and appropriated, individually or collectively. Transformative processes rely, therefore, on periodic experiences, including repetitions, reiterations, cycles, or cadences. When studying the relations between the periodicity of specific patterns (e.g., the exercise of critical self-reflection or dialogue; the alternance between study and work in dual education) and the transformative processes they relate to, period, frequency and tempo have to be considered. Describing the periodic aspects of educational and transformative processes requires one to consider at least three features: what is the duration that separates two occurrences of a similar phenomenon or the completion of a cycle (i.e., its period)? How many times does it occur (i.e., its frequency)? What is the rate of repetition and how does the tempo evolve through time? Some transformative processes are difficult to observe because they are characterized by periodic features that occur too slowly to be perceived; what Jullien (2011) conceives as "silent transformations". Others involve patterns of behavior whose periodic repetition displays a higher level of intensity (short periods of reoccurrence, high frequency or accelerated tempo) (e.g., intensive courses or accelerated learning). From an educational perspective, it is, therefore, critical to question the appropriateness of those temporal features, considering the specificity of the learning involved and the context within which it unfolds. For a specific pattern of activity (e.g., introspection, dialogue, writing, reading), how suitable are the period (too short or too long), the frequency (too high or too low) and the tempo (too fast or too slow; monotonous or fluctuating) that characterize its repetition over time? Furthermore, what are the factors that influence or determine such a periodicity? Who has the capacity to define, legitimize or impose specific periodic features? Where does the pace of the activity come from? And how are periodic features experienced?

The Movement of a Transformation

The movement of a transformation, whether conceived through the history of an institution, the life course of a person or one's everyday life, reveals a third kind of tension. Transformative processes involve variations and inconstancy, as much as they may provoke rupture and disorder. They are usually envisioned through the punctual events that introduce a break within a continuum. Thus, they may involve the capacity to negotiate the meanings, and balance the tensions that characterize the relationships between regularity, irregularity, continuity and discontinuity. Transformative processes can also be interpreted through the experience of syncopes: intervals that provide one with the opportunity to resource, balance or reinvent oneself, and renew social, discursive or embodied rhythms that would have been otherwise lived as too regular, constant, monotonous, foreseeable or standardized. Because the experience of a syncope does not systematically carry transformative effects, it is also critical to question the level of reversibility and irreversibility that characterizes the emergence of a variation, an interval, a crisis, or a disruption. From an educational and developmental perspective, it is relevant to consider that what constitutes the movement of a transformative process (e.g., the experience of a rupture), may also become part of a larger pattern, that may be repeated. For instance, emancipation can be theorized as a rhythmic process that involves the repetition of specific patterns of disruption (e.g., transgressions), whose repetition participates to a movement of detachment and appropriation of one's life (Alhadeff-Jones, 2017). Considering the movements that shape the rhythms of transformation, additional questions may be considered: what does legitimate the experience of continuity or discontinuity? What are the resources required to articulate constancy and rupture? Where does the feeling of irreversibility come from? How is it subjectively and socially defined?

Toward a Rhythmanalytical Conception of Transformative Education

The reflection developed in this chapter started with the description of the dual nature of transformative processes, as they involve both discontinuity (e.g., epiphany, ordeal, disorienting dilemma) and continuity (e.g., frames of reference, ways of being, critical self-reflection, dialogue, developmental phases). Then, lifelong learning and transformation have been envisioned as rhythmic phenomena. Referring to the concept of rhythm appears particularly heuristic, as it constitutes a strategic entry point to conceive the experience of time and the complexity it displays. The value inherent to the concept of rhythm is that it provides us with a renewed vocabulary to deconstruct dominant representations of time in education. Furthermore, it provides us with conceptions that nuance the way we depict and experience the temporalities involved in adult education. Transformative processes can be conceived through patterns, periodicities and movements that compose the social, discursive and embodied rhythms found in life. Furthermore, they can be analyzed through specific features that characterize the rhythms involved in transformations: the level of fluidity of the patterns considered, the duration, frequency and speed that define their reoccurrence, and the levels of continuity/discontinuity, reversibility/irreversibility they display.

The reflection conducted in this chapter should be conceived as a starting point. There are numerous contributions in sciences and philosophy, human sciences and the arts, that could serve to elaborate further a rhythmic theory of adult learning and development, and to define the grounds of a rhythmanalytical praxis. Such a framework may for instance contribute to the renewal of our conception of emancipatory education (Alhadeff-Jones, 2017). From a theoretical perspective, a lot remains to be done to clarify and develop additional resources to analyze, interpret and assess the temporalities involved in adult education and the way they contribute to alienate and/or emancipate learners and educators as well. It seems particularly relevant to pursue such a project and to enrich the initial insights formulated by pioneers around the idea of rhythmanalysis (Bachelard, 1931, 1950; Lefebvre, 1992/2004; Pineau, 2000), and key contributions to the field of adult education (Mezirow, 1991) in order to design further a theory of adult education dedicated to the study of how people learn to discriminate, interpret, evaluate, argue, judge and challenge the nature and the values of the rhythms that shape their lives and the flow of their experiences.

References

Adam, B. (1994). *Time and social theory*. Cambridge: Polity Press.

Alhadeff-Jones, M. (2017). *Time and the rhythms of emancipatory education. Rethinking the temporal complexity of self and society*. London: Routledge.

Ardoino, J. (2000). *Les avatars de l'éducation*. Paris: Presses Universitaires de France.

Bachelard, G. (1931). *L'intuition de l'instant*. Paris: Stock.

Bachelard, G. (1950). *La dialectique de la durée*. Paris: Presses Universitaires de France.

Baudouin, J. M. (2010). *De l'épreuve autobiographique: Contribution des histoires de vie à la problématique des genres de texte et de l'herméneutique de l'action*. Bern: Peter Lang.

Boltanski, L., & Thévenot, L. (2006). *On justification: Economies of worth* (C. Porter, Trans.). Princeton: Princeton University Press. (Original work published 1991).

Gonord, A. (2001). *Le temps*. Paris: Flammarion.

Jullien, F. (2011). *The silent transformations* (K. Fijałkowski & M. Richardson, Trans.). Chicago, IL: Seagull Press.

Lefebvre, H. (2004). *Rhythmanalysis: Space, time and everyday life* (S. Elden & G. Moore, Trans.). London: Continuum. (Original work published 1992).

7 Time and the Rhythms of Transformative Learning   109

Lesourd, F. (2001). Ecoformation et apprentissage au long cours par les rythmes de l'environnement. *Education Permanente, 148*, 255–265.

Martuccelli, D. (2006). *Forgé par l'épreuve*. Paris: Armand Colin.

McDonald, M. G. (2005). *Epiphanies: An existential philosophical and psychological inquiry*. Doctoral dissertation, University of Technology, Sydney.

Mezirow, J. (1991). *Transformative dimensions of adult learning*. San Francisco: Jossey-Bass.

Mezirow, J. (2000). Learning to think like an adult: Core concepts of transformation theory. In J. Mezirow & Associates (Eds.), *Learning as transformation. Critical perspectives on a theory in progress* (pp. 3–34). San Francisco: Jossey-Bass.

Michon, P. (2005). *Rythmes, pouvoir, mondialisation*. Paris: Presses Universitaires de France.

Nohl, A.-M. (2015). Typical phases of transformative learning: A practice-based model. *Adult Education Quarterly, 65*(1), 35–49.

Pineau, G. (2000). *Temporalités en formation. Vers de nouveaux synchroniseurs*. Paris: Anthropos.

Pomian, K. (1984). *L'ordre du temps*. Paris: Gallimard.

Ricoeur, P. (1990). *Soi-même comme un autre*. Paris: Seuil.

Sauvanet, P. (2000a). *Le rythme et la raison (vol. 1) Rythmologiques*. Paris: Kimé.

Sauvanet, P. (2000b). *Le rythme et la raison (vol. 2). Rythmanalyses*. Paris: Kimé.

Slattery, P. (1995). A postmodern vision of time and learning: A response to the National Education Commission Report 'Prisoners of time'. *Harvard Educational Review, 65*(4), 612–633.

8

Communicative Practices in Work and Training Contexts: Exercising Transformative Authority?

Jerome Eneau and Eric Bertrand

Critique, Dialogue and Transformation in Work and Training

Many theories of organisational learning are complementary with the theory of transformative learning (Watkins, Marsick, & Faller, 2012) but there are differences in how authority and power are conceptualised. French critical sociology explores how the exercise of authority and power, both at work and in training, is often linked to domination and coercion (Boltanski, 2009). Although Mezirow (1991) views hierarchies as serious obstacles to transformative learning, we think he can be usefully put into dialogue with this tradition. Indeed, the complexity of training (Alhadeff-Jones, 2012) leads us to reflect on antagonistic and competing logics rooted in the concept of "dialogue" or "experiential dialogism" (Bertrand, 2014a), following the principle of Habermas' "communicative rationality" (Habermas, 1987). Certain conditions of this "communicative rationality" require creating mutual understanding, that

J. Eneau (✉) • E. Bertrand
University of Rennes, Rennes, France
e-mail: jerome.eneau@uhb.fr

© The Author(s) 2019

T. Fleming et al. (eds.), *European Perspectives on Transformation Theory*,
https://doi.org/10.1007/978-3-030-19159-7_8

111

is, for an individual to navigate through three social, objective, and subjective worlds. As we will see, this may transform experiences of domination in vocational training and work contexts into opportunities for transformative learning. But under which specific processes is this possible? And how does this affect the way we think about power and authority?

This chapter will address these issues. We will first present the theoretical framework, methodology and research that have led us to this conclusion. The proposals presented here are the result of studies undertaken over ten years in France in our training programmes in university targeting managers and employees and in professional training, in France. After having briefly presented the literature on the concepts of authority and power and their semantic proximity with the concepts of authorship and autonomy, we will then present ideas to reflect on, and further develop, transformative learning.

From Learning at Work to Transformative Learning

This contribution is in line with the studies undertaken by Argyris and Schön (1996) and Watkins and Marsick (1993, 1996, 2003). It is based on research conducted in France, focusing on the development of transformative learning rooted in work processes (Bertrand, 2014b, 2016). Mezirow (1991) refers to Habermas's theory of communicative action (1987). We will draw on Habermas's concept of "mutual understanding." Drawing on research and action programmes, we seek to develop transformative learning based on work activities around objects such as authority and power that lie at the heart of communicative practices. We believe, however, that this project is possible only when critical and interactionist approaches are used jointly. More particularly, applying critical approaches to management theories (Boltanski & Chiapello, 2011) has made it possible to reflect upon authority and power as the capacity of individuals to become the authors of their lives and actions. Individuals are thus responsible for creating the conditions necessary for work groups to develop this capacity. These two relational concepts, that is, power and authority, notably led to analyse the development of professional training and management practices through a "communication ethics" (Bertrand, 2011).

8 Communicative Practices in Work and Training Contexts... 113

Using a critical approach ultimately means pursuing a reflective course, in one's actions, in the development of thoughts and ideas, and in the production of knowledge. It is an exercise that seeks to avoid all forms of alienation stemming from practices of domination, including those practices imposed on oneself (practitioners, researchers) when one produces his or her own "impediments to reflection" (Bertrand, 2015). Lastly, the critical approach is clearly involved with the objects it analyses: power, authority, and even domination.

Exploring the concept of mutual understanding in work and training contexts suggests that one must observe reality from a holistic approach. This approach often leads down the uncomfortable path of a transdisciplinary epistemology for which working experience "occurs" as much as it is "experienced" between intersubjectivity (Eneau & Labelle, 2008), the blending of social business worlds and the radicalism of the objective world of scholarly knowledge. By drawing on the critical sociology of Habermas (1987), Mezirow's (Mezirow, 1991; Mezirow and Associates, 2000) theory of transformative learning, Barbier's (1996) action research or Hess's (1993) institutional analysis,[1] we will attempt to use this epistemological and methodological framework to analyse how professional situations in work and training are experienced and, reciprocally, the transformation of learning, professional environments and the subjects themselves.

Experimentation and Research: The "Action–Research–Training" Model

The research outlined here was undertaken within a French university setting and was part of a training programme in connection with work contexts and based on an experimental education model we call the "Action–Research–Training" model, which we are continuously seeking to retest (Eneau, Bertrand, & Lameul, 2012, 2014). Like "action research" (Barbier, 1996), this scientific and pedagogical arrangement is aimed at transforming reality and producing knowledge in relation to the changes observed. We are interested in the development of transformative learning in multidisciplinary approaches and those that use qualitative and quantitative approaches both *on* and *for* adult education.

Rather than directly observe organisations, we analysed the careers of the adults we trained through work-linked training activities. These are training spaces called into question by adult learners in learning theories *in* and *through* research. The educational task is to promote the gradual emergence of a practitioner/researcher who is a reflexive and critical thinker during the two-year training programmes (Master's degree in Adult Education at University Rennes 2 and Master's degree in Training Practices and Expertise at University Paris Est).

We also guide professionals engaged in long-term training processes with whom we can analyse the process and meaning that characterises transformative learning through the design and facilitation of training programmes targeting managers (e.g., the training of education managers of the Juvenile Protection Service, interventions for the Centre of Young French Leaders, etc.). In these practices, conditions, processes and the effects of transformative learning are never directly observed from within organisations (local authorities, associations, companies). Rather, these organisations are either spaces where the adult practices we support in the university can be tested or the context in which business leaders or executives can experiment with reflexive practices and transformative learning strategies both for their employees and themselves.

Social Experience: An Individual and Collective Phenomenon

Over the past few years, we have been working on issues related to transformative learning in relation to professional practices in work contexts by analysing social experiences through a matrix with four dimensions in constant interaction: subjects, social groups, organisations and institutions.

This approach to social experience in general and to authority and power in particular makes it possible to examine the relationships of mutual dependence that are involved, in "reproducing" and "transforming institutions" (Castoriadis, 1975). The units of analysis are both social and technical artefacts that shape the institutions of work and training and in which social relations evolve and are reproduced. These are the relations subjects maintain with themselves, others and the world. For the purposes of research and action, it is impossible to support the development of the transformative learning of subjects without placing practices and interactions in the social and historical context of organisations and taking into account their modes of functioning.

How then can one create the conditions for rational dialogue for these unexamined aspects to be expressed and transformed? Reflexivity is a key concept at the heart of Habermas's mutual comprehension process, which is coupled to the concept of decentration. It is impossible to take action and to learn without mutual understanding, that is, without being able to participate in a dual exercise of reciprocal reflexivity (such as the ability to question the just, true and sincere nature of a communicative situation) and decentration. This practice of reflexivity also uses multiple approaches, insofar as action and reflection combine the four dimensions mentioned above. Thus, the critical approach in social sciences highlights the need to design an exercise of collective reflexivity that involves researchers, policymakers and practitioners in three tasks (Boltanski, 2009): (1) first, the pursuit of cognitive goals, the production of knowledge in the identification of genuine psychosocial issues; (2) the identification of "dysfunctions" compared to a given normative framework; and (3) advising and supporting organisations, groups and topics, in line with political, social, personal and professional transformation objectives.

Authority, Power and Transformative Learning in Work Contexts

Authority and power are at the heart of all processes of action and learning, and, indeed, of all social processes. Different disciplines focus on the "functioning of groups and organisations, processes of change, power relations, the management of psychological and social conflicts, and the relationship between research and social practices" (Barus, Michel, & Enriquez, 2002, p. 9). In France, the theories of organisational learning have been examined by social psychologists, educational psychologists and practitioners and researchers in management sciences. Transformation is a central issue in these three perspectives even though the aims and epistemological postures differ.

In adult education and training, authority and power are often examined via the critical theory from Frankfurt school of thought that relies on a *praxis* that can take the form of institutional intervention (Ardoino, 2002). It also establishes that the primacy of speech and of the democratic process in power games and discussion (or even) negation is fundamental. Criticism is impossible without intersubjective practices that make up reality. In addition to these conditions, American studies (Mezirow, 1991, 2009; Mezirow and Associates, 2000; Mezirow & Taylor, 2009; Taylor, 2009; Taylor & Cranton, 2012, 2013; Watkins et al., 2012) have notably shown the importance of awareness-raising processes in transformative approaches.

Authority and power can thus be levers of learning and development insofar as they do not seek, explicitly or implicitly, consciously or unconsciously, to exercise domination in their multiple forms. These forms include economic, administrative, or with its processes of monetisation and bureaucratisation, for example, when domination produces social pathologies and the "colonisation of the worlds experienced" (Eneau et al., 2012, 2014). In France, critical sociology, and Bourdieu's heirs, in particular (Boltanski, 2009; Boltanski & Chiapello, 2011), have analysed the concept of domination when it produces conditions that alienate subjects and reinforces their sense of powerlessness. It is worth mentioning that transformative learning primarily seeks the development of a critical consciousness that thwarts the limits imposed by all forms of ignorance. In this regard, professional training in work contexts has great potential and plays a major role even though these objectives hardly target the development of the critical conscience of actors who, often, are expected to continuously adapt to changes in the work place.

The Transformative Exercise of Authority: Becoming Self

The word "*authority*" has the same prefix as "*autonomy*" and "*author*" (Ardoino, 2002). As its Latin origins suggest (*augere*), the exercise of authority seeks to "augment" others. This "augmentation" is a fundamental transformative practice, which involves disequilibrium for the manager and his or her subordinate as well as for the educator and the learner, ultimately leading to a "boosting" readjustment. The exercise of authority acts jointly on the different processes: facilitating the interlocutor's self-knowledge (personal development); self-control (through education); and control of the world (transformation). As for the educative professions, engaging in relationships in which one must create the conditions for the development of the interlocutor requires a certain psycho-affective maturity which consists in not seeing a threat in the "augmentation" of one's interlocutor (for instance losing control of situations, losing one's place).

Becoming Autonomous: Engaging in Relationships of Mutual Dependence

It is easy to confuse autonomy and independence. In adult education, autonomy is defined as subjects' ability to engage in relationships of mutual interdependence (Bertrand, 2016; Eneau, 2005, 2008). Dependence is not simply the principle that makes one agree against his or her will to any force or any form of false beliefs, obstacles to thinking, epistemic, sociolinguistics, and psychological distortions (Mezirow, 1991). On the contrary, mutual dependence is a principle that "connects" people (Eneau, 2008, 2012, 2017). The real problem of autonomy is related to actors' capacity to act and whether or not they are able to engage in a more or less reciprocal and equal relationship (Bertrand & Cariat, 2017). In this perspective, the project that seeks to make one the subject of his or her narrative in the work place within more or less selected relations expects individuals to accept that others are involved in our own development, our own learning, just as we participate in theirs.

Transformation as a Practice Issue at the Heart of the Exercise of Authority and Power

Work and adult education are two fields of practices involving processes of psychosocial transformations based on four interrelated dimensions (subjects, social groups, organisations, institutions). These processes ensure both the maintenance and transformation of institutions, organisations, social relationships, representations and ideologies. Work and training practices fall within but also participate in these psychosocial dynamics. Authority and power are concepts present in all professional practices. They are always motivated by a will, an intention, and a more or less conscious desire to transform a situation. But should the exercise of power and authority aim to reproduce, control, transform or liberate?

On a pragmatic basis, the exercise of authority and power in the work and training context seeks to create the conditions for the collective achievement of an activity, service, or a manufactured good. This is a tricky exercise because its objective is to drive the reproduction of meaning and processes related to action (for example targeting desired standardisation, notably in the context of the streamlining of both organisations and activities), that is, itself deeply transformative and capable of creating social, cultural or economic value. In parallel and in an iterative and recursive manner, this exercise of authority and power also seeks its own transformation: social, organisational, technical, economic, legal transformations and adaptations to the changes imposed by external and internal constraints. The objectives of mastery, mutual understanding, training, or even emancipation are connected more than they are separated.

However, our studies have frequently revealed that these ways of thinking are often experienced and spoken about in a pre-reflexive manner that perceives them as unsurpassable contradictions. The harmonisation of practices with polarised aims (to control, understand, and emancipate) takes shape once the subjects reflect, take a different view of something (what underlies Habermas's process of mutual understanding) and develop a critical and rational dialogue. In the absence of these conditions, practices are governed by a primarily instrumental act, a manoeuvre which escapes the consciousness of the individual who develops this practice and, sometimes, the consciousness of those to whom it is destined.

Transformative learning works in the background to ensure the coherence of the sense of the experiences of subjects and groups by returning that which was acted out in a non-conscious manner (pre-reflexive) and without critical review to the level of the "represented" and the "representable." This liberating process is stimulated when the emergence of individual and collective subjects is supported because authority, as the etymology of the word *augere* implies, "augments" the other.

Mutual Understanding as Communicative Practices, Which "Authorise"

One of the major problems in the management of actors, activities and organisations arises from the collective daily support and production of ways to surpass apparent paradoxes. These paradoxes are nestled in work density and completion (Morin, 1990). Meaning, its collective elaboration, and how it is put in perspective is at the heart of this psychosocial practice that either denies or relies on the concerns of mutual comprehension. From a critical perspective, how are the sense of action and the projects of actors and organisations formulated?

Three Worlds for Co-construction of Meaning and Mutual Comprehension

From a French-speaking perspective, a review of the literature related to the concept of "meaning" shows some form of inconsistency (Zarifian, 2001). French usually distinguish "*common sense*" (pre-thought, or pre-reflexive according to Mezirow) from "*reflective sense*," which arises from speculation and intellectual constructions. Common sense is associated with authority and power when a practice or a situation appears as normal, occasionally preventing all forms of critical thinking. Common sense can be built on ignorance, personal and collective prejudice, distortions of meaning and other delusions. It may thus become dangerous from a social and psychological perspective. Meaning is a psychosocial construct, which becomes a "given" (common sense), and is called into question once it is subjected to the critical examination of actors. Meaning is also defined as what "steers" a project. It cannot be separated from human experience (Bertrand, 2014a), i.e., from experience in its capitalistic dimension (personal and collective reservoir of knowledge, values, beliefs, etc.). It also involves daily co-elaboration through which subjects deconstruct and reconstruct their representations with more or less skill and flexibility. Finally, these representations are both a process and a result of this process.

From a psychological perspective, meaning also encompasses different models and perspectives. It is an interpretive framework that individuals project onto the world to elucidate it, make it habitable and find their place. The subject is rarely alone in professional situations and meaning is thus the more or less conflictual encounter of different interpretations of situations. These encounters are the result of an intersubjective process in which mutual understanding allows—or not—individuals to commit to a reflexive process of self-questioning. This process of mutual understanding that jointly elaborates the meaning of current and future action also requires mediation, translators, couriers, and social, cultural and technical conditions that we will present. All these conditions and practices of mediation thus constitute, following Habermas (1987), a "communicative practice" (Bertrand, 2016). The conditions of "communicative rationality" then required to create mutual understanding. For an individual to navigate the three social, objective, and subjective worlds, and to be able to identify the types of validity claims and recognise the types of statements for each type of validity, he or she must be able to perform the dual exercise of reflexivity and decentration. Reflexivity in communication is defined here as the questioning of the subject's relationship to others, to the world and to oneself based on an authentic speech: "*what did I say, I say to myself, he tells me, one says, the situation tells me?*" These questions help a subject distinguish the dilemmas emerging from these different yet complementary worlds. This "individuation" takes place when different worlds are compared (*I, you, he* or *she* and *that*), that is, within discussions that refer to situations ("*From where are we speaking— physically, symbolically, biographically—and what are we speaking about?*

How and why do we speak about it?" These questions examine the content, process and premises within the associated experiences.

Supporting Practices of Mutual Understanding: What Does This Mean?

The studies undertaken (Action–Research–Training model) show that mutual understanding is a concept and practice at the heart of all social relationships. From the perspective of the theory of communicative action, this concept relies on language and seeks mutual understanding in the pursuit of a joint project or action. In the midst of the discussion, each language proposal expresses the form and substance of actors' experiences. These experiences may be combined under three sub-worlds: subjective, objective and social worlds. The purposes and modes of communication of these worlds are more or less connected, consistent, and conscious.

The "objective world" corresponds to the world that seeks efficiency, mastery, the quest of that which is "real," that which can be reproduced ad infinitum. The work of *homo faber* is its preferred space. Critical sociology warns us about viewing sciences and techniques as ideology, that is, as the foundation of this world, because there are huge risks of deviance and of alienation (or self-alienation) which inherently present a risk of "commodification" of subjects perceived as objects or things (Honneth, 2000, 2007). When authority, as the exercise of power, responds by pursuing total control, it is a reflection of an ideology of managerialism.

The organisations affected by this managerial trend regulate and sometimes associate it with actions driven by less instrumental, more practical and communicative rationality in the sense that they seek the development of mutual agreement which is necessary for positive work experiences. This can be seen in the organisation and facilitation of the spaces of rational dialogue, based on critical reflexivity and deliberative practices. Indeed, it is a question of discussing these rationalistic aims while taking into account the foundations of the social life of the groups, that is, values, traditions, beliefs and knowledge. These spaces and these moments can thus be defined as the encounter of "social worlds." They are often multiple and correspond to a specific professional sector, profession or social group. The rationality observed in the activity of language within these spaces is less about seeking what is "real" and more about seeking what is "just" (Boltanski & Thévenot, 1991). The space of social interactions symbolises this world (practice of social dialogue, annual appraisal interview, etc.).

The "subjective world" is the world to which only subjects have access. Synonymous with interiority, this world is sometimes foreign to the subjects themselves when they have not had the opportunity to engage in activities seeking personal development and self-awareness. It creates favourable conditions for critical reflection and self-directed learning. Mutual understanding occurs when subjectivities and intersubjectivity meet. The validation of the meaning produced by language does not seek the "real" or the "just" even though it takes its inspiration from this. Rather, it seeks "sincerity" as the reflection of what subjects are really thinking when they say that they are "saying something to themselves." In France, the spaces and moments of training which are often found outside the workplace as part of university courses or professional training programmes are privileged moments where subjectivities can interconnect and come together.

The exercise of authority involves developing synergy between the role of subjectivity, the implementation of conditions for subjects' self-realisation, and a communicative rationality to regulate instrumental rationalities. The combination of these three worlds explains one way of reflecting on the real, to "take action" and produce knowledge.

Designing Spaces of Intermediation?

Ultimately, communicative management can be based on a mutual understanding language practice that seeks the encounter, confrontation and transformation of experienced worlds. It is based on the principles of parity, reciprocity and mutual dependence. Meetings and individual or collective appraisals are some of the different formal moments during which it is exercised in the work context and where learners implement it. To summarise, our analysis, from previous research (Bertrand, 2014a,

8 Communicative Practices in Work and Training Contexts... 123

2014b; Eneau et al., 2012), reveals that language content in the spaces of intermediation can be classified into three groups:

* Content in line with related projects, action, issues, priorities, et cetera. This content responds to the question of "why and why should we do it together?" It mobilises three subsets of "experienced worlds." When the project of an organisation, its functioning and its managerial practices create the conditions for collective and reflective activities on this theme, then subjects and the organisation learn to learn. This category corresponds to double loop learning (Argyris & Schön, 1996). The exercise of authority gives subjects the power to position themselves to appropriate, challenge and influence the meaning of collective action.
* The second category includes all the language content in relation to the formal and informal and negotiable and non-negotiable rules that shape, guarantee, and support the meaning of individual and collective action. It responds primarily to the "how" of action. It mobilises in priority the objectives of the social and objective worlds experienced. Working together on appropriation and on the constructive criticism of rules said to be "negotiable" also makes it possible to gain access to a communicative management that is both empowering and transformative. This is related to double loop learning but is less powerful in terms of organisational learning, especially when actors are invited to work on the issue of methods without questioning the meaning of actions or projects. The third category of contents of language activities concerns relationships and interrelationships. It concerns the principles of "living together at work." It primarily mobilises the social and subjective worlds and gains by sometimes reverting to the objective dimension of activity, and is often one in which a number of tensions and conflicts crystallise. This category of language content is to make subjects "speak" and to ensure discussion and coherence with the content relating to the meaning of collective action and to the rules that govern it. Our Action–Research–Training of managers and business leaders shows that managers address the meaning of the action and rules in a frequently disconnected manner. Our findings suggest that this is a common mistake that slows down the process of mutual understanding.

Note

1. Institutional analysis, in France, is the result of what is referred to the *"Ecole de Vincennes,"* an experimental university founded in 1968 and dismantled in 1980, which was led by researchers such as Deleuze, Lapassade, Lourau or Foucault.

References

Alhadeff-Jones, M. (2012). Transformative learning and the challenges of complexity. In E. Taylor & P. Cranton (Eds.), *The handbook of transformative learning: Theory, research and practice* (pp. 178–194). San Francisco: Jossey-Bass.

Ardoino, J. (2002). Autorité. In M. Barus, E. Enriquez, & A. Lévy (Eds.), *Vocabulaire de psychosociologie* (pp. 61–64). Toulouse: Érès.

Argyris, C., & Schön, D. (1996). *Apprentissage organisationnel: Théories, méthodes, pratiques.* Bruxelles: De Boeck.

Barbier, R. (1996). *La recherche action.* Paris: Anthropos.

Barus, M., Michel, J., & Enriquez, E. (2002). Le pouvoir. In M. Barus, E. Enriquez, & A. Lévy (Eds.), *Vocabulaire de psychosociologie* (pp. 212–221). Toulouse: Érès.

Bertrand, E. (2011). De l'expérience du management au management de l'expérience à La Poste: penser l'agir communicationnel en entreprise. *Pratiques de formation/Analyses- Former les managers* n°60–61, 99–120.

Bertrand, E. (Dir.). (2014a). Formation expérientielle et intelligence en action. (Construire l'expérience 3). *Éducation permanente, Parution n° 198.* http://www.education-permanente.fr/public/articles/articles.php?id_revue=1727.

Bertrand, E. (2014b). Quelles pratiques managériales dans les métiers de l'aide à domicile? In M. Delaloy, M. Foudriat, & F. Noble (Eds.), *Le management des chefs de service dans le secteur social et médico-social: Repères, enjeux, perspectives* (pp. 274–301). Paris: Dunod.

Bertrand, E. (2015). De l'épreuve de la critique à la critique de l'épreuve au travail et en formation. Contribution à la théorisation de la formation expérientielle des adultes. *Pensée plurielle, 3*(40), 85–96.

Bertrand, E. (2016). La compétence communicationnelle au cœur du pouvoir d'agir des chefs de service. In D. Argoud & F. Noble (Eds.), *Pouvoir et autorité des chefs de service: Dans le secteur social et médico-social* (pp. 32–60). Paris: Dunod.

8 Communicative Practices in Work and Training Contexts... 125

Bertrand, E., & Cariat, I. (Eds.). (2017). *Empowerment, le pouvoir d'agir des chefs de service en action sociale et médico-sociale.* Paris: Dunod.

Boltanski, L. (2009). *De la critique: Précis de sociologie de l'émancipation.* Paris: Gallimard.

Boltanski, L., & Chiapello, E. (2011). *Le nouvel esprit du capitalisme.* Paris: Gallimard.

Boltanski, L., & Thévenot, L. (1991). *De la justification: Les économies de la grandeur.* Paris: Gallimard.

Castoriadis, C. (1975). *L'institution imaginaire de la société.* Paris: Seuil.

Eneau, J. (2005). *La part d'autrui dans la formation de soi: Autonomie, autoformation et réciprocité en contexte organisation.* Paris: L'Harmattan.

Eneau, J. (2008). From autonomy to reciprocity or vice-versa? French personalism's contribution to a new perspective on self-directed learning. *Adult Education Quarterly, 58*(3), 229–248.

Eneau, J. (2012). Educational reciprocity and developing learner autonomy: The social dimension of self-directed learning. In K. Schneider (Ed.), *Becoming oneself: Dimensions of "Bildung" and the facilitation of personality development* (pp. 29–54). Wiesbaden: VS Verlag.

Eneau, J. (2017). From self-directed learning to self-formation: Transforming the self through Bildung. In A. Laros, T. Fuhr, & E. W. Taylor (Eds.), *Transformative learning meets Bildung: An international exchange* (pp. 165–178). Rotterdam: Sense Publishers.

Eneau, J., Bertrand, E., & Lameul, G. (2012). Se former et se transformer: Perspective critique et formation universitaire aux métiers de la formation. *Revue internationale de pédagogie de l'enseignement supérieur.* Retrieved from http://ripes.revues.org/585

Eneau, J., Bertrand, E., & Lameul, G. (2014). Le stage en formation alternée: Pour quel développement professionnel? Le cas d'une formation universitaire aux métiers de la formation. *Éducation and Socialisation, n° 35 – Phronesis, 3*(1–2), 38–48.

Eneau, J., & Labelle, J. M. (Eds.). (2008). *Apprentissages pluriels des adultes.* Paris: L'Harmattan.

Habermas, J. (1987). *Théorie de l'agir communicationnel: Pour une critique de la raison fonctionnaliste, l'espace du politique – Tome 2.* Paris: Fayard.

Hess, R. (1993). *L'analyse institutionnelle.* Paris: Presses Universitaires de France.

Honneth, A. (2000). *La lutte pour la reconnaissance.* Paris: Cerf.

Honneth, A. (2007). *La réification: Petit traité de théorie critique.* Paris: Gallimard.

Mezirow, J. (1991). *Transformative dimensions of adult learning*. San Francisco: Jossey-Bass.

Mezirow, J. (2009). Transformative learning theory. In J. Mezirow, E. W. Taylor, & Associates (Eds.), *Transformative learning in practice: Insights from community, workplace and higher education* (pp. 19–31). San Francisco: Jossey-Bass.

Mezirow, J., & Associates. (2000). *Learning as transformation: Critical perspectives on a theory in progress*. San Francisco: Jossey-Bass.

Mezirow, J., & Taylor, E. W. (2009). *Transformative learning in practice: Insights from community, workplace and higher education*. San Francisco: Jossey-Bass.

Morin, E. (1990). *Introduction à la pensée complexe*. Paris: Le Seuil.

Taylor, E. W. (2009). Fostering transformative learning. In J. Mezirow & E. W. Taylor (Eds.), *Transformative learning in practice. Insights form community, workplace and higher education* (pp. 3–17). San Francisco: Jossey-Bass.

Taylor, E. W., & Cranton, P. (Eds.). (2012). *The handbook of transformative learning: Theory, research and practice*. San Francisco: Jossey-Bass.

Taylor, E. W., & Cranton, P. (2013). A theory in progress? Issues in transformative learning theory. *Journal of Research on the Education and Learning of Adults, 4*(1), 33–47.

Watkins, E., & Marsick, V. (1993). *Sculpting the learning organization*. San Francisco: Jossey-Bass.

Watkins, E., & Marsick, V. (Eds.). (1996). *In action: Creating the learning organization*. Alexandria, VA: ASTD Press.

Watkins, E., & Marsick, V. (2003). Making learning count! Diagnosing the learning culture in organizations. *Advances in Developing Human Resources, 5* (2). Thousand Oaks, CA: SAGE.

Watkins, E., Marsick, V., & Faller, P. (2012). Transformative learning in the workplace: Leading learning for self and organizational change. In E. W. Taylor & P. Cranton (Eds.), *The handbook of transformative learning: Theory, research and practice* (pp. 373–387). San Francisco: Jossey-Bass.

Zarifian, P. (2001). Evènement et sens donné au travail. In G. Jeannot & P. Veltz (coord.) (Ed.), *Le travail: Entre l'entreprise et la cité* (pp. 109–124). Paris: Presses Universitaires de France.

Part II

Connecting Theory with Educational Practice

9

Introducing the Method *Transformation Theory in Educational Practice*

Alexis Kokkos

Seeking Educational Practices of Transformative Learning

Since Mezirow introduced his seminal view on transformative learning (TL), a rapid growth of interest and research followed, focusing on the processes through which we question and reassess the problematic assumptions we have endorsed through prior learning. Melacarne (2018) found that over 3000 articles published since 1991 are described by the authors themselves as related to TL. As a consequence of this development, the field of TL has become a continually expanding area of research and practice, which, as it has been substantiated by Cranton and Taylor (2012), constitutes a blessing and a problem at the same time. On the one hand, an increasing number of alternative perspectives of TL have emerged, offering new insights and research opportunities. On the other hand, since the various alternative conceptions often differ from each other, there is a growing incidence of fragmentation, dichotomies and confusion about the identity of TL. According to Cranton and Taylor

A. Kokkos (✉)
Hellenic Open University, Athens, Greece

© The Author(s) 2019
T. Fleming et al. (eds.), *European Perspectives on Transformation Theory*,
https://doi.org/10.1007/978-3-030-19159-7_9

(2012), this situation becomes even more complicated when it comes to teaching practices attempting to foster TL within educational settings. A great proportion of these practices are not consistently associated with and/or significantly shaped by a concrete theoretical orientation as regards TL, therefore they are ill-defined, have shortfalls and lead to a kind of "teaching arbitrary" (p. 15).

This conclusion is probably associated with two other observations reported by Taylor and Laros (2014). Very few recent articles framed by TL have a defined methodology section where practices of fostering TL are presented. Moreover, there is often a lack of clarity when the authors refer to their practices. For instance, they provide little explanation of what these practices look like and how the students and the educators themselves engage in them. Finally, through an extensive literature review, Taylor (2008, 2009) concluded that there are few clear signposts or guidelines which may shed light on how the practices of transformative educators might be connected to a relevant theoretical framework. Therefore, he argued, it becomes difficult for educators "to get a handle on how it plays out in the classroom" (Taylor, 2009, p. 3) so they "have to trust their teaching instincts" (p. 14).

However, some notable exemplars which consistently link a TL theoretical view with educational practices can indeed be identified in the literature. For example, Freire (1970) pursued the aim of conscientization through an effective problem-posing educational method within which, while engaging in an open dialogue with the educator, the learners become co-researchers of the reasons of their socio-cultural oppression and realize their capacity toward changing the societal status quo. Brookfield (2012) associated his orientation of challenging the dominant ideology with a range of teaching techniques that promote critical thinking. Cranton (2002) described a number of teaching strategies that correspond to each of the facets of TL. Yorks and Kasl (2002), building on Heron, introduced a theoretical and practical approach to *Whole-Person Learning*, involving the interaction between affective, imaginal, conceptual, and practical ways of knowing. O'Neil and Marsick (2007) elaborated on a model of action learning grounded in the Critical Reflection School, which aims to challenge practitioners' assumptions underlying their actions.

Nevertheless, these few integrated exemplars do not seem to be able to ameliorate the general impression that there is a wide range of studies dealing with the development of TL in classrooms which, most probably, are random and weakly supported by sound theoretical assumptions.

The Emergence of a Teaching Method

The aforementioned situation appears to be even more problematic as regards the relevance of educational practices to Mezirow's Transformation Theory. This is due to three basic reasons.

First, Mezirow did not put a great deal of emphasis on ways of fostering TL. His primary concern (Mezirow, 1991, 1996) was to describe a comprehensive general learning theory explaining the process through which dysfunctional frames of reference may be challenged and transformed. Therefore, his work focused on the philosophical, pedagogical, epistemological and socio-cultural exploration of the transformational process and the analysis of its components, rather than on the practical aspects of this process. It focused, for instance, on critical reflection, discourse, the forms of TL (transformation of meaning perspectives/habits of mind and transformation of meaning schemes/points of view), as well as on the connection of TL with individual and social action, the role of educators, and so forth. In this respect, in Mezirow's work, we can only find a general description of the variations of the transformation phases of habits of mind and a number of recommendations related to the ways of designing adult education programs and fostering learners' self-directedness.

Finally, Mezirow himself did not describe instructional methods that may foster TL; rather, he edited a volume (Mezirow and Associates, 1990) where seventeen authors presented a collection of typical transformational techniques. However, even though they do describe transformative processes, the texts of that volume are not purposefully associated with the aspects of Transformation Theory.

Second, as Taylor and Laros (2014) persuasively argue, critical reflection, which constitutes the core element of Transformation Theory, is rarely deconstructed by the researchers who deal with its educational

132   A. Kokkos

implementations. Particularly, most studies overlook the importance of Mezirow's conceptualization (1991) concerning the three forms of critical reflection: (a) *content reflection*, which relates to what we perceive, think, feel, or act upon, (b) *process reflection*, referring to how we perform these functions, and (c) *premise reflection*, involving becoming aware of the biographical, cultural and societal factors that have contributed to shaping how we make meaning and behave.

Third, it seems that, within TL literature, little attention is given to the connection of educational practice with an aspect of Mezirow's perspective which I consider to be very important, namely the forms that TL may take. The first form entails the reconstruction of a point of view, which constitutes one of the specific expressions that compose a habit of mind, referring to a broad predisposition we use to interpret experience. The second form refers to the transformation of a habit of mind. Some varieties of habits of mind are, according to Mezirow (2000), the sociolinguistic, moral-ethical, epistemic, philosophical, psychological and aesthetic ones. For instance, *ethnocentrism* is a habit of mind of a sociolinguistic nature. Some points of view that constitute this habit of mind include, for example, that our people belong to a conspicuous, superior nation, that all other nations are inferior, that immigrants and refugees are a hazard and menace to society, that we have nothing to benefit from them, and so forth. For Mezirow (1991, 2000), consequent changes in a series of dysfunctional points of view may possibly lead to a transformation of the broader habit of mind. Accordingly, the most significant and emotionally demanding transformations are those that involve challenging a habit of mind. Mezirow also stressed (Mezirow, 1991, 1997) that habits of mind are highly durable and require the activation of all three forms of critical reflection in order to be transformed. On the contrary, points of view "are more accessible to awareness and to feedback from others" (Mezirow, 1997, p. 6) and are subject to changes that may occur every day, and, therefore, content and/or process reflection is enough for their transformation to occur.

Taking all the above into consideration, I cannot help but point out the fact that neither Mezirow's work nor the relevant TL publications include sufficient sources in order for a thorough response to be offered to a sequence of questions that are often raised by educators who wish to involve the ideas of Transformation Theory in their teaching practice. Such questions include: *How is this theory conceptualized in practice? How could an educator act when he/she notices that the participants have espoused a range of distorted assumptions? How may he/she prioritize the targets of transformation and include them in the available time schedule? How could he/she attune them with the learning objectives that are associated with the educational program?*

It is for these reasons that I argue that it would be worthwhile to structure a teaching method grounded in the perspective and facets of Transformation Theory while also integrating ideas of TL scholars which are congruent with and may even enrich Mezirow's view. The seven-stage method I have developed to this end is called *Transformation Theory in Educational Practice*. The main aspects of this method are discussed here as they were implemented in a pilot training program.

Pilot Implementation

The method was piloted in the context of a training program for adult educators which the Greek Ministry of Labor recently launched. The development and implementation of that program was entrusted to the Hellenic Adult Education Association (HAEA), the leading members of which are experienced adult educators espousing the TL perspective. In total, 260 people employed in public sector organizations participated in it. Most of them were experienced school teachers who, nevertheless, had not yet been involved in adult education, nor had attended a relevant training program in the past. According to the requirements set by the Ministry, the program consisted of 300 hours covering a time period of six months. One hundred hours involved in-person meetings with the participants, while the remaining 200 hours involved distance learning, based on study materials that had been specifically developed for this program, as well as the completion of three assignments. The participants formed groups, each of which comprised 20 members and was facilitated by a HAEA adult educator.

The aims of the program, as specified by the Ministry, included helping the participants enhance their knowledge and skills with regard to: (a)

134 A. Kokkos

using innovative educational methods; (b) establishing effective educator–learners communication; (c) designing appropriate instructional sessions. The seven stages of the method under discussion and the way each of them was implemented in this program are described below.

Stage One: Determining the Need for Transformative Learning

This stage involves an exploration by the educator of the participants' need for critically assessing their own problematic assumptions. The exploration may take two forms: It may be an intentional investigation of the learners' underlying assumptions through an open discussion with them or through analysis of written texts on a certain issue they are asked to produce. Alternatively, the exploration may be initiated due to a particular incident which may have occurred during the everyday educational practice (e.g., the fact that the participants expressed views illustrating certain dysfunctional assumptions regarding the subject-matter, or a specific event involving, for instance, discrimination, indifference to learning, etc.).

Once the educator identifies the dysfunctional assumptions on an issue, he/she facilitates the learners' participation in a process aiming to trigger a disorienting dilemma (Mezirow, 1991), that is, their realization that their current ideas are unjustified, and their concern regarding the need to critically explore them. Indicatively, Cranton (2002) claims that, in order for this process to be achieved, the educators might activate a "catalyst," such as exposing the learners to views, texts or works of art that include ideas alternative to their own. McGonigal (2005) describes how in Stanford University, a number of professors who framed their work in TL theory helped students recognize the limitations of their current knowledge and articulate its underlying assumptions.

In the pilot program described above, the educators, at this stage, realized during their initial discussions with the participants that the latter held strong preconceptions illustrating the perception of informative and instrumental learning which is dominant in Greece, that is, that mere presentation of new information is enough for optimal learning to be

9 Introducing the Method *Transformation Theory...* 135

achieved. Indeed, one of the educators involved in the implementation of the program noted the following: "A great difficulty for me is that many of the participants have been profoundly affected by the 'school' perception of education. 'Liberating' a teacher from the typical education model is very hard."

The leaders of the program concluded that the participants needed to reflect critically on their own assumptions related to their educational role, while, at the same time, feeling that the significance of their efforts and achievements throughout their educational and professional lives thus far was acknowledged and taken into account. This idea was discussed among the groups and, although some of the participants did initially express hesitation or objections, they all agreed to be engaged in a further exploration of the topic.

Stage Two: Participants Express Their Ideas

At this stage, the educator asks the learners to respond—in writing or in small groups—to one or two open-ended questions, so that he/she is able to understand thoroughly their way of thinking about the issue at hand. In the context of the pilot program, the questions were: *"What is the role of the adult educator as far as you are concerned?"* and *"What kind of activities do/would you engage in so as to perform, in practice, the role you described earlier?"*

Stage Three: Identifying the Transformational Strategy

At this crucial stage, the educator, with the active involvement of the participants, analyses their responses to the questions posed during the previous stage and accurately identifies and prioritizes the targets of transformation. In order for this task to be achieved, it would be helpful for the educator to consider two of Mezirow's ideas (1991, 1997) regarding the nature of and the dialectical relationship between points of view and habits of mind. First, as previously stated, the points of view may be changed more easily than a habit of mind. Second, a series of

136   A. Kokkos

transformations in interrelated points of view may progressively lead to a reframe of a relevant habit of mind. These considerations might offer educators a compass for designing teaching strategies aiming to help participants gradually reassess their distorted assumptions, starting from points of view and moving progressively, if consensus and adequate time exist, toward the relevant habit of mind. Specifically, after assessing the personal abilities and inclinations of the participants, their life conditions, their own convictions, their potential resistance to transformation, the learning atmosphere created in class, as well as the time available, educators reflect on the following questions:

> *Should I facilitate a process aiming at the transformation of certain points of view? If so, which ones and how might they be selected?*
> *Should I focus, if there is adequate time, on the transformation of a whole habit of mind? If so, which points of view does it contain? In what order may I attempt to facilitate the transformation of the points of view, aiming potentially at the transformation of the habit of mind? In what ways could this endeavor incorporate Mezirow's view about the transformation phases of a habit of mind?*
> *Within the content of which sections of the curriculum (if there is any) will the transformational process take place? How might this process be linked to the initial teaching aims of the course?*

In the pilot program, the problematic habit of mind which was identified referred to the teacher-centered approach to education. The main participants' points of view through which it was demonstrated involved the following:

(a) The role of the adult educator primarily consists in guiding the learners, who are not capable of taking responsibility for decisions related to their own learning.
(b) The educator teaches the learners mainly through lectures which sometimes could be accompanied by experiential methods.
(c) It is useful to establish creative relationships in the classroom but the educator does not need to emphasize this dimension because his/her role is primarily to enhance the learners' knowledge and skills.

9 Introducing the Method Transformation Theory... 137

(d) As a component of education, critical reflection is synonymous to thoughtful thinking; more specifically, framing critical reflection within the limits of thoughtful thinking, the participants defined it in terms of adequate acquisition and processing of knowledge, without appreciating that an essential dimension of this concept (Cranton, 2006; Mezirow, 1991) lies in questioning learners' problematic assumptions, feelings and actions, with a view to transforming them toward a more functional orientation.

(e) Finally, ongoing learning is not essential; in this regard, the participants believed that they themselves did not particularly need to continue learning since, as they claimed, they had already acquired all essential pedagogical knowledge and had educational experience.

Afterwards, the leaders of the program formulated the strategy which would be implemented. It was decided that the achievement of the program's objectives should be attempted in such a way that the participants would not only upgrade their knowledge and skills as adult educators but, also, they would have the opportunity to critically reflect on their educational role and, further on, to undertake relevant action, as identified by Mezirow (1991, 2000) in his description of the phases of transforming a habit of mind (see analytically in Stage Four below). The ultimate aim was to cause a series of transformations in their points of view, which could potentially lead, by accretion, to the transformation of their habit of mind and the subsequent educational practice.

To that end, the order in which each of the problematic points of view would be challenged was first determined. It was considered more prudent to start by focusing on the points of view which related to educational methods and the educator–learners relationship. This is because, during the initial stages of the program, the participants did not appear to be strongly opposed to experiential learning and the development of a creative learning environment. Therefore, involving them in critically assessing their hesitations regarding these issues seemed relatively less demanding compared to challenging the rest of their points of view.

Afterwards, as expected, emphasis could be placed on helping the participants question their perceptions regarding the concept of critical reflection and the ways it functions within the educational process.

Finally, when there was enough time available, the educators could focus on engaging the participants in approaching critically the last two points of view which seemed to be at the core of their habit of mind, referring, correspondingly, to the guiding role of the educator and their disposition toward their own continuous learning and personal development. Based on the extent to which these ultimate goals are approached, it is argued that the reframe of the whole teacher-centered habit of mind and the resulting practice will be attempted.

It should be noted, at this point, that, according to the rationale of the method, the fact that there is a kind of order in which the points of view would be critically approached does not necessarily imply that a linear process has to be followed. Instead, that order just provides an indication regarding the issue that each transformational endeavor needs to focus on each step of the program, depending on the learning conditions that had been created in each group.

Stage Four: Identifying Educational Practices and Materials

This stage involves designing a variety of teaching activities and materials, through which the strategy identified in the previous stage is specified. In fact, a variety of educational practices which are consistent with the rationale of the present method can be found in the literature. Indicatively, such practices may include critical questioning, incident tasks, role playing, problem solving, life histories, journal writing, criteria analysis, metaphor analysis, imagining alternatives, simulation, critical debate, brainstorming, use of aesthetic experience, whole-person learning strategies, debriefing and so forth (see, e.g., Brookfield, 2012; Cranton, 2006; Freire, 1970; Kokkos, 2010; Mezirow & Associates, 1990; Mezirow & Taylor, 2009; Yorks & Kasl, 2002). When, especially, the transformation of a habit of mind is being attempted, a range of specific practices should be designed drawing on the phases described by Mezirow (1991, 2000), which come after the critical reflection phase. These include:

9 Introducing the Method *Transformation Theory...* 139

* Acquisition of knowledge and skills for implementing a plan.
* Exploring of options for new roles, relationships and actions.
* Trying new roles/Building competence and self-confidence in new roles and relationships.
* A reintegration into one's life on the basis of conditions dictated by one's new perspectives.

In the context of the pilot program, most of the mentioned teaching activities were integrated within face-to-face meetings, study materials and assignments. According to the rationale of the method, emphasis had been placed on the use of art. Our contact with significant works of art—as argued by major scholars such as Adorno (1970/1986), Dewey (1934/1980), Greene (2000) and Marcuse (1978)—can offer alternative ways of making sense, as well as serve as triggers for critical reassessment of our dysfunctional perspectives. This happens because these works of art, due to their unconventional character and the holistic, integrated quality of their content and structure, may contribute in unearthing perceptions and feelings that are distinct from the dominant ones and challenge the beliefs and norms of the established state of affairs. Dewey (1927/1985) argued characteristically that "The function of art has always been to break through the crust of conventionalized and routine consciousness" (p. 183).

Hereby, the educator of the program used works of art, such as *The Class* by Laurent Cantet, *Poetry* by Chang-Dong Lee and Raphael's *School of Athens*, aiming to reconsider the participants' assumptions on issues regarding how we learn, how an educator can handle competing interests while promoting critical reflection, as well as how learners might progressively take control of their choices and actions.

What was highly important as far as the in-person meetings are concerned was that they included two microteaching sessions, a pilot and a final one. In these sessions, each participant presented a short teaching lesson (30 minutes), where he/she acted as an adult educator, the rest of the group acted as learners and, at the end, there was a constructive exchange of views about the common experience. The microteaching sessions aimed at helping the participants develop knowledge, skills and self-confidence, as well as reflect critically on their own educational practices and options, through a balance of recognition of the significance of their endeavors and provision of valuable feedback.

Along the same lines, the assignments and the study materials, in general, had been developed in such a way so as to provide the learners with the opportunity to reflect critically on the subject-matters of the curriculum, as well as on their own educational role. For instance, in order to encourage the participants to reflect on and consolidate the new knowledge, skills and dispositions they were acquiring, the third assignment consisted of the following open-ended questions: *"Did you possibly think of or 'learn' anything 'new' during the program? If so, what was that? Are you going to incorporate it in your practice as an adult educator? If so, how? What kind of difficulties might you encounter and how are you going to overcome them? What 'steps', if any, do you intend to take in the future, as regards your development as an adult educator?"*

Concerning the participants' encouragement to search for new roles, relationships and actions, the program included a range of educational visits to adult education organizations where TL was being implemented. Moreover, progressively encouraging the participants to create individual plans for further learning and personal development was considered crucial, so that they integrate their newly acquired perspectives in their lives.

Stage Five: Applying Transformational Education

This stage involves appropriately implementing in class and monitoring all the practices that have been designed throughout the Stages Three and Four. Furthermore, within the framework of the pilot program, the participants applied their new roles within the real conditions of their own classrooms.

Stage Six: Reflecting on the Experience

At this stage, the educator facilitates a process during which the participants reflect critically and holistically on the experience occurred throughout the previous stages, as well as on their insights resulting from it.

Moreover, the educator and the participants discuss the extent to which, and the reasons why, the reconsideration of the group's assumptions was realized. In the specific framework of the pilot program, reflective groups, in-depth interviews and reflective questionnaires were employed to that end. In his questionnaire responses, a participant shared the following thoughts, illustrating how his awareness of the reasons underlying his assumptions and actions was raised through the program:

> One of the most important conclusions I have reached is that the effectiveness of learning largely depends on the educator's inner desire, ability and willingness to 'give the floor' to the learners themselves (their experience and interests). It depends on the extent to which he [sic] truly wants to listen to their views, incorporate them creatively in the learning process and, when necessary, juxtapose them with the theoretical background. Adults need a different approach from what even we, the educators, have got used to at school or the university. (P.L., participant)

Stage Seven: Defining Next Steps

Given that the transformational endeavor is a long one, the educator, at the end of the process, might discuss with the learners certain actions aiming at the continuance of the elaboration of the issues at hand. Indicatively:

* They might form a plan of "next steps," such as the critical study of texts, the assessment of similar others' experience, or the formation of synergies among peer groups, so that topics continue being discussed and practices are expanded.
* The educator makes himself/herself available to the learners so as to keep on collaborating with them.

After the completion of the pilot program, self-study groups were formed consisting of prior participants and educators, who kept meeting each other with a view to further exploring their experience and knowledge. Several of the participants also became members of the Hellenic Adult Education Association, in the context of which they currently

142   A. Kokkos

collaborate with colleagues who share similar views on adult education and transformative learning.

Further Remarks

On the basis of the discussion in the previous sections, the core concepts of Transformation Theory, as earlier described, should permeate all seven stages of the method. This approach could even be enriched with compatible contributions put forward by scholars of learning for change, particularly as regards issues about which Transformation Theory is not likely to offer much guidance regarding the educational practice. For instance, Fleming (2018) suggests that paying attention to *recognition*, referring to an interpersonal process of caring and support which develops reciprocal self-respect, self-esteem and self-confidence, might "soften" Mezirow's emphasis on the rational dimension of TL process. One may also benefit from Taylor and Cranton's (2013) view that the ability of learners and educators to comprehend each other's perspective (*empathy*) may contribute to the evolution of transformative experiences. From my own perspective, what is worth noting, as well, is that we, adult educators, ought to be aware of group dynamics, which can indeed provide us with further insights in terms of building relationships in the classroom, dealing with complexity and unpredictability, taking advantage of group diversity and exploring the right blend of challenge and encouragement the learners should be provided with.

Conclusion

Most of the existing TL literature does not provide sufficient guidance concerning the ways in which the various TL theoretical views could be conceptualized in the educational practice. This appears more problematic as regards the implementation of Mezirow's Transformation Theory, even though this particular perspective is the most cited one within TL literature (see Chap. 2 of this book). Aiming at facilitating educators' endeavors to apply Transformation Theory, while also enriching their practices with insights offered by other TL scholars, the teaching method *Transformation Theory in Educational Practice* was discussed in this Chapter, with reference to its pilot implementation in a training program.

References

Adorno, T. (1970/1986). *Aesthetic theory*. New York: Kegan and Paul.
Brookfield, S. (2012). *Teaching for critical thinking*. San Francisco: Jossey-Bass.
Cranton, P. (2002). Teaching for transformation. In J. M. Ross-Gordon (Ed.), *Contemporary viewpoints on teaching adults effectively* (pp. 63–71). New Directions for Adult and Continuing Education, No. 93. San Francisco: Jossey-Bass.
Cranton, P. (2006). *Understanding and promoting transformative learning*. San Francisco: Jossey-Bass.
Cranton, P., & Taylor, E. W. (2012). Transformative learning theory: Seeking a more critical theory. In E. W. Taylor & P. Cranton (Eds.), *The handbook of transformative learning: Theory, research and practice* (pp. 3–20). San Francisco: Jossey-Bass.
Dewey, J. (1927/1985). *The public and its problems*. Athens, OH: Swallow.
Dewey, J. (1934/1980). *Art as experience*. New York: Perigee Books.
Fleming, T. (2018). Critical theory and transformative learning: Rethinking the radical intent of Mezirow's theory. *International Journal of Adult Vocational Education and Technology, 9*(3), 1–13.
Freire, P. (1970). *Pedagogy of the oppressed*. New York: Herder and Herder.
Greene, M. (2000). *Releasing the imagination*. San Francisco: Jossey-Bass.
Kokkos, A. (2010). Transformative learning through aesthetic experience: Towards a comprehensive method. *Journal of Transformative Education, 8*, 153–177.
Marcuse, H. (1978). *The aesthetic dimension*. Boston: Beacon Press.
McGonigal, K. (2005). Teaching for transformation: From learning theory to teaching strategies. *Newsletter on Teaching, 14*(2), 1–5. Stanford University.
Melacarne, C. (2018). *Where the literature and the research perspectives on TLT are going to: A meta-analysis based on ERIC*. Proceedings of the 3rd Biennial Conference of ESREA's Network "Interrogating Transformative Processes in Learning and Education: an international dialogue," Milan, Italy 28/06/2018-01/07/2018.

144   **A. Kokkos**

Mezirow, J. (1991). *Transformative dimensions of adult learning*. San Francisco: Jossey-Bass.

Mezirow, J. (1996). Contemporary paradigms of learning. *Adult Education Quarterly, 46*, 158–172.

Mezirow, J. (1997). Transformative learning: Theory to practice. In P. Cranton (Ed.), *Transformative learning in action: Insights from practice* (pp. 5–12). New Directions for Adult and Continuing Education, No. 74. San Francisco: Jossey-Bass.

Mezirow, J. (2000). Learning to think like an adult. Core concepts of transformative theory. In J. Mezirow & Associates (Eds.), *Learning as transformation: Critical perspectives on a theory in progress* (pp. 3–33). San Francisco: Jossey-Bass.

Mezirow, J., & Associates (Eds.). (1990). *Fostering critical reflection in adulthood*. San Francisco: Jossey-Bass.

Mezirow, J., & Taylor, E. W. (2009). *Transformative learning in practice: Insights from community, workplace, and higher education*. San Francisco: Jossey-Bass.

O'Neil, J., & Marsick, V. (2007). *Understanding action learning*. New York: AMACOM.

Taylor, E. W. (2008). Transformative learning theory. In S. Merriam (Ed.), *Third update on adult learning theory* (pp. 5–15). New Directions for Adult and Continuing Education, No. 119. San Francisco: Jossey-Bass.

Taylor, E. W. (2009). Fostering transformative learning. In J. Mezirow & E. W. Taylor (Eds.), *Transformative learning in practice: Insights from community, workplace, and higher education* (pp. 3–17). San Francisco: Jossey-Bass.

Taylor, E. W., & Cranton, P. (2013). A theory in progress? *European Journal for Research on the Education and Learning of Adults, 4*(1), 33–47.

Taylor, E. W., & Laros, A. (2014). Researching the practice of fostering transformative learning: Lessons learned from the study of andragogy. *Journal of Transformative Education, 12*(2), 134–147.

Yorks, L., & Kasl, E. (2002). Toward a theory and practice for whole-person learning: Reconceptualizing experience and the role of affect. *Adult Education Quarterly, 52*(3), 176–192.

10

Disorienting Dilemmas and Irritations in Professional Development: A Longitudinal Study of Swiss Teacher-Students

Anna Laros and Julia Košinár

Introduction

Being a teacher presents young professionals with a myriad of challenges: full responsibility for the students' learning and development, communicating with parents, extended lesson planning, and classroom-management, just to name a few. During practical training, teacher-students can start engaging with their new roles[1] within the safe space of only partial responsibility for a predetermined, and limited, period of time before they are fully responsible after their career entry. Engaging with their new roles often causes teacher-students to experience a disorienting dilemma. On the one hand, coping with the dilemmas can trigger (future) teachers to change their pedagogical habits and to experience processes of professionalization (Košinár, in press). On the other

---

A. Laros (✉) • J. Košinár
University of Applied Sciences and Arts, Northwestern Switzerland, Windisch, Switzerland
e-mail: anna.laros@fhnw.ch; julia.kosinar@fhnw.ch

© The Author(s) 2019
T. Fleming et al. (eds.), *European Perspectives on Transformation Theory*,
https://doi.org/10.1007/978-3-030-19159-7_10

hand, it can trigger them to develop a more integrated and inclusive perspective and to experience transformative learning processes (Mezirow, 1991). Processes of professionalization as well as transformative learning processes are the two foci of this chapter.

Teacher-trainees at the University of Applied Sciences and Arts, Northwestern Switzerland study for three years for their Bachelor of Arts degree and afterward teach at a primary school as full professional teachers. Field experience plays a major role in the curriculum of teacher education in Switzerland.[2] The outsized importance of field experience led to our longitudinal qualitative research project "Challenges for Future and Beginning Primary Teachers" (PH FHNW 2014–2017). This project aims to identify how primary teacher-students perceive and cope with profession-related crises[3] and challenges during practical training and post career entry. The occupational-biographical perspective that describes teachers' professional development as lifelong experience-based process is used as a theoretical frame to shed light on the structure of the processes of professionalization (Košinár, 2014). For the project, we interviewed teacher-students twice: first at the end of their study and again one-and-a-half years post career entry. By using the Documentary Method, we reconstructed four different types of professionalization (Bohnsack, 2014). Our differentiated analysis of cases from these types hints that some interviewees experience transformative learning processes on their way of becoming teachers (Mezirow, 1991, 2000). As stated by King (2000), life changes, such as starting at a new workplace, can trigger transformative learning processes. Accordingly, our results indicate, that becoming a teacher can accompany transformative learning processes (see Laros & Košinár, 2016). With the following chapter, we would like to shed light on these (possible) transformative learning processes by further looking at individual learning processes.

In our contribution, we will describe our first theoretical focus on professionalization. This is followed by an overview of our project "Challenges for Future and Beginning Primary Teachers". We will then describe our second theoretical focus on transformative learning theory. With Mezirow's ten steps as a heuristic, our findings will be outlined by using three contrasting cases. We will then discuss the interaction between processes of transformation and processes of professionalization. We will conclude with the next steps of our research.

Professionalization

As mentioned above, our project's theoretical framework is centered on the occupational-biographical approach. In this perspective of teacher professionalization, (future) teachers meet various requirements that they need to cope with in order to develop competencies and identity formation as teacher (Hericks, 2006). The concept of requirements (Keller-Schneider & Hericks, 2011) identifies four developmental tasks for teachers: (1) identity forming role-taking, (2) respectful classroom-management, (3) suitable instruction, and 4. participating cooperation. On the basis of our own studies, we can add a fifth developmental task for teacher-trainees: Being in a training situation (Košinár & Laros, 2018).

But what leads or "forces" (future) teachers to deal with requirements and to search for solutions? According to the theory of experiential learning (Combe, 2015), the starting point is a crisis where subjects experience for example, a limit of autonomy to act or a limit of understanding a problem. This can lead to two different reactions (mostly prereflexive): (1) avoiding the crisis by assessing the situation/the problem as "irrelevant" or—due to a lack of resources—as "unresolvable," (2) engagement with the situation/the problem with the aim to learn from this experience (Dewey, 1994).

From these conceptual perspectives, mastering developmental tasks can be described as an experiential process dependent on the subjective interpretation of the situation and its handling. The assessment of the situation is based on personal conditions like knowledge and resources but depends also on institutional (the concrete school and pupils) and social conditions (the support by the mentor or the colleagues). For the reconstruction of our case studies, the combination of these two concepts turned out to be a helpful structure.

It became visible that crises can have the force to irritate students' meaning perspectives (see 4). In the process of accepting and engaging with such deep irritations, transformative learning processes can occur.

This is recognizable in changes of habits and acting. But a transformation of meaning perspectives is not automatically accompanied by professionalization. At the same time, we expect processes of professionalization to go along with a transformation of perspectives. With the following contribution, we decided to further look at potential transformative learning processes.

Project Overview

The project "Challenges for Future and Beginning Primary Teachers" aims at identifying key moments and critical incidents that trigger future and young primary teachers to engage with professional requirements and to consequently experience processes of development that lead to their professionalism.

In our longitudinal qualitative study, at two different points in time, teacher-trainees (t1, n = 25) and two years later young professionals (t2, n = 12) participate in narrative interviews. The selection of the sample is based on highly contrasting characteristics of the interviewees on the one hand and on their decision to start teaching after finishing their studies on the other.

Data were analyzed with the Documentary Method (Bohnsack, 2014; Nohl, 2017). By using this method, the implicit meaning of interviewees' narratives regarding their field of practice, the so-called "frames of orientation," can be reconstructed. The frames of orientation can be described as the inner structure or habits of a person—or what Mezirow (1991) calls frames of reference. With our analysis, we developed four types of professionalization along diverse dimensions that were found in the data (e.g., the handling of requirements, the role of the mentor). They were named: 1. self-fulfillment, 2. development, 3. avoidance, 4. probation.

Due to (work-) life changes (e.g., critical incidents), the frame of orientation can (partly) change. Such changes become obvious when looking at the relational typology in a longitudinal comparison. They give hints that transformative processes have occurred on an individual level. With this contribution, we aim to gain further insights into such possible transformative processes by focusing on case studies.

Transformative Learning

According to Mezirow (1991, 2000), in a transformative learning process, individuals triggered by a crisis (disorienting dilemma) become irritated by their existing meaning perspectives. They find their existing perspectives to be insufficient for interpreting a new experience. This is usually paired with negative emotions, such as guilt or shame. Consequently, individuals start searching for alternative interpretation frames. Within this search, they start an exchange with others and explore and try out new roles, which accompany "new" framings, gathering competence and self-confidence along the way. Eventually, they integrate their new perspective into their worldview. After this integration, individuals tend to internalize the change, and their future action is guided by their new perspective. In other words, transformative learning has occurred.

Mezirow (2000, p. 22) has described an ideal-typical transformative learning process as one that happens within these ten phases:

1. Disorienting dilemma;
2. Self-examination with feelings of fear, anger, guilt, or shame;
3. A critical assessment of assumptions;
4. Recognition that one's discontent and the process of transformation are shared;
5. Exploration of options for new roles, relationships, and actions;
6. Planning a course of action;
7. Acquiring knowledge and skills for implementing one's plans;
8. Provisional trying of new roles;
9. Building competence and self-confidence in new roles and relationships;
10. A reintegration into one's life on the basis of conditions dictated by one's new perspective.

Later studies that work with Mezirow's model outlined that transformative learning processes do not necessarily include all ten steps and that the steps' logic tend to be circular rather than linear (e.g., Laros, 2015).

In the following, Mezirow's ten steps will be used as a heuristic (Mezirow, 1991) for answering the following questions:

1. Do students or young professionals experience transformative learning processes while they are engaging with their (new) role as teachers?
2. If so, how does the transformative learning start and how much have students progressed one-and-a-half years post career entry?
3. What is hindering and what is facilitating their transformative learning?

Findings—Transformative Learning of Becoming a Teacher—Contrasting Cases

In the following, we will look deeper into these cases and analyze how the theory of transformative learning can further inform the processes on how interviewees learn to become teachers.

During practical training, students make experiences they cannot interpret with their existing assumptions. They experience disorienting dilemmas while working with pupils as well as while collaborating with their mentor or with other teachers. Students handle these crises differently. Students of the type "development" consequently start to cope with crises by trying out their new role authentically—without feeling restricted by the structure of practical training and in full responsibility of their actions. Simultaneously, they are running through various steps of a transformative learning process (case Pia). Others try out their "new" role as teachers only to a limited extent. For the type "probation," the mentor, who is accompanying and evaluating the student-teachers, plays a central role. Being closely oriented to the mentor, leads these students to place their status as interns in the foreground (case Karin). For students of the type "avoidance," a close orientation to the mentor can also lead to a lack of engagement with a transformative learning process. This is the case, when the mentor's evaluation is the student's main concern, which is then determining their course of action (case Natasha).

10 Disorienting Dilemmas and Irritations in Professional... 151

Alongside their career entry, young professionals face many requirements and consequently experience disorienting dilemmas and crises. Those who are far into experiencing transformative learning processes seem more advanced and are able to not only try out the new role but also build competencies and self-confidence in the new role (Pia). Others experience first steps of transformative learning processes but ostensibly stagnate at an early stage—stopping short of critically examining their existing beliefs (cases Karin, Natasha). Why this happens appears to fall into one of two categories: sometimes teachers overburden themselves which results in them quickly feeling demoralized. As a result, it is difficult for them to try out and find themselves in their new role. Alternately, young teachers sometimes seem to question whether they fit into their profession, effectively stunting their orientation with categories relevant to professionalization (case Natasha).

In the following, we will outline students' possible courses of transformative development by using three contrasting cases. Each case will be analyzed from a longitudinal perspective, using data from t1 and t2.

Pia

During her internship, Pia begins to intensively and authentically try out her new role as a teacher and continues this learning process post career entry. Her narration gives hints that she has made much progress in her transformative learning process already during practical training. The first steps of a transformative learning process become obvious in the following excerpt, when her mentor obliges her to sing a song with the pupil. Since Pia, according to her own statement, "cannot sing well," this duty becomes a disorienting dilemma. She engages herself with this requirement and accepts the crisis. She does not persist in her assumption that she "cannot sing well" but starts exploring courses of actions that enable her to overcome the crisis.

Pia: I did not choose music during my studies, I cannot sing well, singing does not make me feel comfortable. I was preparing at home and recorded my singing with my phone and I had to laugh, it was very special, and I was not sure how to do it in class. I then chose a song that was more a rap, and it went great. I managed to be self-confident in front of the class. But I was not as comfortable as usual.

Pia feels the limitations of her course of action and starts to work on them. She puts across to pupils that she is a learner as well, even though she is teaching them. The structures of her practical training (the mentor evaluates her and is present in the class) do not limit her actions. She takes full responsibility for herself already during her practical training.

> **Pia**: I thought I do not want to seem insecure in front of the kids. But I told them frankly that I'm not the most talented singer but together we can surely sing a great song. They took it positively cause the kids like it when the teacher sometimes does not know how to do something…and I looked at my mentor and had to smile.

The excerpts outline that Pia is starting to experience first steps of a transformative learning process during her practical training. By viewing herself as learner and exploring new courses of action (choosing a rap song), she starts reinterpreting two assumptions: 1. that music education always includes the introduction of songs that are sung and 2. that she cannot sing and eventually gains new self-confidence.

Post career entry, Pia at first experiences being a teacher as being "thrown into cold water"—a metaphor she repeats several times. She starts coping with this crisis and further continues the transformative process of learning her new role as teacher. She progresses by actively engaging with new requirements. Pia emphasizes that she is now the one responsible for decision-making.

While (transformative) learning her role, Pia is reflecting about new courses of action that she has tried out so far. In doing so, she is balancing out her high self-expectations on the one hand and challenges she has to cope with on a daily basis on the other hand.

> **Pia**: How did I solve new requirements? Just do it. There is no recipe. I profit from my experiences; I check out what others are doing; this is what I do—there is no recipe. The curriculum does not tell you how to do it.

10 Disorienting Dilemmas and Irritations in Professional...   153

Alongside, Pia pays attention to her well-being and manages to avoid feeling overburdened. Even though she calls her career entry a "strict time," she seems to have made sure that she is "never doing bad."

It becomes obvious that Pia's transformative learning process of becoming a teacher has already started during her practical training. At this early stage, she starts to intensively engage with and tries out her new role as a teacher—before she even has her teaching diploma. During her following career entry, new requirements seem to overwhelm her at first and she experiences a crisis ("cold water"), but she faces it head-on and starts to cope. One-and-half years after her career entry, she seems to have progressed in her transformative process. She continues to explore and try out her new role, plans courses of action, acquires new knowledge and continuously tries out and critically examines her experiences and builds competence (steps 5–9 of Mezirow's model).

Karin

Karin also starts to engage with her new role during practical training. But, in contrast to Pia, only to a limited extent because her status of being an intern stops her from moving toward a profound learning process. The following excerpt is an example on how she begins engaging with her new role during practical training by acquiring new knowledge through experienced teachers. Her status as novice who needs to be led by experts seems to be central for her.

> **Karin**: It was great that I was well accepted by the mentors in every practical training. I could ask them anything concerning school and they gave me answers. I was allowed to try out things and they encouraged me and that was great.

On the other hand, the hierarchy in a practical training (the mentor is evaluating and present) seems to limit Karin's ownership over her new role. She tries to act in a manner that she thinks her mentors are expecting from her.

154   A. Laros and J. Košinár

> **Karin:** That is difficult. In every practical training, you do it the way the mentor wants it. Of course, sometimes you are trying, a little bit, things out but you are taking over the mentor's structures. Now I know things I would not do the same way or do differently.

Post career entry, Karin seems to feel overwhelmed by the disorienting dilemma that goes along with taking on the new role. She seems to overuse her resources in a way that inhibits her from finding herself in her new role. This is underlined by her use of the terminology "being shot into cold water," which harkens back to Pia's expression. But, when facing the crisis, she starts to critically examine her assumptions. Consequently, she does not succeed in balancing her high self-expectation with her limited available resources. As a result, she does not cope with her disorienting dilemma in a way that advances a transformative learning process. This is exemplified in the following excerpt: feeling overburdened leads her to externalize her crisis—she starts to question the profession and her choice of profession.

> **Karin:** I would like to… reflect on how I could didactically do a great lesson but there is not enough time somehow. Maybe the profession needs to be changed. Or I don't know what. An additional person would be needed who has this time. I don't know.

During her practical training, Karin started to tackle her role as a burgeoning teacher. However, her beginning transformative learning process, which seemed to be triggered during her career entry, seems to stagnate at the early stage of the critical assessment of her own assumptions (step 3): Karin's high self-expectation along with her high use of resources keep her away from exploring options for new roles (step 4) and progressing in finding herself within her new role.

Natasha

Within her practical training, Natasha does not authentically try out her new role as a teacher—she rather seems to feel distanced from the teaching profession. Her mentors' evaluation is central for Natasha. This seems

10 Disorienting Dilemmas and Irritations in Professional... 155

to be the reason why Natasha aims at rather creating a positive image of herself as a teacher (in front of her mentor) instead of authentically trying out the role of a teacher.

> **Natasha**: Yes, sometimes you feel like a master of ceremonies. During practical training, you would like to show how awesome you are, and this is a challenge.

Natasha seems not to identify herself with the teaching profession—that might be another reason why it is challenging for her to really try out her new role. Her distance becomes obvious in the way she downgrades standards of her profession as unnecessary "details."

> **Natasha**: I think when something goes really wrong, feedback is needed and reflections are needed. But because of every single detail like "you haven't used the red pen but an orange one." Such things. This is not my world, but I figured holding onto such details is this primary schooling level.

Post career entry, it seems to be challenging for her to start exploring new roles and actions concerning her "attitude" as a teacher as well as concerning her question whether or not she can find a fit in the profession. The following excerpt highlights her difficulties in identifying with the profession.

> **Natasha**: My attitude towards the profession, in general, is challenging because you do not have a reputation in front of society, you do not have a reputation in front of the parents and the only thing that you can say and that I am convinced by is that school is needed because it is obligatory.

Natasha seems to be aware of her non-conformist attitude. Furthermore, she starts critically assessing her "attitude." She recognizes a need for change and, therefore, seems to be standing at the beginning of a transformative learning process. Her learning stage becomes obvious when she is reflecting about her participation in team meetings.

> **Natasha**: Team meetings within our internal formation are interesting, but I am flying pretty fast into my previous role of being a pupil, that makes

me start thinking "Oh, this is bullshit."... I would like to be more constructive concerning co-working or other themes and prove my new attitude.

While Natasha was avoiding teachers' requirements during practical training, she is starting to critically engage with her "attitude" post career entry. But it seems to be impossible for her to go beyond a critical assessment (step 3).

Discussion and Outlook

Looking at the whole learning processes from the end of students' studies up until one-and-half years post career entry, it becomes obvious that the students experience disorienting dilemmas in the process of becoming teachers. As we could show along the case of Pia, some of them are progressing pretty far into their transformative learning processes as they take on their new role, by running through various steps of Mezirow's ideal-typical learning process. Others seem to start a transformation but stagnate at the early stage of critically assessing their assumptions. They seem to be incapable of going beyond this stage—even though they start to recognize that their existing assumptions are insufficient when they are trying to frame their new roles as teachers. In the following, we discuss whether the outlined (potential) transformative learning processes lead to the development of professionalism.

From the beginning of her study, Pia is engaging in new requirements and reflecting about new courses of action that she has tried out so far. The example proves that she is willing to take risks in trying out new courses of action, but simultaneously she is seeking a suitable way for her pupils to follow her instructions. At the same time, she defines her role as a learner and as a teacher. Post career entry, the necessity of dealing with requirements, duties and expectations leads her to her limits. In engaging with requirements, she seems to be oriented toward categories relevant for professionalization. The example with the rap song first proves her awareness of the necessity of building up a working relationship with the pupils, which is a substantial part of the quality of teaching (developmental task: suitable instruction). Secondly, Pia continuously shows a highly developed reflexivity and a sensible use of her own resources (developmental task: identity forming role-taking). Thus, processes of transformation and of professionalization seem to occur simultaneously.

Also, Karin is oriented on categories relevant for professionalization. In her critical search for an authentic way to decide and act in class, a reflective attitude emerges. According to Helsper (2018), this is the basis for the development of a professional habitus. Karin seems to have the potential of being a teacher with high professional standards, but she does not succeed in progressing through further steps of a transformative learning process when her high self-expectations collide with the real conditions during career entry. This experience leads her to an "avoidance" (Košinár, 2014) of any further dealing with challenges. Here, her behavior has to be interpreted as a kind of self-protection, a (temporary) state in which any professional progress stagnates.

In the case of Natasha, a first concern with the developmental task "identity forming role-taking" can be identified in her critical self-assessment one-and-a-half years post career entry. But in this state, taking into account her (subjective) lack of fitting into this profession, it is unpredictable whether any further professional development can be expected.

Resuming the findings out of the present cases, the stagnation of a transformative learning process can be located on a spectrum: Due to high standards and despite an engagement in professional requirements, the feeling of being overburdened can hinder young professionals from truly arriving in the new role (Karin). On the other hand, the experience of a lack of fitting into the teaching profession can hinder one from exploring ways of finding their footing. This is what keeps one at a distance from the new role (Natasha).

However, those who have progressed very far in their transformative learning processes are those who authentically cope with the disorienting dilemmas they experienced at an early stage of professional development. This early engagement seems to work as a "setting the stage" (Laros, 2015) for the following transformative process (Pia). Others, whose transformative processes do not go beyond a critical assessment of assumptions, have not been engaged during practical training in the same way (Natasha) or only in a limited scope with the structure of the practical training in the foreground (Karin).

Further analysis will clarify how the transformative elements that were outlined by looking at individual cases could further inform our types of professionalization that were reconstructed in our longitudinal study for t1 and t2.

Notes

1. The terminology "learning a role" is used according to Mezirow in a rather unspecific way and focuses on how a change of perspectives accompanies interviewees' processes of mentally arriving in their profession. From a profession-theoretical viewpoint, learning the role of a teacher focuses on engaging with (profession-related) requirements in one's profession-biographical process.
2. The teacher-students fulfill four phases of practical training during their studies (in sum 16 weeks, partly in the form of day placements over a year). During each of these placements, two students work with an experienced teacher in their class as "assistant teachers."
3. The terminology "crisis/crises" and what Mezirow calls "disorienting dilemma" is being used synonymously.

References

Bohnsack, R. (2014). *Rekonstruktive Sozialforschung: Einführung in qualitative Methoden*. Opladen: Barbara Budrich.

Combe, A. (2015). Dialog und Verstehen im Unterricht. Lernen im Raum von Phantasie und Erfahrung. In U. Gebhard (Ed.), *Sinn im Dialog. Zur Möglichkeit sinnkonstituierender Lernprozesse im Fachunterricht* (pp. 51–66). Wiesbaden: Springer VS.

Dewey, J. (1994). *Erziehung durch und für Erfahrung*. Stuttgart: Klett-Cotta.

Helsper, W. (2018). Lehrerhabitus. In A. Paseka, M. Keller-Schneider, & A. Combe (Eds.), *Ungewissheit als Herausforderung für pädagogisches Handeln* (pp. 105–140). Wiesbaden: Springer VS.

Hericks, U. (2006). *Professionalisierung als Entwicklungsaufgabe*. Wiesbaden: Springer VS.

Keller-Schneider, M., & Hericks, U. (2011). Beanspruchung, Professionalisierung und Entwicklungsaufgaben im Berufseinstieg von Lehrerinnen und Lehrern. *Journal für Lehrerinnen und Lehrerbildung, 11*(1), 20–31.

King, K. P. (2000). The adult ESL experience: Facilitating perspective transformation in the classroom. *Adult Basic Education, 10*, 69–89.

Košinár, J. (2014). *Professionalisierungsverläufe in der Lehrerausbildung. Anforderungsbearbeitung und Kompetenzentwicklung im Referendariat.* Opladen: Barbara Budrich.

Košinár, J. (in press). Habitustransformation, Wandel oder kontextinduzierte Veränderung von Handlungsorientierungen? In R.-T. Kramer & H. Pallesen (Eds.), *Lehrerhabitus. Theoretische und empirische Beiträge zu einer Praxeologie des Lehrerberufs.* Bad Heilbrunn: Julius Klinkhardt.

Košinár, J., & Laros, A. (2018). Zwischen Einlassung und Vermeidung – Studentische Orientierungen im Umgang mit lehrberuflichen Anforderungen im Spiegel von Professionalität. In T. Leonhard, J. Košinár, & C. Reintjes (Eds.), *Zwischen Einlassung und Vermeidung – Praktiken des Umgangs mit lehrberuflichen Anforderungen.* Bad Heilbrunn: Julius Klinkhardt.

Laros, A. (2015). *Transformative Lernprozesse von Unternehmerinnen mit Migrationsgeschichte.* Wiesbaden: Springer VS.

Laros, A., & Košinár, J. (2016). Transformative learning processes in practical trainings? Students on their way of becoming primary teachers. *Proceedings of the 2nd ESREA-network conference: Interrogating Transformative Processes in Learning and Education* (p. 20). Athens.

Mezirow, J. (1991). *Transformative dimensions of adult learning.* San Francisco: Jossey-Bass.

Mezirow, J. (2000). Learning to think like an adult. Core concepts of transformation theory. In J. Mezirow & Associates (Eds.), *Learning as transformation* (pp. 3–33). San Francisco: Jossey-Bass.

Nohl, A.-M. (2017). *Interview und Dokumentarische Methode: Anleitungen für die Forschungspraxis (Qualitative Sozialforschung).* Wiesbaden: Springer VS.

11

New Scenario for Transformation: How to Support Critical Reflection on Assumptions Through the Theatre of the Oppressed

Alessandra Romano

Introduction

The chapter describes and analyses the use of Theatre of the Oppressed in Higher Education programmes. The Theatre of the Oppressed (TO) is a form of popular and participatory theatre that fosters democratic and cooperative forms of interaction in order to spark processes of personal and collective reflections (Boal, 1985, 1996). The epistemological framework underpinning TO relies on Freirean practices of transformative learning through the use of the 'pedagogy of the oppressed' based on popular education principles (Freire, 1970). We think this Freirean tradition can be usefully supplemented by also drawing on Mezirow's theory to answer a key question: how can the creative and embodied activities used in TO create opportunities for 'reflective discourse' leading to a critical assessment of their assumptions and an examination of alternative perspectives (Mezirow, 2000)? Embodied knowledge is a type of knowledge where the body knows how to act (e.g., how to walk,

---

A. Romano (✉)
University of Siena, Siena, Italy

© The Author(s) 2019
T. Fleming et al. (eds.), *European Perspectives on Transformation Theory*,
https://doi.org/10.1007/978-3-030-19159-7_11

161

run, etc.) and asserts that the body, not the mind, is the knowing subject. Embodied knowledge is not confined only to motor skills, as all experiences share the property of doing without representing. Representation is not necessary because there is a pre-reflective correspondence between body and world. Embodied knowledge is beyond the Cartesian mind–body dualism and requires an embodied view of mind (Tanaka, 2011). Mezirow did not take account of embodied knowing in his theory. Starting from this question, the chapter aims at studying how experience-based and performative art-based learning can be connected to transformative learning theory in Higher Education contexts.

In the first half, I will outline what is involved in TO and offer some theoretical reflections based on my experience as a practitioner. The second part of the chapter will explore the impact of TO empirically through data gathered longitudinally in two 'laboratories', in which different TO methods were used with cohorts of Bachelor's and Master's Degree students and teachers. This involved qualitative (narrative accounts) and quantitative tools (Learning Activities Survey—see below for full outline). Based on this data, the chapter argues that TO experience-based learning encourages critical reflection on assumptions in students and teachers in training about their professional identity and role. On the basis of our practice and research of TO, we believe there is a clear rationale for incorporating arts-based practices and TO to support an experience-based transformative approach to teaching and learning in Higher Education (Ferguson, Romano, Bracci, & Marsick, 2018).

The Theatre of the Oppressed: Dialogue, Play and Learning Leadership

TO is a practice which builds directly on Paulo Freire's approach (Freire, 1970), which promotes a transformative model of learning based on dialogue. In TO, dialogue is brought about through the creation of a playful environment in which people express, analyse and collectively change

11 New Scenario for Transformation: How to Support Critical...

aspects of their reality according to their desires (Boal, 1985, 1996). Play is designed to activate a 'problem-posing' learning process where participants examine and analyse their reality starting from a situation of personally lived oppression and/or injustice. Boal (1985) states that TO has two fundamental principles: (1) to help the spectator become a protagonist in the dramatic action so that s/he can then (2) apply those theatrically practiced actions s/he in real life situations. Participants create scenes based on their own direct experiences and explore unresolved conflicts stemming from political or social problems. Each story represents the perspective of an oppressed protagonist actively engaged in implementing a strategy for the resolution of a conflict. When the protagonist fails to resolve the conflict participants analyse the power relations and the causes of oppression. Finally, they act to transform the situation according to their vision of possible alternatives.

In TO, thinking, language and gesture are unified through a holistic and embodied practice of collective story-telling. The purpose is to move from oppressor/oppressed dichotomies, otherness and simplistic solutions to explore the true complexity of social systems. This perspective is influenced by understanding community as an integrated living organism (Diamond, 2007) and by placing a strong focus on relationships.

Participants' leadership skills, including their internal beliefs that they can successfully effect change or engage in a leadership process, determines whether or not they take on leadership roles. Creating a 'brave space' (Dugan, Turman, Barnes and Associates, 2017, p. 422), where participants can rehearse how to address problems, challenge oppressive behaviours or envision how to engage in a leadership process, can positively impact both on leadership efficacy and capacity. According to this framework, leadership is based on relationships—a collaborative process where people intend to effect changes for the common good. The ultimate goal of this method is to empower participants to take action, to engage in leadership for emancipatory social change, to explore the root causes of inequalities and injustice, and to collaborate with others, as a group, to resolve them.

Participation, Problem Posing and Critical Reflection

Everybody who attends a Forum Theatre session participates. The joker, who facilitates discussion, frequently interrupts the scene during the performance and asks the audience to recognize and problematize the situation of oppression and to try to identify an oppressed and an oppressor. Through questions, participants speculate about the situation performed and begin to encode and decode that reality represented in the stage action. The audience is asked: *'if you were the oppressed, what would you do? How would you react? What would you think of doing to resolve the conflict?'* The joker opens a dialogue on why oppressive conditions exist and how they can be changed. Participants explore rigid patterns of perception that generate miscommunication and conflict, as well as ways of transforming them.

By also drawing on Heron (1992), TO methods facilitate learners in discovering ecologically embedded, embodied, symbolic and presentational ways of knowing. Through the body, people bring the whole self into their learning experience: they bring mind, soul, body and spirit into learning. It allows the collective reflection about what holds someone and about what aspects hold/prevent someone from doing something, from imaging and practising a diverse reality, a transformed reality. In a recursive process of action–discussion–reflection–transformative action, Theatre Forum combines theorizing and being active (Lundgren et al., 2017). This promotes the kind of deep learning that can also support societal change.

In this way, TO is a preparation for the implementation of cultural change to address injustice, inequality and oppression. But a key assertion of this chapter is that we enhance our understanding of these processes if we also examine the process of change and transformation using Mezirow's (1991) concepts and theory. We think this dialogue—and theoretical synthesis—between TO and Mezirow will help sensitize practitioners and research to the full range of modes of critical thinking and development which avoids cognitivism (Dirkx, 2012) and articulates transformative learning within an emancipatory, collective and embodied framework (Fabbri & Romano, 2017). This will enhance the ability of teachers to support a more comprehensive and multi-faceted understanding of learning.

Researching the Transformative Potential of the Theatre of the Oppressed

The purpose of the cross-case study *TOTP: Transformative Potential of the Theatre of the Oppressed* (Romano, 2014, 2016) described below is to 'test' these claims in a systematic way and to explore if, and under what conditions, the adoption of the TO methods in Higher Education with students and teachers in training is helpful in promoting critical reflection related to the framework of transformative learning (Marsick, 2015; Mezirow, 2000).

The research was conducted in the academic years 2013/2014 and 2014/2015 at the University of Naples, Italy. Higher Education students engage in a Forum Theatre workshop over two days, which aims to support them to actively explore in body-based practices how development unfolds across multiple domains (social constraints, personality growth, etc.) and how their personal identity and professional identities are shaped and shapes socio-cultural norms in a society where, cultural and political forces, intragroup and intergroup dynamics are continuously evolving (Wijeyesinghe & Bailey Jackson, 2012).

In the first meetings, a set of exercises and techniques aimed to encourage creativity, self-expression and improvization were used with the students. Warm-up activities that help creating a safe and trusting environment and make participants familiar and comfortable with embodied learning and that begin to explore issues of power and oppression are used (Boal developed a wide range of scenarios and practices to do this). Then, students are divided into two groups. As was mentioned above, each group is asked to write a story of oppression, violence or injustice that they had experienced. They create together a plot and are asked to perform it in front of their colleagues. One group, for example, represents the story of abuse and violence in a couple engaged to be married: they stress characters' powerless conditions and social pressures on them. In the story represented by the cohort of teachers in training, meanwhile, the public/personal dimensions of the role of the teachers are stressed.

Participants

The research used intentional sampling (Creswell, 2007). The three groups who participated in the research were:

* 145 students doing a Bachelor's Degree in Psychological Sciences
* 87 students doing a Master's Degree in Clinical and Community Psychology
* 100 teachers in training enrolled on a Certified Special Course,

Data were gathered at the end of the laboratories. Participants were required to write narrative accounts and fill out two surveys.[1]

Data Analysis

The first type of analysis conducted is the phenomenological analysis of all the narrative accounts. For the phenomenological analysis (Creswell, 2007), a panel of independent researchers was asked to analyse the data (see Chart 11.1): they first worked individually and then compared and discussed their findings. Through phenomenological analysis we (a) identified core categories which featured strongly in the narrative 'reports' produced by participants, and then (b) measured the frequency and occurrences of each core category.

The software NVivo was used to do open and selective coding. The researcher worked with the narrative data fracturing and analysing it, initially through open coding for the emergence of core knots and categories. Subsequently, in the phase of axial coding, we undertook theoretical sampling and selective coding of data and identified the emergence of core concepts. Theoretical 'saturation' is achieved through constant comparison

11 New Scenario for Transformation: How to Support Critical... 167

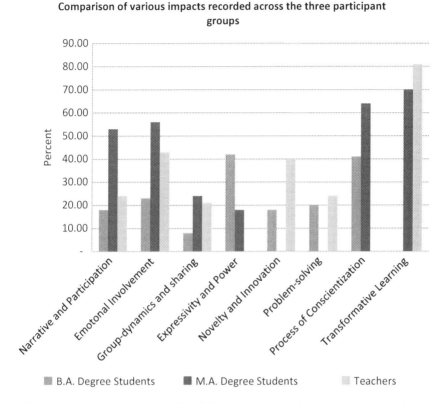

Chart 11.1 Comparative analysis of the three groups showing frequency of categories in percentages

of incidents (indicators) in the narratives to elicit the properties and dimensions of each category (codes) (Creswell, 2007; Holton, 2007).

Later, the researcher analysed the responses of each participant to the Learning Activity Survey questionnaire in order to evaluate changes in meaning perspectives These sources allowed me to assess for each participant what if any transformative learning had occurred using four criteria (Marsick, 2015) asking if:

1. A process of questioning and critical reflection is present?
2. A change of meaning perspectives is discernible?

168   A. Romano

3. More inclusive, open and differentiating perspectives are shown?
4. New pattern of actions thanks to this transformation are in evidence?

In the next phase of the analysis, all the participants are stratified into three groups, rated by the scoring of the Perspective Transformation Index (PT-Index, see note 1) as well as the narrative report to assess if a person exhibits:

1. *High Level of Transformation: evidence of all four criteria;*
2. *Low-Level Transformation: people with only two of four criteria;*
3. *No Transformation: people who do not show any criteria for transformation.*

Research Outcomes

We conducted a comparative analysis for each group of participants (Bachelor's Degree students, Master's Degree students, Teachers in training) based on the narrative reports.

Based on this analysis TO had a significant impact and encouraged deep critical thinking and new forms of praxis (although as I discuss below this was certainly not the case for all participants). The representation on stage of autobiographical experiences, encouraged them to work in an analytical way. This presents them with disorienting dilemmas that encourages teachers in training to critically examine their previous assumptions and to (at least partially) change them. One participant (22) reflected:

> *TO allows us to make "visible" the daily oppression; create a unifying symbolic object, a social ritual of community, to get used to reacting with discomfort to change; have a solidaristic and collective dimension; create links for new actions in people lives; emotional and energetic activation, as well as the intellectual side [..] to address the problems and test possible changes; projection into the future through visions, can reveal and shake what is the individual and collective imagination, powerful means of prefiguration of the future.*

11 New Scenario for Transformation: How to Support Critical... 169

Another participant (10) noted:

> *The theatre of the oppressed allowed me to process so many humiliations and to represent my idea of being professor and director who is not founded on the power games but on dialogue [...]. I went through a real catharsis*

When we explore these changes for the different groups, we see that TO sparks change and even transformative learning but not in a uniform way as the chart below illustrates.

The most prominent category in the three groups of participants is the 'change in perspectives and disorienting dilemma.' This category occurs in 82% of the journals of teachers in training, in 70% of journals of Master's degree students and in the 35% the journals of Bachelor's Degree students. This is the strongest evidence in the narratives of the protagonists that a change in meaning perspectives, which can be interpreted through the schemes of the transformative learning theory, occurred. One participant (30) said:

> *During the various scenes I changed my viewpoints. Thanks to the comparison with the other guys I realized that I could do something to address situations, I could transform the class and be the agent of change simply by changing myself.*

Despite the variegated impact of the process, the research indicates that the power of TO is such that it frequently led to a form of reflexive awareness that goes beyond the forms of instrumental and technical knowledge that are often taught in university classrooms. Future psychologists and future teachers learn performative and art-based methods that will be of use for their professions. Through the sequential and systematic use of other forms of presentational knowledge (Heron, 1992), such as theatre, metaphor, dramatic action, followed by the writing of the narrative journals and the discussion, students and teachers challenge their assumptions, making them explicit and forcing them to review and process them through critical and complex collective ways of thinking. Significantly these transformations, the data indicate, is never just cognitive, it is also always affective and emotional, partly empathetic. However, as can be seen in Chart 11.1, evidence of conscientization is missing in the self-report of the teachers in training, and transformative learning is not evident in the self-reports of Bachelor's Degree students.

The Findings of the Phenomenological Cross-Group Analysis

The cross-group analysis sought a deeper understanding of the experiences of the participants. 332 participants are divided into three categories:

The High Level of Transformation (N = 151; 44% of the total sample) are participants that in their narrative journals discuss changes which match the four criteria for transformative learning discussed above (Marsick, 2015; Mezirow, 1991). They describe the TO as prompting them to explore previously unquestioned premises, to try new strategies and approaches and to access a new understanding of values, beliefs, assumptions about themselves and their world.

The group with low-level transformation, composed by learners who gained a score of 2 PT-Index Questionnaire to LAS (King, 2009), is the smallest group (N = 53; 18% of the total sample). These subjects put into question their meaning schemes, their world views, but do not show new, open, inclusive and permeable prospects of meaning or attempts to create new social roles and new patterns of actions. For example, one of the teachers-in training speaks about the importance of analysing power dynamics that are often hidden in the school organization. She describes how she thinks she will now, following the laboratory, interact in a more empathetic way with her Principal, linking the story represented on stage with her personal stories. But she never presents herself as an active part of the power dynamics or explores *her* perspective on the relationship between the Principal and the teachers, or, much better, on how the perception of this relationship as oppressive impacts on the way she relates to her students in her classroom.

The group with No Transformation, with a score of 1 to PT-Index Questionnaire LAS, is the second group by number (N = 128; 38% of the total sample). They are participants who do not describe a transformation process in their self-reports and do not show any one of the criteria for transformative learning. They do not show any change (N = 101; 79% of the entire group No Transformation) and persist in keeping their perspectives and assumptions; there are subjects who do not show a change in meaning perspectives in their self-report (N = 27; 21% of the group No Transformation), even if Learning Activity Survey (King, 2009) responses confirm that there is a learning experience that can be considered a challenge in meaning schemes (Mezirow, 2000). The comparison with the responses to the Theatre of the Oppressed survey triangulates the cross-case analysis and the stratification into the three groups (High, Low, No Transformation) and gives more information to validate the criteria for the scoring and the discussion of the outcomes.

Formalizing Transformative Learning

I want to now build on the earlier theoretical reflections and the empirical analysis. The results of the cross-group analysis indicate that it is useful to view critical transformative learning as an understanding of social agency and collective empowerment that occurs through an embodied dialectical process. In the model of critical transformative learning (see Fig. 11.1), it is possible to track the dialectical tension between the phases of the TO methods and the steps of the transformation of meaning perspectives. The process of collective reflection and critical dialogue unfolds across the criticism of the previous beliefs, the participation into a disorienting practice-based learning experience, the identification of needs and expectations and the testing of new schemes of actions and strategies for problem-solving.

In the model of critical transformative learning, the embodied dimension missing in Mezirow's work (Mezirow, 1991), is reported in terms of embedded and performed dialogue among participants able to activate processes of critical collective reflections (Romano, 2018). As Mezirow himself said: 'when learners come to identify with others who have been similarly oppressed, collective social action may develop and it is desirable and appropriate that it do so' (Mezirow, 1989, p. 172). The centrality of conscientization and the importance of entrenched power and

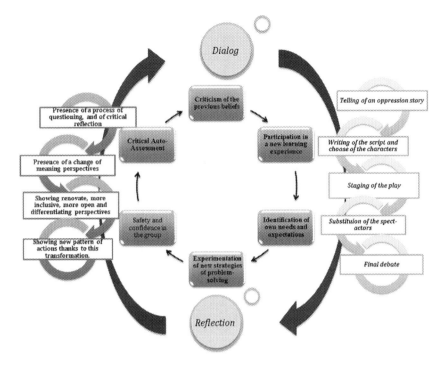

Fig. 11.1 The model of critical transformative learning. How the process of change of meaning perspectives unfolds across the Theatre of the Oppressed steps

agency in community and professional identity development are here fostered through the Theatre of the Oppressed.

In the cross-case study described, students and teachers in training are supported to (a) surface tacit beliefs, implicit expectations, feelings and judgments that unconsciously direct and shape their representations of professional identity; (b) collectively recognize and critically interrogate shared problems and underlying assumptions; and (c) speak out against oppression, exclusions and injustice and reaffirm commitment to a just and equitable society.

The TO dialogical practices and performative methods help to develop collective reflection processes *in*, *on* and *through* action; to challenge and resolve personal and collective disempowerment; and to imaginatively

11 New Scenario for Transformation: How to Support Critical...

explore "what if" and "what could be" possibilities for social change and effective interventions.

Through the lens that takes into account individual, group and transformational learning processes (Lawson, Blythe, & Shaw, 2014; Marsick & Neaman, 2018), including these methods in class offers an emancipatory transformative standpoint that allows learners to:

(a) Explore the relationship between knowledge and power, eliciting critical examination of how as knowers they are positioned in a network of human and non-human power arrangements that constrain or enable their lives (Gherardi, 2017).
(b) Re-elaborate their life and social experiences, and the way these influenced and determined reproductive tendencies and distortions of perspectives about gender, relationships and politics.
(c) Work on professional identity and empowerment issues, developing creativity and fostering autonomy and self-awareness.

Within this backdrop, TO methods facilitate students in discovering ecologically embedded, embodied, symbolic and presentational ways of knowing (Gherardi, 2017; Heron, 1992). The entire workshop experience of TO is characterized as a disorienting dilemma. The transformation of assumptions (Mezirow, 2000) is achieved through the development of self-criticism, awareness and reflection on oneself and on others as well as through the development of a capacity for ethical behaviour, and of collective reflective dialogue on the dynamics of oppression. These results call for conception transformative learning that moves the theory (and the research) away from cognitive-centred abstraction and separations of the body (Dix, 2016; Hoggan, 2016).

Understood within this context, TO can support groups and organizations to engage in essential debate over strategy and process to work for social change and collective perspective transformations, and to enhance their learning into a revolutionary praxis, a critical praxis that encompasses reflection, dialogue, action and transformation in an ongoing alliance.

Note

1. The Learning Activity Survey (LAS) is a questionnaire constructed and tested by the research group directed by King (2009). The LAS has two major purposes: identifying whether adult learners had a perspective transformation in relation to their educational experience; and if so, determining what learning activities have contributed to it (King, 2009, p. 14). The assessment tool has four major parts. Part one identifies the stages of perspective transformation and asks participants for a brief description of their experience. Part two determines which learning experiences have promoted a perspective transformation. Part three is a series of questions determining the learning activities in which respondents were involved. Lastly, Part four collects information on demographic characteristics.

    In the LAS survey, items 1–5 guide the respondent to reflect on an experience of change and delve into what exactly it was, how it happened, and what contributed to its occurrence. The educator uses the information from these items to determine a score for each participant on a scale from one to three. This PT-Index scale indicates whether learners had a perspective transformation, in relationship to their education, PT-Index = 3; whether they had one not associated with their education, PT-Index = 2; or whether they did not have a perspective transformation experience, PT-Index = 1 (King, 2009, p. 16). The PT-Index provides three concise categories for representing who have experienced perspective transformation and who have not. More details about the survey can be found in Romano (2018).

References

Boal, A. (1985). *Theatre of the oppressed* (C. A. McBride and M. O. Leal McBride, Trans.). New York: Theatre Communications Group.

Boal, A. (1996). *The rainbow of desire: The Boal method of theatre and therapy.* London: Routledge.

Creswell, J. W. (2007). *Qualitative inquiry and research design: Choosing among five approaches* (2nd ed.). Thousand Oaks, CA: Sage.

Diamond, D. (2007). *Theatre for living: The art and science of community-based dialogue.* Victoria, BC: Trafford.

Dirkx, J. M. (2012). Self-formation and transformative learning: A response to "calling transformative learning into question: Some mutinous thoughts," by Michael Newman. *Adult Education Quarterly, 64*(2), 399–405.

Dix, M. (2016). The cognitive spectrum of transformative learning. *Journal of Transformative Education, 14*(2), 139–162.

Dugan, J. P., Turman, N. T., Barnes, A. C., & Associates. (2017). *Leadership theory: A facilitator's guide for cultivating critical perspectives.* San Francisco: Jossey-Bass.

Fabbri, L., & Romano, A. (2017). *Metodi per l'apprendimento trasformativo: Casi, modelli, teorie* [*Methods for transformative learning: Cases, models, theories*]. Roma: Carocci Editors.

Ferguson, J., Romano, A., Bracci, F., & Marsick, V. (2018). Enacting transformative community through theatre of the Oppressed in higher education. In M. Welch, V. Marsick, & D. Holt (Eds.), *Building transformative community: Enacting possibility in today's times. Proceedings of the XIII Biennial Transformative Learning Conference* (pp. 281–284). New York: Teachers College.

Freire, P. (1970). *Pedagogy of the Oppressed.* New York: Herder and Herder.

Gherardi, S. (2017). What is the place of affect within practice-based studies? *Management, 20*(2), 208–220.

Heron, J. (1992). *Feeling and personhood: Psychology in another key.* Newbury Park, CA: Sage.

Hoggan, C. (2016). Transformative learning as a metatheory: Definition, criteria and typology. *Adult Education Quarterly, 66*(1), 57–75.

Holton, J. A. (2007). The coding process and its challenges. In A. Bryant & K. Charmaz (Eds.), *The Sage handbook of grounded theory* (pp. 265–289). Thousand Oaks, CA: Sage.

King, K. (2009). *The handbook of the evolving research of transformative learning based on the learning activities survey.* Charlotte, NC: Information Age Publishing.

Lawson, R., Blythe, J., & Shaw, G. (2014). Alternative stories: Creating liminal space for transformative learning in police education. *Proceedings from the 11th International Conference for Transformative Learning*, pp. 148–154. New York: Teachers College.

Lundgren, H., Bang, A., Justice, S. B., Marsick, V. J., Poell, R. F., & Yorks, L. (2017). Conceptualizing reflection in experience-based workplace learning. *Human Resource Development International, 20*(4), 305–326.

Marsick, V. (2015). *Transformative learning. Key concepts.* Class lecture, Fall 2015. New York: Teachers College, Columbia University.

Marsick, V., & Neaman, A. (2018). Adult informal learning. In N. Kahnwald & V. Täubig (Hrsg.), *Informelles Lernen* [Informal learning]. Berlin: Springer.

Mezirow, J. (1989). Transformation theory and social action: A response to Collard and Law. *Adult Education Quarterly, 39,* 169–175.

Mezirow, J. (1991). *Transformative dimensions of adult learning.* San Francisco: Jossey-Bass.

Mezirow, J. (2000). Learning to think like an adult. In J. Mezirow & Associates (Eds.), *Learning as transformation: Critical perspectives on a theory in progress* (pp. 3–33). San Francisco: Jossey-Bass.

Romano, A. (2014). Promoting reflexivity through drama: Educational practices of the Theatre of the Oppressed. *Educational Reflective Practices, 1,* 131–145.

Romano, A. (2016). *Il palcoscenico della trasformazione: Processi di apprendimento nel Teatro dell'Oppresso* [The stage of transformation: Learning processes in the Theatre of the Oppressed]. Milano: FrancoAngeli.

Romano, A. (2018). Transformative learning: A review of the assessment tools. *The Journal of Transformative Learning, 5*(1), 53–70.

Tanaka, S. (2011). The notion of embodied knowledge. In P. Stenner, J. Cromby, J. Motzkau, J. Yen, & Y. Haosheng (Eds.), *Theoretical psychology: Global transformations and challenges* (pp. 149–157). Concord, Canada: Captus Press.

Wijeyesinghe, L. C., & Bailey Jackson, W. (Eds.). (2012). *New perspectives on racial identity development: Integrating emerging frameworks.* New York: New York University Press.

12

Promoting Transformative Learning Through English as a *lingua franca*: An Empirical Study

Nicos C. Sifakis and Stefania Kordia

Introduction

Since Jack Mezirow first introduced his transformation theory in 1978, there has been a growing interest in exploring the transformative processes adults may go through in their attempt to achieve greater agency and autonomy. Within this framework, a great amount of research, both in the field of adult education and other related disciplines, has focused on the ways in which transformative learning (TL) could be fostered in practice (Taylor, 2008; Taylor & Cranton, 2012). Despite the emphasis being placed on this area of study, there is still much uncertainty and ambiguity in the existing literature, particularly when it comes to describing effective TL practices along the lines of Mezirow's theory. Indeed, as Taylor and Laros (2014, p. 139) highlight, there is, more often than not,

---

N. C. Sifakis (✉) • S. Kordia
School of Humanities, Hellenic Open University, Patras, Greece
e-mail: stefania.kordia@ac.eap.gr

© The Author(s) 2019
T. Fleming et al. (eds.), *European Perspectives on Transformation Theory*,
https://doi.org/10.1007/978-3-030-19159-7_12

'little explanation' of what TL may actually look like in an educational setting, as well as of the activities an educator may carry out to facilitate TL. What is more, 'little actual data' (Taylor, 2000, p. 295) are still offered in many TL studies to support their findings. One key reason behind this situation is that, while Mezirow's theory (Mezirow, 1991, 2000) offers a clear depiction of the processes whereby dysfunctional habits of mind and relevant points of view may be challenged and, eventually, replaced, it provides few clarifications as to how these processes may be translated into actual educational practice.

In the light of the above, the contribution that this chapter seeks to make to TL research is twofold. On the one hand, the chapter aims at providing a comprehensive picture of how TL, as defined by Mezirow (1991, 2000), could be fostered in English language teacher education, which remains a relatively understudied territory as far as TL is concerned (but see, for example, DeCapua, Marshall, & Frydland, 2017). To this end, it focuses on professional development programmes for teachers of English as a foreign language (EFL) which revolve around the current function of English as a lingua franca (ELF). Broadly defined as the language of communication among people with different mother tongues (Seidlhofer, 2011), ELF, in fact, presents unique TL challenges for teachers which only recently have been highlighted (but see Sifakis, 2007). In essence, it calls them to transform the way they perceive and perform their teaching role in classrooms. In the first section, after briefly discussing the essence of the 'problem' which ELF generates for EFL teachers, Sifakis (2014, 2019) describes the core elements of an original teacher education model he has developed. The model adopts Mezirow's transformation theory and aims at the development of what has been termed 'ELF awareness' (Sifakis & Bayyurt, 2018). This involves a continuous process of critical reflection on one's deep assumptions related to using, teaching and learning English nowadays, as well as the construction of action plans to integrate ELF in one's classroom. In this respect, emphasis is placed on the activities a teacher may carry out to facilitate TL, as Taylor and Laros (2014) suggest.

This chapter also seeks to shed light on what TL may actually look like in practice and contribute to bridging the gap between TL theory and practice (cf. Taylor & Laros, 2014)—in this case, as far as ELF awareness is concerned. Kordia (2015, 2018) focuses on her transformative journey throughout an ELF-aware teacher education programme. She presents indicative data extracted from the reflective journal she kept during that programme and discusses them along with the core elements of Sifakis' teacher education model and the ten phases of transformation, as originally described by Mezirow (1991, 2000). In this regard, her data also illustrate the perspective she had, as a teacher, prior to her engagement in TL (cf. Taylor, 2000), which, eventually gave rise to a new perspective as an ELF-aware teacher.

Challenges and Implications of ELF for Teacher Education

ELF and the 'Problem' It Generates for EFL Teachers

Over the past few decades, the unprecedented dominance of English as an international language (EIL) and the corresponding rapid increase of non-native speakers (NNSs) around the world has become a major area of concern for applied linguists. One of the most widely discussed topics, in this regard, is that EIL 'calls for a critical revisiting' of various well-established notions (Sharifian, 2009, p. 2), most significantly the traditional view of the native speaker (NS) as the ideal communicator. This need has become even more evident in recent years due to the findings of research on ELF, a 'specialized branch' of EIL pertaining to communication mainly among NNSs.

Indeed, one of the key research findings is that, while employing it in countless domains of social and professional life, NNSs have, over the years, appropriated (or else, 'transformed') the language to suit the particular demands of each interaction they participate in. Such linguistic appropriation has occurred to an extent that, to date, there are non-native 'varieties' of English that merge features of local languages and dialects in very creative ways. Discourse analysts studying NNSs' discourse in various contexts highlight the inherently fluid nature of ELF (e.g., regarding its linguistic and cultural elements), as opposed to the relatively stable Standard English varieties (e.g., British and American English). They point out that effective communication in ELF is determined by factors other than those traditionally assumed. Most importantly, the widespread perception that the NS provides the 'gold standard' against which successful communication is gauged does not correspond to reality any longer. Instead, they emphasize the importance of interactional skills for the development of a shared understanding, the preserving of intelligibility through negotiation of meaning, and recourse to other linguistic codes mutually known to interactants, also known as 'translanguaging' (Jenkins, 2015; Jenkins, Baker, & Dewey, 2018).

The developments in ELF research, as briefly described above, have enormous implications for EFL teachers. Where English-medium communication involves increasingly more NNSs than NSs, they, first, imply that English 'is not just a foreign language like any other' (Widdowson, 2013, p. 192). Instead, it is 'a language that has been de-foreignized to become common property', meaning that the commonly-held belief that it is 'owned by its native speakers' alone is, in essence, unjustified (Widdowson, 2013, pp. 192–193). Second, they imply that the traditional definition of the 'skilled' user of English is highly problematic and needs to be reconceptualized. Research has shown that, in international communication, a successful interactant is 'no longer someone who has mastered the forms of a particular native variety, but someone who has acquired the pragmatic skills needed to adapt their English use' in ELF contexts (Jenkins, 2011, pp. 931–932). This is where the 'problem' for EFL teachers lies, in that, by disproving the validity of the linguistic assumption that the NS is the only 'owner' and 'ideal' user of English, ELF seriously challenges a range of assumptions which have traditionally been at the core of the theory and practice of English language teaching (ELT) and, by and large, have shaped the way teachers typically perceive and enact their professional role.

These assumptions relate to 'native-speakerism', a 'pervasive ideology within ELT', according to which the NS represents the only legitimate target model for learners and the most appropriate teacher (Holliday, 2006, p. 385). This ideology permeates various highly popular EFL approaches and methods around which most pre- and in-service training seminars and courses revolve, as well as the curricula and courseware employed in EFL classrooms for decades. It is also reflected in the dominant narrative in EFL contexts which compels learners to sit high-stakes proficiency exams that are predominantly NS-oriented (see Sifakis et al., 2018). Having been 'bombarded' by the native-speakerist discourse ever since they were learners themselves, EFL teachers tend to force their learners to conform to the hegemonic native-speaker model and, worse still, to act as custodians of 'proper English' and as the official representatives of the 'ideal NS' in their classroom (Sifakis, 2009).

Some of the most typical native-speakerist points of view underlying EFL teachers' way of thinking and acting include:

(a) that the more convincingly a learner can imitate the linguistic and cultural behaviour of a NS, the better learner he/she is; therefore, 'good teaching' requires prioritizing the acquisition of NS linguistic and cultural norms (e.g., sounds and idiomatic phrases of NS varieties, even though, in reality, they may not play an important role in effective communication—cf. Jenkins et al., 2018);

(b) that every 'deviation' from the norms of NS varieties constitutes an undesired 'error' (rather than a potentially appropriate form in a given interactional context—cf. Seidlhofer, 2011); therefore, 'good teaching' requires preparing the learners to produce 'proper' and 'error-free' language (even when this implies suppressing their creativity in real-life ELF interactions);

(c) that successful learners are those who can employ the language appropriately with NSs (although most interactions they have nowadays involve other NNSs, for example, in online gaming and social networks—cf. Vettorel, 2014); therefore, good teaching requires engaging the learners in so-called authentic NS communicative contexts and avoiding the inferior NNS discourse as much as possible (even though this may help them develop essential ELF-related interactional skills);

(d) that learners need, above all, a teacher who can show them what a 'real' NS is like; therefore, being a 'good teacher' means being a NS yourself or, at least, being able to sound and act like one. For NNS teachers, this, in turn, may imply overlooking one's own NNS identity (even when their own example may be more relevant to the learners—cf. Llurda, 2018) and promoting the NS 'ideal' even harder, so as not to 'lose face' in front of the class, colleagues and society, in general (Sifakis, 2009).

TL and ELF Awareness

Taking into consideration the serious challenges that ELF poses for EFL teachers, special emphasis has been placed on the need for *change* in ELT. As has often been argued, teachers need to be empowered to integrate ELF in their classrooms, which requires engaging them in 'a radical re-appreciation of [their] beliefs about their long-established practices' (Sifakis & Bayyurt, 2018, p. 457), through critical reflection on their deeply rooted native-speakerist assumptions. It goes without saying, however, that such a change is anything but straightforward. It demands *transformative learning* in the sense that Mezirow has given to this term, that is:

(a) critically assessing the validity of and, when necessary, reconstructing a range of *points of view*, namely specific 'beliefs, feelings, attitudes and judgments' resulting from a *habit of mind* (Mezirow, 2000, p. 18)—in this case, a native-speakerist sociolinguistic habit of mind which shapes the way one interprets and performs his/her role as a teacher;

(b) going through the various phases of the transformation of a habit of mind (Mezirow, 1991, 2000), from a disorienting dilemma to exploring, planning and implementing a new course of action and, then, to building competence and self-confidence in new roles—in this case, a new role as a teacher who is liberated from the native-speakerist ideology and can determine why, when and how ELF can be integrated in one's classroom.

Along these lines, Sifakis has put forward a comprehensive model for teacher education, which draws heavily on Mezirow's theory and aims at the development of what has been termed 'ELF awareness' (Sifakis, 2007, 2014, 2019; Sifakis & Bayyurt, 2018). This refers to the process whereby the transformation of the native-speakerist habit of mind results from an accretion of transformations in relevant points of view (Mezirow, 1997). This process involves, first, identifying, questioning and reconceptualizing one's points of view and, thereby, developing a new understanding of one's professional role in view of ELF. Then, it involves designing, implementing and evaluating action plans that integrate ELF in one's classroom,

12 Promoting Transformative Learning Through English... 183

in a way that is relevant to one's specific context and, of course, compatible with one's new perspective as a teacher (Sifakis & Bayyurt, 2018). In this sense, ELF awareness includes the following components (Sifakis, 2019):

(a) *awareness of language use* (of the role of NNSs nowadays, the competences of successful English users, the forces that have framed one's definition of the 'skilled' communicator, etc.);
(b) *awareness of instructional practice* (of the target model one promotes while, for instance, correcting the learners' discourse, how one's background as a learner and trainee-teacher may have influenced his/her practices, etc.);
(c) *awareness of the learning process* (of what one's learners actually need to learn, how their own experiences as users influence their learning, etc.).

On this basis, the ELF-aware transformative model includes three main phases (Sifakis, 2014; Sifakis & Bayyurt, 2018). The first phase ('Exposure') entails an initial exploration of teachers' perceptions about key issues related to the spread of EIL, the use of ELF and, of course, ELT, through exposure to real-life ELF discourse, videos and selected extracts of EIL/ELF literature. Discussion of the points illustrated therein is essential in terms of acquiring knowledge of *language use*, as well as generating a disorienting dilemma that may trigger the transformative process. Moreover, keeping, right from the start, a reflective journal where one may respond to progressively more demanding reflective questions is important. For example, some reflective questions based on a video illustrating a NS-NNS interaction could be: *Which of the speakers uses 'proper' English, in your opinion? What does 'proper English' mean to you? Why? Would you ever show this video to your learners? Why/Why not?*

The second phase ('Critical awareness') includes more systematic exploration of worldviews and practices, through content, process and premise reflection (Mezirow, 1991). Therefore, it is devoted to helping teachers critically engage with their native-speakerist points of view about *language use, instructional practice* and *the learning process*, and assess their validity, in relation to: (a) new information about EIL and ELF, (b) their context and their current teaching practices, (c) their own previous experiences as users, learners and trainee-teachers. Finally, at the third phase ('Action plan'), teachers are prompted to design, implement and evaluate original lessons for their classes, illustrating their own understanding of ELF and, if this is indeed the case, their altered or enriched ELT perspectives. This phase is more than significant so as to help them explore, try out and build self-confidence in new roles as teachers and, eventually, develop as 'autonomous, responsible thinkers' (Mezirow, 1997, p. 8), free from native-speakerist constraints.

Since 2012, this model has been implemented in various programmes, including the online self-study 'ELF-TEd Project' at the Boğaziçi University, in Istanbul (Bayyurt & Sifakis, 2015). Being one of the first participants of this programme, Stefania narrates, in the following section, her personal transformative experiences.

Stefania's Transformative Journey

To shed light on what TL may look like in practice regarding ELF awareness, I am presenting, in this section, an overview of my own development throughout the 'ELF-TEd Project' (also see Kordia, 2015, 2018). For the purposes of this chapter, content analysis of the data included in the reflective journal I kept since its beginning, in September 2012, and for approximately nine months, has been carried out. The codes and categories employed have been drawn from the theory of ELF awareness (e.g., the three components mentioned earlier) and Mezirow's theory (as regards the phases of a habit of mind transformation; Mezirow, 1991, 2000), both of which have been included in my research interests since the completion of the programme.

Along these lines, my experiences are here explored from the perspective of both the researcher and the researched. My narrative follows the three phases of Sifakis' ELF-aware teacher education model and illustrates (albeit rather briefly, due to space constraints) the transformation of a range of points of view, leading to a reinterpretation of my role as a teacher. While all of the ten phases of a transformation of a habit of mind are evident in my data, the process has been found to be 'more recursive, evolving, and spiraling in nature' (Taylor, 2000, p. 290).

Phase 1: Exposure to the Current Realities in English Language Use

When embarking on this journey at the age of 32, I had particularly high self-esteem as a teacher. I had already been teaching for 10 years, I had completed a Master's degree with flying colours and I had attended various other training programmes which had convinced me that my teaching practices had all of the characteristics of 'good teaching', as usually defined. Participating in 'ELF-TEd' was, in short, a way to reconfirm and reinforce my "good teacher" status, by enriching my practices with new information about ELF. Little had I known, back then, that this involved arriving at a new definition of 'good teaching' itself.

An introductory video I was invited to watch at the outset of the programme proved highly important in terms of initiating the transformative process. In this video, emphasis was placed on the idea that radical changes in education always come from grassroots movements, namely from teachers themselves, rather than from policy-makers. This view was fairly new to me and made me wonder whether I was indeed part of such a movement. In fact, even though, at that point, I could not really understand what true change meant, the idea that, as a teacher, I might not be as successful as I thought was quite unsettling. Signifying the emergence of a *disorienting dilemma* which would eventually bring me into conflict with several of my prior convictions, it was this thought that made me consider the possibility of looking at my knowledge and experience from a different angle. Regarding my role as a possible agent of change, I wondered:

> Why hadn't I thought about that before? Perhaps I should […] start thinking about what exactly I have done to make things better… I should be 'part of the solution, not the problem', but what exactly does this entail?

While reading (e.g., Sharifian, 2009) about the spread of EIL to raise my *awareness of language use* around the world, the nature of the 'problem' as regards my own role as a teacher became more and more obvious to me. The fact that the vast number of NNSs using English today essentially implies that it is them, rather than the NSs, who are responsible for the evolution of the language, seemed so striking and so reasonable to me

186   N. C. Sifakis and S. Kordia

that made me embark, even at this initial stage, on a process of *critical assessment of the assumptions* I held about the 'ideal' NS. This, in turn, led to some quite comforting moments of *recognition that my discontent over those assumptions was shared* by the authors whose work I read:

> A language becomes global due to the power of the people who speak it [...]. I had never thought [of] that. The language does not belong any longer only to its native users [...]. It is remarkable, if I was asked to define a 'native speaker' before, I would have included almost all of the features traditionally associated with this term [...]. I can't but agree with [the authors' criticism on] the alleged superiority of native speakers.

Phase 2: Critical Awareness

As my work on the programme progressed, more systematic *critical assessment of the assumptions* I had about *language use, instructional practice* and *the learning process* took place, involving *self-examination* as regards the factors that had possibly reinforced them. Critical reflection on the way I had been trained as a teacher and, earlier, as a learner of the language made me, in fact, view my University courses and, then, the native-speaker teacher who taught me when I was young, from a different, more accurate perspective:

> [At a course] we were involved in 'learning' how to pronounce English words 'properly' [...], exactly the way British people [do]. I couldn't [and] I remember [...] the feelings of inferiority I had. [However] to my mind, that was the modern way to teach, the way that people 'who knew better' taught.

> [My teacher] seemed 'exotic' to my eyes [...], she was the 'representative' of the culture which I could only have a taste of through books, pictures, and her, of course. I even tried to imitate her behavior [...] because, I guess, I thought that was part of the process of learning the language.

The realization that my educational background had actually promoted a native-speakerist mindset was indeed highly shocking and, in a sense, liberating, evoking feelings of enthusiasm and optimism. While, though, I had managed to identify the sources, for instance, of my former point of view that any 'deviation' from NS norms constitutes an 'undesired error', a crucial question had been generated, pertaining to my future *instructional practice*:

> As most, if not all, of my colleagues, I think I have been brainwashed [...]. I find it pretty amazing; long, well-established, traditions are being challenged here and, most importantly, it feels that they deserve to be challenged [...]. I think I [have] also had the tendency to regard all features which do not conform to NS norms as 'errors' [...]. [However], what the target model would be [now]? [The] 'native speaker' in the traditional sense is certainly no longer appropriate.

Finding an appropriate answer to this question essentially entailed reframing my definition of the 'skilled' English user. Therefore, studying the findings of ELF research was significant not only in terms of *acquiring knowledge* (or else, raising my awareness of *language use*) about what being a competent communicator actually meant in today's globalized world, but also in terms of *exploring options for my new roles and actions* as a teacher:

> I am VERY surprised and OF COURSE there are implications for teaching. The [research] results show that our approach to teaching [pronunciation], grammar and vocabulary should be redirected if our aim is to prepare students to communicate effectively in lingua franca contexts. [We should] take them into consideration when determining teaching objectives and selecting/adapting/producing [instructional] materials.

Nevertheless, the more knowledge I gained about ELF discourse, the more evident it became that there was a striking discrepancy between my own teaching practices and the current realities in language use. The nature of the 'problem' and its possible 'solution' which had puzzled me since the beginning of this journey had thus now acquired new dimensions. With respect to my former points of view that learners should be exposed only to NS interactions and learn how to produce error-free language, I wrote the following:

What kind of 'real life communicative situations' have we been talking about? BBC world news? That's exposing them to native-speaker contexts of use alone, when 80 or so percent of communication nowadays takes place in lingua franca contexts [...]. I think I have 'suppressed' my students' creativity to a large extent by insisting on conventional use of language reflecting NS norms.

In fact, exploring the consequences of my native-speakerist points of view and, more specifically, whether what I had been teaching my learners matched the profile of a competent ELF speaker, was definitely not an easy task. It involved, probably for the first time throughout my transformative journey, *self-examination with feelings of anger, guilt and shame*, which resulted in an honest admission of the need to truly change myself:

> Even though I always considered my teaching to be aiming at developing communicative competence, I never really helped my students [...], which, as I see it now, is quite disappointing, if not unprofessional. [A] transformation in my [teaching] is necessary; that would be highly beneficial not only for my students, but also for myself [...] in terms of the ethical satisfaction associated with 'doing your job right'. I am not yet sure how I can do that.

As illustrated in the quote above, my self-confidence had been considerably shattered, as I realized I was not as 'good' a teacher as I thought. Although I did appreciate the need to integrate ELF in my teaching, confusion as to how this could be done in practice, however, prevailed.

Phase 3: An ELF-Aware Action Plan

Focusing on the pedagogical implications of ELF research as described in the literature (e.g., Seidlhofer, 2011) and trying to determine their relevance to my own teaching situation played a crucial role in helping me *plan a course of action* so as to bring about change in my teaching. While preparing, therefore, the action research which the third phase of the programme involved, various ideas came to me pertaining to the implementation of ELF-aware teaching in my classroom:

[The author suggests] providing the opportunity to negotiate meaning […] the way that speakers do in real life. This is a very interesting idea; I could give it a try. [Moreover] I could expose [my learners] to various NSS-NSS interactions and […] elicit the various negotiation strategies that successful communicators use.

In this regard, the close examination of the characteristics of my context, including the current and future needs of my learners, led to the conclusion that another significant parameter had to be taken into account. Based on my own experience as a learner in 'ELF-TEd', raising the learners' awareness of their own assumptions was, I thought, essential. After several months, I had thus found a 'solution' to the real 'problem' that was caused by perceiving myself as a custodian of 'proper' NS English:

The way I see it now, the very first step involves […] determining what exactly my students think about all this. […] I feel that most of them also regard native speaker competence as the benchmark of perfection, [and] this is one of the most important challenges: being able to adapt your teaching […] both according to your specific teaching situation, as well as in response to the status of English as an international language.

Being, therefore, aware of the challenges, as well as the opportunities, of ELF-aware teaching, I proceeded to explore my learners' worldviews and, then, to design and implement two ELF-aware lessons tailored to their own particular needs (cf. Kordia, 2015, 2018). It was actually this *provisional trying of my new role* as a teacher which not only helped me *build competence and self-confidence* in this new role but also realize that becoming an autonomous and responsible ELF-aware thinker is, in essence, a never-ending process. *Reintegration* into my teacher life on the basis of my new perspective included, in this sense, an awareness of what true development involves:

As for my own transformation […], no matter how uncomfortable, and even painful at times, that experience was, it was worth all the while. Moreover, I don't think it's over; you can never claim that you have utterly and completely been transformed into a successful ELF-aware teacher—it's a journey with a very clear destination but also a journey without ending, much like education itself.

Conclusion

The purpose of this chapter has been to discuss the significance of the theory of TL in ELF-aware teacher education. After briefly describing the challenges which the ELF phenomenon poses for teachers, it was highlighted that, in order for them to modify their teaching in line with the current realities in language use, they need to become aware of and replace some of their deepest native-speakerist points of view. On this basis, we described the main aspects of the ELF-aware teacher education model, based on Mezirow's transformation theory. Aiming at illustrating the effects that a programme adopting this model had in her worldviews Stefania provided, afterwards, an overview of her own transformative journey. Her discussion demonstrates that critical reflection was crucial in terms of determining what her old and her new role as a teacher involved, as well as in raising her competence and self-confidence in implementing ELF-aware teaching. Her experience also highlights that ELF-aware transformation needs to be viewed as a recursive, ongoing process which may entail feelings of disappointment and self-doubt.

References

Bayyurt, Y., & Sifakis, N. (2015). ELF-aware in-service teacher education: A transformative perspective. In H. Bowles & A. Cogo (Eds.), *International perspectives on English as lingua franca: Pedagogical insights* (pp. 117–135). Basingstoke: Palgrave Macmillan.

DeCapua, A., Marshall, H. W., & Frydland, N. (2017). The transformational learning journey of a novice ESL teacher of low-literate adults. *Journal of Transformative Education, 16*. Advance online publication. https://doi.org/10.1177/1541344617704645.

Holliday, A. (2006). Native-speakerism. *English Language Teaching Journal, 60*(4), 385–387.

Jenkins, J. (2011). Accommodating (to) ELF in the international university. *Journal of Pragmatics, 43*, 926–936.

Jenkins, J. (2015). Repositioning English and multilingualism in English as a lingua franca. *Englishes in Practice, 2*(3), 49–85.

Jenkins, J., Baker, W., & Dewey, M. (Eds.). (2018). *The Routledge handbook of English as a lingua franca*. London: Routledge.

Kordia, S. (2015). From TEFL to ELF-aware pedagogy: Lessons learned from an action-research project in Greece. In K. Dikilitaş, R. Smith, & W. Trotman (Eds.), *Teacher-researchers in action* (pp. 235–261). Kent: IATEFL Research Special Interest Group.

Kordia, S. (2018). ELF-aware teaching in practice: A teacher's perspective. In N. C. Sifakis & N. Tsantila (Eds.), *ELF for EFL contexts* (pp. 53–71). Bristol: Multilingual Matters.

Llurda, M. (2018). English language teachers and ELF. In J. Jenkins, W. Baker, & M. Dewey (Eds.), *The Routledge handbook on English as a lingua franca* (pp. 518–529). London: Routledge.

Mezirow, J. (1991). *Transformative dimensions of adult learning*. San Francisco: Jossey-Bass.

Mezirow, J. (1997). Transformative learning: Theory to practice. In P. Cranton (Ed.), *Transformative learning in action: Insights from practice. New directions for adult and continuing education, no.74* (pp. 5–12). San Francisco: Jossey-Bass.

Mezirow, J. (2000). Learning to think like an adult: Core concepts of transformation theory. In J. Mezirow & Associates (Eds.), *Learning as transformation: Critical perspectives on a theory in progress* (pp. 3–34). San Francisco: Jossey-Bass.

Seidlhofer, B. (2011). *Understanding ELF*. Oxford: Oxford University Press.

Sharifian, F. (2009). English as an international language: An overview. In F. Sharifian (Ed.), *English as an international language: Perspectives and pedagogical issues* (pp. 1–18). Bristol: Multilingual Matters.

Sifakis, N. C. (2007). The education of the teachers of English as a lingua franca: A transformative perspective. *International Journal of Applied Linguistics, 17*(3), 355–375.

Sifakis, N. C. (2009). Challenges in teaching ELF in the periphery: The Greek context. *English Language Teaching Journal, 63*(3), 230–237.

Sifakis, N. C. (2014). ELF awareness as an opportunity for change: A transformative perspective for ESOL teacher education. *Journal of English as a Lingua Franca, 3*(2), 317–335.

Sifakis, N.C. (2019). ELF awareness in English language teaching: Principles and processes. *Applied Linguistics, 40*(2), 288–306.

Sifakis, N. C., & Bayyurt, Y. (2018). ELF-aware teacher education and development. In J. Jenkins, W. Baker, & M. Dewey (Eds.), *The Routledge handbook on English as a lingua franca* (pp. 456–467). London: Routledge.

Sifakis, N. C., Lopriore, L., Dewey, M., Bayyurt, Y., Vettorel, P., Cavalheiro, L., et al. (2018). ELF-awareness in ELT: Bringing together theory and practice. *Journal of English as a Lingua Franca, 7*(1), 155–207.

Taylor, E. W. (2000). Analyzing research on transformative learning theory. In J. Mezirow & Associates (Eds.), *Learning as transformation: Critical perspectives on a theory in progress* (pp. 285–328). San Francisco: Jossey-Bass.

Taylor, E. W. (2008). Transformative learning theory. In S. Merriam (Ed.), *Third update on adult learning theory* (pp. 5–15). San Francisco: Jossey-Bass.

Taylor, E. W., & Cranton, P. (2012). Transformative learning theory: Seeking a more critical theory. In E. W. Taylor & P. Cranton (Eds.), *The handbook of transformative learning: Theory, research and practice* (pp. 3–20). San Francisco: Jossey-Bass.

Taylor, E. W., & Laros, A. (2014). Researching the practice of fostering transformative learning: Lessons learned from the study of andragogy. *Journal of Transformative Education, 12*(2), 134–147.

Vettorel, P. (2014). *English as a lingua franca in wider networking*. Berlin: Mouton deGruyter.

Widdowson, H. G. (2013). ELF and EFL: What's the difference? Comments on Michael Swan. *Journal of English as a Lingua Franca, 2*(1), 187–193.

13

The Theory and Practice of Evaluating Transformative Learning Processes

Claudio Melacarne

The Globalization of Transformative Learning (TL) Across Cultures and Disciplines

The concept of transformative learning (TL) refers to the process and the educational conditions that can facilitate the development of more inclusive, open, and critical perspectives. Inspired by the original definition of Jack Mezirow, learning can be defined as the process in which the adult uses a previous interpretation to build up a new interpretation of his/her experience and to be able to guide and self-direct future actions (Mezirow, 1994).

Starting from a constructivist perspective, Mezirow (2000) argues that the worldview of a subject is not determined only by the frames of reference or assumptions that form the basis of thought, beliefs, values and actions. What we think is actually the result of a sociocultural conditioning that becomes tacit over time. A fundamental precept in all of

---

C. Melacarne (✉)
University of Siena, Siena, Italy
e-mail: claudio.melacarne@unisi.it

© The Author(s) 2019
T. Fleming et al. (eds.), *European Perspectives on Transformation Theory*,
https://doi.org/10.1007/978-3-030-19159-7_13

194   C. Melacarne

Mezirow's work is that collectively assimilated values and cultural beliefs, can limit individuals' power to use critical thinking in the analysis of their own experience or, more generally, the context in which they are surrounded. Mezirow (1990, p. 4) states:

> Meaning perspectives are, for the most part, uncritically acquired in childhood through the process of socialization, often in the context of an emotionally charged relationship with parents, teachers, or other mentors. The more intense the emotional context of learning and the more it is reinforced, the more deeply embedded and intractable to change are the habits of expectation that constitute our meaning perspectives. Experience strengthens, extends, and refines our structures of meaning by reinforcing our expectations about how things are supposed to be.

These tacit structures restrict the individual's ability to produce new meanings and inhibit processes of emancipation and social change. This builds on the ideas of Freire (1970). Thus, people can produce many actions in their lives, have exciting and diverse experiences, while never changing the meanings they use to interpret those actions and experiences.

A Dynamic and Growing Field of Research on Transformative Learning

Research on transformative theory is growing exponentially, both in terms of number of publications and contents. Taylor (2007) points out that there was not only a quantitative increase, but also an expansion and hybridization of the constructs underlying the theory (Taylor, 2007, 2014; Taylor & Cranton, 2012a). For example, think of how the critique of Mezirow's rationalist and cognitivist orientation has led to the enrichment of the field through the development of new theories and practices. As a result of this, Taylor (2014) argues that, in addition to the central concepts of "critical reflection" and "experience," there are two more equally important constructs to keep in mind to understand how adults learn: that of "emotion" and that of "relationship."

Mezirow's work is now used and connected with many other theoretical perspectives, such as that of communities of practice (Bracci, 2017;

Fabbri, 2011; Wenger, 1998), studies on performative methodologies (Kokkos, 2012, 2014; Perkins, 1994; Romano, 2014) and organizational studies (Marsick, 2009). In this way, Transformative Learning Theory (TLT) is now changing itself through the action of the communities of researchers who stretch the "original" version (Mezirow, 1978) in various ways and explore it in relation to other intellectual and research traditions and a variety of methodological approaches.

For instance, in Italy, where I am based, many studies inspired by Mezirow's theory are using mixed methods and new theoretical syntheses such as on collaborative research (Fabbri & Bianchi, 2018), organizational development research (Melacarne, 2018), studies of social inclusion practices (Striano, 2010), whole-person approach to learning (Formenti & Dirkx, 2014) and of career development (Cunti, 2014; Fedeli & Coryell, 2014).

As Fabbri (2018, p. 1) notes:

after its first formulation, for over thirty years, TLT has been elaborated and modified by various scientific communities, belonging to different geographical areas, intercepting challenges certainly related to adult education but also to professional development, to the innovation of teaching and learning methodologies and to organizational innovation. We are talking about trajectories which can be traced back to transcultural and transdisciplinary processes. The theoretical constructs related to TLT are contaminated by theories concerning other theoretical and methodological frameworks, hence leading to new perspectives and applications to be translated or transferred to new research avenues anchored to traditions, cultures and epistemologies belonging to that context.

Transformative Learning Theory is becoming more open and what exactly constitute its core ideas is more uncertain. This theory is living the transformation of itself through the "process of translation" (Latour, 1978, p. 266). Latour (1978, p. 269) explains very well what can happen to a theory when it moves across multiple networks:

Each of the people in the chain is not simply resisting a force or transmitting it in the way they would in the diffusion model; rather, they are doing something essential for the existence and maintenance of the token. In

196 C. Melacarne

> other words, the chain is made of actors—not of patients—and since the token is in everyone's hands in turn, everyone shapes it according to their different projects. This is why it is called the model of translation. The token changes as its moves from hand to hand and the faithful transmission of a statement becomes a single and unusual case among many, more likely, others. (Latour, 1978, p. 268)

This is not a negative thing but has opened up new paths in practice and use of research methodologies, not least in the context of the assessment of transformative learning (Cox, 2017). Theoretical hybridization of the theory is also accompanied by an interesting increase of the tools available to evaluate the process or the outcomes of the experiences of transformative learning. The growing interest in these assessment tools demonstrates how important it has become to produce data on the impact of transformative processes, both at the individual or organizational level. Further, these tools can serve to improve accountability during research conducted for companies and organizations. Assessment tools can also provide practitioners with information to deepen learning processes of both participants and practitioners asking them to reflect on these data at the end of a lesson or a workshop.

The following sections will describe some tools used to evaluate transformative learning process connected with Transformative Learning Theory but with other theories also. The aim is to contribute to the debate by providing a classification of the assessment tools, underlining the different perspectives used to develop them and their possible applications.

Assessment of Transformative Learning

Some recent studies have tried to systematize the discussion of the assessment of transformative learning (Cranton & Hoggan, 2012; Romano, 2017; Stuckey, Taylor, & Cranton, 2013). For example, Cranton and Hoggan (2012) identify ten approaches used to evaluate transformative learning: self-evaluation, interviews, narrative accounts, observations, surveys, checklists, journals, metaphor analysis, conceptual mapping and arts-based techniques. These approaches aim at responding to different needs, such as a) understanding whether or not transformative learning has occurred, b) what level of reflection a specific type of disorienting experience generates, c) what has generated a transformative learning experience.

There is also a concern in these studies to assess if the understanding of transformative learning underpinning evaluation tools is consistent with Mezirow's approach. The studies on assessment of the transformative learning process or outcomes are also clearly linked to theoretical debates and knots related to the evolution of Transformative Learning Theory. Answering to the problem "what are we to evaluate," the debate on assessment had to define what transformation is and how Jack Mezirow's theory is changing and being adapted over time.

For example, three of these tools are analyzed in detail by Romano (2017). All of them have been designed and constructed based on Mezirow's theory. The first, the *Learning Activities Survey* (King, 2009) attempts to operationalize transformative learning through a rational model (Mezirow, 1991). In this case, the unit of evaluation is the process of thinking how the psychological categories change the way we interpret the experience. The second is the *Transformative Learning Survey* created by Stuckey et al. (2013). This tool allows the users to have a feedback on the different transformations that a specific experience generated. Also, it is interesting to study what type of experience precipitates a transformation because the tool collects data on the users' transformational experience and nature of their disorientating dilemmas. The study of Romano also discusses a third tool, the *Student Transformative Learning Record* (Romano, 2017). This was applied to a large sample of students with the aim of evaluating their progress in higher educational programs. It is particularly interesting for managing teaching and learning processes within the classroom and in higher educational settings. The *Student Transformative Learning Record* introduces a new point of view into the debate on assessment of transformative learning. The idea is that transformative learning and its evaluation is connected to a specific situation, context and target. This tool uses items elaborated with a language close to the experience of the students and calibrated to the educational setting. In this way, the transformation is not so much a property of the mind but what happens in a situated context.

198   C. Melacarne

Following these assessment studies, more recently, an article has been published by Cox (2017) on this topic. He has elaborated the *Transformative Outcomes and Processes Scale questionnaire* (TROPOS), trying to capture the main aspects of the theory of transformative learning. It is not based only on the ten phases outlined by Mezirow in his analysis of transformative learning processes. TROPOS is based on the elaboration of indicators constructed using developments and debates in contemporary transformation theory, using and putting together established theoretical ideas and new critical perspectives. Cox's goal is to assess transformative learning and move toward a unified framework. Cox's tool seeks to extend the research of Stuckey, Taylor and Cranton by including transversal ideas and create a tool able to assess transformative education.

Two additional pilot tools have been tested in the professional field and in the higher education setting. Based on collaborative research (Fabbri & Bianchi, 2018), the first is the *Doctors' Perspective Inventory* (DPI) (Melacarne & Romano, 2018). The DPI has been developed to be used in professional training programs by doctors in order to identify the areas of development of personal perspectives of meaning, in self-training or in classroom settings. The second tool is the *Reflective Learning Journal Survey* (RLJS), based on Barbara Bassot's reflective journal model (Bassot, 2013), Action Science Theory (Argyris & Schön, 1978), and Mezirow's theory (Mezirow, 1991). A first version of RLJS has been designed. This version has been used in the Department of Educational Sciences, Humanities and Intercultural Communication at the University of Siena with 80 undergraduate and graduate students and their internship mentors. This tool assesses both outcomes and learning processes. The *Reflective Learning Journal Survey* was created to help students and tutors manage their internship experiences in a reflexive manner.

Another quantitative tool that has emerged in the literature is the *Questionnaire for Reflective Thinking* (QRT) (Kember, Leung, Jones, & Loke, 2000). Within this questionnaire, Kember has identified four constructs that cover a broad spectrum of reflective thinking. They include: habitual action, understanding, reflection and critical reflection. These constructs have been derived from the literature on reflective thinking and the work of Mezirow (1991). This work is also complemented by the work of Baxter Magolda (1992), who focuses on the way in which beliefs and values underpin action.

A broad spectrum of tools has been used, as for instance interviews, student biographies, surveys, open-ended survey questions, portfolios, logs, student journals and concept maps. However, these tools mostly relate to courses, rather than to complete programs. Land and Meyer (2010) point out that evaluation of transformative learning needs to be studied and that in online programs additional challenges arise, especially in higher education settings. For example, in the field of online education, the tools tested and used are different. An important part of these tools is built in the form of e-portfolios (Land & Meyer, 2010). An example of an e-portfolio inspired by the theory of transformative learning is described by Arnold and Kumar (2014). They describe two qualitative approaches experimented within university courses. The first is based on the structure of a portfolio, while the second requires students to construct an artifact. In both cases, the material is interpreted by instructors through the reading grids derived from textual analysis (Carley, 1993). Instead, Meerkerk uses the logbook to work in a transformative key with a group of teachers, showing how "the solicited logbooks participants to shape their contributions according to their personality, their role in the process, and the context in which the events took place" (Meerkerk, 2017, p. 6).

Some of these tools are coherent with the original Mezirow's theory, while others incorporate different nuances, thus enriching transformative theory and producing indicators derived from different theoretical perspectives. We can discern a trend here in the evolution of the theory and the tools. There is a relationship between the evolution of Mezirow's theory, from an individual-rational-perspective toward a social–emotional perspective which is reflected in the type of tools that have been constructed the past decades. If at the beginning, the tools have been made to study the transformative learning process and to support transformative learning, but now many tools are made to support emancipatory processes in groups, communities or organizations. In the assessment approaches and in the tested methods as well, there is an evident heterogeneity in the use of background constructs, because the problem of transformation is shifting from an individual educational challenge to a

200   C. Melacarne

social challenge. The question is not any more "how to supporting the personal transformation of the perspectives" but "how to supporting personal transformation to transform the setting where this transformation can be stabilized." Below is a summary table of the tools examined. The criteria to classify the tools refer to Chapters 2 and 32 of the *Handbook of Transformative Learning* (Taylor & Cranton, 2012b). This table could be useful to choose what type of tools could be used to promote or study different type of learning (Chart 13.1).

Discussion

The chapter has discussed how transformative learning theory is changing over time and this evolution impacts on the way scientists construct and justify the tools to assess transformative learning.

On a theoretical level, an embryonic line of research has emerged: transformative learning has become the object of study for the construction of instruments of assessment. The tools and methods collected are both descriptive (how does the process of transformative learning develop?) and educational (can such as assessment process or outcomes become an occasion to support self-directed learning tool?). Cranton and Hoggan (2012) warn that in the absence of a unanimous definition of the term "transformation" and of agreement on how to support the process of critical elaboration of experience, it is necessary to pay great attention when choosing to use some of these tools or others. More than measuring an outcome, these tools should allow a subject or a community to reflect on their practices or to think deeper about how they reason or do things. Cranton and Hoggan (2012) state:

> Emancipatory knowledge cannot be predetermined, predicted, or set up as an objective for a course. Educators can create the environment, but they cannot make it happen. It can be evaluated in the same way that you have experienced in a particular setting, context, or program and every time. Shift in their perspectives on themselves or the world around them. But in the literature we have paid virtually no explicit and direct attention to the process of evaluating transformative learning. (pp. 437–438)

13 The Theory and Practice of Evaluating Transformative... 201

Title	Target	Unit of work	Only qualitative	Only quantitative	Mix qualitative and quantitative	Emotions /relation ship	Sociality /ethics
Learning Activities Survey	All	Subject			Yes	No	No
Transformative Learning Survey	All	Subject			Yes	Yes	No
Student Trasformative Learning Record	Students	Subject			Yes	Si	No
Transformative Outcomes and Processes Scale	All	Subject/ practices		Yes		No	Yes
Doctors' Perspective Inventory	Doctors	Subject		Yes		No	Yes

Chart 13.1 Characteristics of the tools for assessing transformations

Reflective Learning Journal Survey	Students	Subject/ practices			Yes	No	No
Question naire for Reflective Thinking	All	Subject			Yes	No	No
e-portfolio	All	Subject			Yes	Yes	No

Chart 13. 1 (continued)

Taylor and Cranton (2012a) suggest to pay attention to the risk of using transformative learning as a "foundation" rather than a "research field" and not to lose the opportunity to use the data we collect to also support social and situated learning. The next steps in assessment research on transformational processes may focus on the social impact of the use of these tools.

Therefore, there is a challenging openness and willingness in recovering the pedagogical and ethical nature of transformative learning theory and assessment strategies. This perspective of analysis would meet the interest of many researchers also within the European context that can boast a wide body of literature tackling these issues, starting from the studies on the autobiographical approaches or the phenomenological studies. Recently, the book *Transformative Learning meets Bildung* (Laros, Fuhr, & Taylor, 2017) has contributed to this line of study, underling an interesting theoretical golden thread that runs between two traditions. The first one is focused on the learning process, the second one is focused on the process of being a whole person. An interesting collection of research has recently been published, showing different approaches and perspectives that introduce examples and methods in this field (Neal, 2018). From a methodological point of view, it appears we are at the beginning of a new interesting shift from a cognitive-individual to a whole-person social way to interpret Transformative Learning and to develop strategies for evaluating and supporting it (Neal, 2018). The development and formalization of qualitative assessment tools is one of the areas in which further research could be undertaken, as well as the development of tools for the assessment of transformative learning in online training settings.

The digital record of students' work and interactions provide rich sources of data to be analyzed. In addition, researchers can learn from online study programs over multiple semesters and years, using assessment methods that can be built into the courses as "jewels in the curriculum" and using digital tools that help students "externalize" their thinking processes (Land & Meyer, 2010, p. 75). The online programs are growing in many countries and fields and they are planned to develop instrumental and complex thinking also. This phenomenon suggests paying attention to the connections between Transformative Learning Theory, methods and tools for assess it in an online environment.

Finally, the revision of the instruments could suggest to extend some of those that have already been tested in order to make them more inclusive and open to take new indicators into consideration. Only some of the tools focus on the social, relational, emotional and ethical variables of transformative learning processes. These indications could lead to further thinking on how the theory of transformative learning can still stimulate and generate new research paths, especially with reference to the European literature on emancipation processes, social change and recovering materialist theories (Fenwick, 2003).

References

Argyris, C., & Schön, D. (1978). *Organizational learning: A theory of action perspective*. New York: McGraw-Hill.

Arnold, P., & Kumar, S. (2014). Crossing professional thresholds with networked learning? An analysis of student e-portfolios using the Threshold Concept Perspective. In S. Bayne, C. Jones, M. de Laat, T. Tyberg, & C. Sinclair (Eds.), *Proceedings of the 9th International Conference on Networked Learning* (pp. 9–16).

Baxter Magolda, M. B. (1992). Students' epistemologies and academic experiences: Implications for pedagogy. *Review of Higher Education, 15*(3), 265–287.

Bassot, B. (2013). *The reflective journal.* London: Palgrave Macmillan.

Bracci, F. (2017). *L'apprendimento adulto. Metodologie didattiche ed esperienze trasformative.* [In English]. Unicopli: Milano.

Carley, C. (1993). Coding choices for textual analysis. A comparison of content analysis and map analysis. *Sociological Methodology, 23*, 75–126.

Cox, R. C. (2017). *Assessing transformative learning: Toward a unified framework.* Doctoral dissertation. Retrieved from http://trace.tennessee.edu/utk_graddiss/4616

Cranton, P., & Hoggan, C. (2012). Evaluating transformative learning. In E. W. Taylor & P. Cranton (Eds.), *The handbook of transformative learning: Theory, research, and practice* (pp. 37–55). San Francisco: Jossey-Bass.

Cunti, A. (2014). *Formarsi alla cura riflessiva. Tra esistenza e professione.* Milano: FrancoAngeli.

Fabbri, L. (2011). Trajectories of professional culture transformation. Fostering learning stories through reflective conversations. *Educational Reflective Practices, 1–2*, 37–55.

Fabbri, L. (2018). Transformative learning and transdisciplinary connections: Towards a situated critical reflection. In L. Fabbri, L. Formenti, A. Kokkos, C. Melacarne, & A. Nicolaides (Eds.), *Transformative learning approaches beyond transformative learning theory.* Proceedings of 3rd Biennial Conference: Contemporary Dilemmas and Learning for Transformation (ESREA).

Fabbri, L., & Bianchi, F. (Eds.). (2018). *Fare ricerca collaborativa. Vita quotidiana, cura, lavoro* [Doing collaborative research: Daily life, care, and work]. Roma: Carocci.

Fedeli, M., & Coryell, J. (2014). Investigating teaching and learning methods in Italian universities and beyond: The quest to improve and share practices and strategies in the international higher education context. *Educational Reflective Practices, 1–2*, 35–50.

Fenwick, T. (2003). *Learning through experience: Troubling assumptions and expanding questions.* Malabar, FL: Krieger.

Formenti, L., & Dirkx, J. (2014). A dialogical reframing. *Journal of Transformative Education, 12*(2), 123–133.

Freire, P. (1970). *Pedagogy of the oppressed.* New York: Herter and Herter.

Kember, D., Leung, D., Jones, A., & Loke, A. Y. (2000). Development of a questionnaire to measure the level of reflective thinking. *Assessment and Evaluation in Higher Education, 25*, 380–395.

King, K. (2009). *The Handbook of the evolving research of transformative learning based on the learning activities survey*. Charlotte, NC: Information Age.

Kokkos, A. (2012). Transformative learning in Europe: An overview of the theoretical perspectives. In E. W. Taylor & P. Cranton (Eds.), *Handbook of transformative learning: Theory, research and practice* (pp. 289–303). San Francisco: Jossey-Bass.

Kokkos, A. (2014). Could transformative learning be appreciated in Europe? *Journal of Transformative Education, 12*(2), 180–196.

Land, R., & Meyer, J. (2010). Threshold concepts and troublesome knowledge: Dynamics of assessment. In J. Meyer, R. Land, & C. Baillie (Eds.), *Threshold concepts and transformational learning* (pp. 53–64). Rotterdam, NL: Sense Publishers.

Laros, A., Fuhr, T., & Taylor, E. W. (Eds.). (2017). *Transformative learning meets Bildung: An international exchange*. Rotterdam, Netherlands: Sense.

Latour, B. (1978). The power of association. *The Sociological Review, 32*(1), 264–280.

Marsick, V. (2009). Toward a unifying framework to support informal learning theory, research and practice. *Journal of Workplace Learning, 21*(4), 265–275.

Meerkerk, E. (2017). Teacher logbooks and professional development: A tool for assessing transformative learning processes. *International Journal of Qualitative Methods, 16*, 1–8.

Melacarne, C. (2018). Supporting informal learning in higher education internship. In B. Vanna & M. Fedeli (Eds.), *Employability and competences. Innovative curricula for new professions* (pp. 51–63). Firenze: Firenze University Press.

Melacarne, C., & Romano, A. (2018). Theory and practice for understanding process and outcomes of transformative learning. *Educational Reflective Practices, 10*(2), 214–233.

Mezirow, J. (1978). Perspective transformation. *Adult Education Quarterly, 28*(2), 100–110.

Mezirow, J. (1990). *Fostering critical reflection in adulthood: A guide to transformative and emancipatory learning*. San Francisco, CA: Jossey-Bass.

Mezirow, J. (1991). *Transformative dimensions of adult learning*. San Francisco: Jossey-Bass.

Mezirow, J. (1994). Understanding transformation theory. *Adult Education Quarterly, 44*(4), 222–232.

Mezirow, J. (2000). Learning to think like an adult. In J. Mezirow & Associates (Eds.), *Learning as transformation: Critical perspectives on a theory in progress* (pp. 3–33). San Francisco: Jossey-Bass.

Neal, J. (Ed.). (2018). *Handbook of personal and organizational transformation.* New York: Springer.

Perkins, D. (1994). *The intelligent eye: Learning to think by looking at art.* Santa Monica, CA: The Getty Education Institute for the Arts.

Romano, A. (2014). Promoting reflexivity through drama. Educational practices of the Theatre of the Oppressed. *Educational Reflective Practices, 1*, 131–145.

Romano, A. (2017). The challenge of the assessment of processes and outcomes of transformative learning. *Educational Reflective Practices, 1*, 184–219.

Striano, M. (2010). *Pratiche educative per l'inclusione sociale.* Milano: Franco Angeli.

Stuckey, H. L., Taylor, E. W., & Cranton, P. (2013). Developing a survey of transformative learning outcomes and processes based on theoretical perspectives. *Journal of Transformative Education, 11*(4), 211–228.

Taylor, E. W. (2007). An update of transformative learning theory: A critical review of the empirical research (1999–2005). *International Journal of Lifelong Education, 26*(2), 173–191.

Taylor, E. W. (2014). Empathy: The stepchild of critical reflection and transformative learning. *Educational Reflective Practices, 2*, 5–22.

Taylor, E. W., & Cranton, P. (2012a). Transformative learning theory: Seeking a more critical theory. In E. W. Taylor & P. Cranton (Eds.), *The handbook of transformative learning: Theory, research, and practice* (pp. 3–20). San Francisco: Jossey-Bass.

Taylor, E. W., & Cranton, P. (2012b). *The handbook of transformative learning: Theory, research, and practice.* San Francisco: Jossey-Bass.

Wenger, E. (1998). *Communities of practice: Learning, meaning and identity.* Cambridge: Cambridge University Press.

14

Sustainability, Reflection, Transformation and Taking Back Our World

Ian Jasper

The origins and the development of this chapter were drawn from the experience of teaching a module entitled "Sustainability" on an undergraduate degree course. Reflection on this experience raised a number of complex issues centred on the problem of the ethics of teaching and the obligations and responsibilities of "teachers" to present to their students the most "truthful" picture of the subject being taught, even when this runs counter to official narratives. Thinking about these two issues in the context of the experience of teaching the "Sustainability" module has led to a reconsideration of what is meant by the idea of transformative learning.

When, more than a decade ago, the "Sustainability" module was first introduced onto the Bachelor of Arts Education and Professional Training (BA EPT) eyebrows were raised. This degree course is aimed at teachers working in what in Britain is called the "Further Education" sector which caters for young people who are over sixteen years of age and are working towards professional and vocational qualifications. More than a few times

---

I. Jasper (✉)
Canterbury Christ Church University, Canterbury, UK
e-mail: ian.jasper@canterbury.ac.uk

© The Author(s) 2019
T. Fleming et al. (eds.), *European Perspectives on Transformation Theory*,
https://doi.org/10.1007/978-3-030-19159-7_14

we have been asked "Why do you want to teach about sustainability on a degree like this?" The implication being that teachers and students in professional and vocational education need not concern themselves with perhaps the gravest threat facing humanity.

The BA Education and Professional Training is an honours degree for adults who are teaching in vocational education. Most of the students enter the programme in their thirties or considerably later, most left formal schooling and entered the world of work at the first legal opportunity. In many cases school was at best a disappointing experience, at worst a harrowing time of life. In many cases students entering the BA do so almost reluctantly many years after revising their originals vows never to return to education.

Later the idea of "alienation" will be discussed in more detail. For the moment the reader will be asked to consider just how "alienated" one needs to be to believe that students such as ours need not take "sustainability" to be germane to their work in education.

When educators talk about "reflection" and "transformation" there is perhaps a tendency to do so a little glibly, at least in the sense that sometimes we tend to take for granted the processes and their importance whilst overlooking the problems. In the case discussed here, the experience of "transformative learning" led to the students facing new challenges and dilemmas. It seems reasonable to assume that any real "transformative" educational process, whatever its benefits, must involve the negotiation of new challenges. I found that my reflections led to me developing a new understanding of the processes involved in "transformative learning"; not least as I began to think about my own activity as a teacher in a changed way.

It is sometimes argued that a key difference between education and training is that the former necessarily implies transformation whereas the latter does not. This claim becomes stronger still if we allow for the possibility that "training" which foments "transformation" becomes "education." In reverse, some activities which are officially designated as "education" but which stymie or prevent any meaningful "transformation" are in fact only forms of training. When we talk about "transformative learning," are we not also talking about "transformative teaching"? If

14 Sustainability, Reflection, Transformation and Taking Back... 209

this is the case, then the teacher who reflects upon their experience and develops because of that reflection must also be changed.

The experience of reflecting on teaching the "Sustainability" module led to me reconsidering and revitalising my own understanding of Marx's work on alienation. In turn, this led to the idea that "transformative learning" itself can be very usefully considered from the viewpoint afforded by an understanding of "alienation." The reflections discussed here in relation to teaching the "Sustainability" module allowed for the development of ideas I had originally encountered many years back, but which were given new life when applied to personal experience. Three texts were particularly important for my "reflection." The first was Karl Marx's *Economic and philosophic manuscripts of 1844* (Marx, 1975, pp. 280–400).

The concept of "alienation" is key to understanding Marx's entire oeuvre; it is ever present in his work though in the texts produced after the 1850s it is rarely mentioned explicitly. Despite Marx not explicitly mentioning "alienation" in his later work it is an ever-present theme. Alienation, its origins and its consequences permeate all Marx's work and most certainly does so in the very important texts of *Capital* (Marx, 1976–1981) and the *Grundrisse* (Marx, 1973). It could certainly be argued that in many ways *Capital* is Marx's attempt to fully explore and explain alienation. The most sustained explicit elaboration of the idea of alienation is to be found in the text known as *Economic and philosophic manuscripts (1844)* a text unpublished in Marx's life (Marx, 1975, pp. 280–400). This text written in 1844 requires the reader to do a fair bit of work to develop an understanding of the idea the author wishes to communicate. In the *Manuscripts*, Marx outlines his understanding of alienation and how this represents both, a break with, and a development of, the idea as it had previously appeared within the German philosophical tradition. This combination of "break with" and "development of" the concept of alienation contributes to the difficulty of fully understanding Marx's writing on the subject. In his early writings, he is both looking back and subjecting to a critique the idea as it had appeared in various "idealist" forms within German philosophy whilst looking forward to the development of the concept of alienation as it appeared in a society dominated by capitalist relations. These difficulties are compounded by

210   I. Jasper

translation problems between English and German. The English words "alienation" and "estrangement" are used to translate German words the meanings of which carry and complex connotations, not exactly coincidental with their closest English equivalents. A further difficulty arises because in the *Manuscripts*, Marx views alienation from the viewpoint of the productive processes of capitalism, hence the use of the term "estranged labour" in the title of the section (Marx, 1975, p. 322). Although "estranged labour" lies at its heart, "alienation" can only be fully understood as something which pervades all social life.

Because Marx's particular concern in the *Manuscripts* is with the treatment of "estranged labour" within the context of political economy, much of what is said about alienation cannot be mechanically applied to education; however, a more creative interpretation of "estranged labour" provides a philosophical illumination in the light of which education in general, and the education of adults in particular can be viewed with great insight. Marx presents a picture of how under capitalism humans become estranged from their "species life" (Marx, 1975, p. 328). As Marx puts it:

> For in the first place labour, *life activity, productive life* itself appears to man only as a means for the satisfaction of a need, the need to preserve physical existence. But productive life is species-life. It is life-producing life. The whole character of a species, its species character, resides in the nature of its life activity, and free conscious activity constitutes the species character of man. Life itself appears only as a *means of life*. (Marx, 1975, p. 328)

Here it should be noted that for Marx "free conscious activity" is an essential part of what it means to be truly human. To live in accord with our species character is to overcome alienation. The argument of this chapter is that the experience of teaching and studying a module titled "Sustainability" on the BA, in a very modest way, works towards this end.

The other two texts, which structured my own reflections, were written with the intention of developing Marx's idea of alienation in the context of education. The first of these is by the philosopher Istvan Meszaros. In his seminal work on "Marx's Theory of alienation" a chapter is specifically devoted to what the author sees as "Alienation and the crisis of education" (Meszaros, 2005). Meszaros' work is very rich in insights but two in particular are relevant here. The first is the idea that "alienation" is learnt through social processes of education. Meszaros points out that what he calls "formal education," typically school, college or university is "but a small segment of the overall process" (Meszaros, 2005, p. 289). Much more is learnt from the wider processes of living in the world. Within these educational processes individuals "interiorise" the conditions of their social world which, in a capitalist society, are alienated. Meszaros points to how education also offers the opportunity of escape from alienation as "the positive transcendence of alienation is, in the last analysis an educational task, requiring a radical 'cultural revolution' for its realization" (pp. 289–290). For Meszaros as for Marx the development of "free conscious activity" is an integral part of transcending alienation; clearly, a link may be made between this and learning which is transformative.

The third crucial text was Stephen Brookfield's article "Overcoming alienation as the practice of adult education" in which he considers how the intellectual contribution of the Marxist psychologist Erich Fromm might be utilised by adult educators (Brookfield, 2002). Brookfield's approach is more closely linked to the practice of education and as a very experienced adult educator who has written extensively on "reflective practice" (Brookfield, 1995), his work is intended to offer practical advice. In the article, Brookfield challenges teachers to stake "everything on helping adults overcome the alienation inherent in capitalist society" (Brookfield, 2002, p. 110). It is inconceivable that any process of "overcoming alienation" through educational practice could be disassociated from transformative education. Below the argument is set out that transformative education which is positively developmental is itself, necessarily, a process of overcoming alienation.

Here it is not possible to explore in any depth the work of the French sociologist Pierre Bourdieu and his work on education and alienation, but it is appropriate to draw attention to a very important way in which his work is in contrast to that of Brookfield and Meszaros. Bourdieu produced some magisterial work on education and alienation. Unfortunately reference to his work is not always a result of it being carefully studied, and his use of the term "capital" in ways very different to that of Marx are not troublesome (Fine, 2001, pp. 53–65). Both Meszaros and Brookfield see education not only as processes of inculcation to an alienated world but very importantly they also see education as a potential, or actual arena in which estrangement can be contested. It would be very difficult for a reader of at least two of Bourdieu's seminal texts on education (1977 and 1996) to draw any conclusion other than that education is indeed alienating. What is not offered by Bourdieu but is present in the work Meszaros and Brookfield is a positive vision of human agency.

Much discussion about "transformative learning" appears to assume that the idea is self-evidently understandable when this is far from being the case. An immediate problem is to assess the extent of "learning," which needs to take place in the learner or teacher for it to be deemed as significant as to cross the threshold of being transformative. A person who passes a driving test will almost certainly find that their life changes very significantly. Learning to drive is certainly life changing but it would not generally be argued that it represents "transformative learning." When learning is described as "transformative" we are referring to something which is supposed to change the "identity" of the learner. Indeed, in both very well-known definitions of transformative learning given below there is an explicit reference to changed identities.

The "identity" aspect of transformative learning is of great importance to the argument which is developed in this chapter because it takes identity to be wholly social although it also has a "personal" dimension. For Marxists the "personal" dimension of identity is itself social. Identity can only be formed by, and understood through, participation in a social culture. The different and divergent aspects of identity are conditioned by the social and cultural conditions in which they form and develop. If the Marxist idea of alienation in capitalist society is accepted, then the development of a genuinely human identity, an identity shaped by "free conscious activity," is inseparable from the struggle to overcome alienation. "Free conscious activity" can only happen when there is sufficient understanding of the real-world circumstances in which it might be exercised. Within education, the facilitation, as far as possible, of an understanding of the real world offers the possibility of a basis for the exercise of "free conscious activity." Therefore, Marxism holds that freedom must be based in the recognition of necessity. For contemporary humanity the

14 Sustainability, Reflection, Transformation and Taking Back... 213

recognition of the gravity of the "sustainability" crisis, we are confronting is a compelling necessity.

For Jack Mezirow, justifiably considered by many to be the doyen of the theory and practice of transformative learning is premised on the idea that it follows discernible stages. The first phase of the process corresponds to the learner being confronted with a "disorientating dilemma" (Mezirow, 2000, pp. 22–23). The learner then assesses and reflects on this dilemma. The learning process proceeds through a variety of stages from which a transformed learner emerges. The learner develops new "roles, relationships and actions" (p. 22), and in one way or another, these are integrated into the learner's changed life activity. When this happens, "transformative learning" is held to have taken place. It is fair to say that for Mezirow and most adherents of his model of transformative learning, it is assumed that new "roles relationships and actions" represent a positive process of development within the transformed learner's life. There is a problem here; we know that in real life "disorientating dilemmas" which lead to the adoption of "new roles relationships and actions" can be transformative, and even developmental in negative ways. Losing employment or one's home are common disorientating dilemmas which millions of adults must deal with and are decidedly negative and transformative. For many people, education, especially their experience of school, is itself is a source of negative transformative experiences. It is not unusual for educators to find that successful adult education is predicated on the transcendence of just such a negative school experience.

Knud Illeris in a development of, and a departure from, Mezirow's formulation has argued for a definition of transformative learning which he believes incorporates in a more integrated way the "emotional," "social," and "societal" dimensions of the identity which is transformed within "transformative learning." Illeris offers the following definition, "The concept of transformative learning comprises all learning that implies change in the identity of the learner" (Illeris, 2014, p. 40). It should be noted that Illeris is quite clear that not all transformative learning is developmental in a positive direction, and he points out that in certain quite easily understood circumstances the transformation might be "regressive" (pp. 93–97). Whilst Illeris's definition allows for transformation being negative, it does not solve at root the problem outlined in

Mezirow's model. The problem remains is one of formulating criteria by which to judge what is, and what is not positive "transformative learning." Here what will be argued is that genuinely positive "transformative learning" is inseparable from the "recognition of necessity" and overcoming "alienation."

Two questions immediately emerge. Firstly, how might transformative learning be adjudged to be either positively or regressively developmental? Following logically on from this the second question to be asked is whether such a judgement necessarily involves an ethical dimension? This second question can be answered quite quickly with a simple "yes." The implications of the answer are far from simple as it is impossible to judge "transformative learning" as being developmental or regressive without that judgement having an ethical dimension.

It has already been stated that genuinely "transformative learning" involves "identity," "personality," and their "development," these are thoroughly social things. It follows logically therefore that the only ethical basis on which to judge transformative learning as being positive or negative is inescapably "social."

So far, the argument being put forward has been developed along the lines of logic, as such it might not be controversial, but it is now about to take a slightly different turn. The claim will be advanced that the combination of social and ethical considerations into a viewpoint is nothing less or more than humanism, and that it is exactly this humanist perspective which must be brought to bear on an understanding of "transformative learning." For Marxists, humanism has a meaning which is very much related ideas of overcoming the alienation of humans from their *species being*. It has often been argued that the idea of species being implies an understanding of "human nature" of the type which features in some of the more jejune discussions of "nature versus nurture." In the *Manuscripts* Marx rejected the idea of human nature being either "innate" or divinely ordained. Instead he argued that human nature was historically conditioned and should be seen as arising from the relationships which humans must enter within society. Writing in 1859 Marx describes this historically conditioned consciousness in the following terms:

In the social production of their existence, men inevitably enter into definite relations, which are independent of their will, namely relations of production appropriate to a given stage in the development of their material forces of production. The totality of these relations of production constitutes the economic structure of society, the real foundation, on which arises a legal and political superstructure and to which correspond definite forms of social consciousness. (Marx, 1970, p. 20)

Elsewhere Marx states clearly that "the human essence is no abstraction inherent in each single individual. In its reality it is the ensemble of the social relations" (Marx & Engels, 1974, p. 122). The idea of human nature being based in and arising from the social and cultural relations in which we all live allows for the possibility of our first of all understanding these relationships and then secondly through the exercise of our "free conscious activity" finding ways to shape these relations so that they allow for the development of our humanity. Education must clearly play a part in the development of an understanding and the genuinely human development of these relationships, from a Marxist perspective this constitutes truly transformative education.[1]

Teaching the "Sustainability" Module and Overcoming Alienation

It is not easy to present "alienation" in such a way as to make the concept easily accessible. To develop an understanding of what Marx first outlined in the *Manuscripts* certainly requires effort and thought; a process sometimes made harder by expositions of "alienation" which present it as though it was something deeply mysterious or other worldly.

Teaching the sustainability module offered an opportunity to observe a perfectly "this worldly" example of students struggling with issues connected with alienation. If alienation is real, we must be able to observe it in the real world. The sociologist Liz Stanley makes a very important and similar point when discussing biographical approaches to sociology. She quite simply states the rather obvious (with hindsight) truth that anything sociological must be observable in the lives of real people or it is very difficult indeed to count it as a real theory. As Liz Stanley explains, the biographical approach in sociology was founded in principle on "The recognition that if structural analyses do not work at the level of particular lives they do not work at all" (Stanley, 1992, p. 5). The converse of this is also true, what happens in the lives of individuals can be theorised. These principles can, and must, be applied to the practice of reflective teaching a large part of which involves theory informing practice, and even more importantly, practice informing theory.

The theoretical premise from which the "Sustainability" module proceeds is the perfectly reasonable, scientifically established proposition that on present trends the "unsustainability" of the human and natural world presents an existential threat to humankind. This proposition is more than a thesis, the great weight of evidence on which it is based means that genuine contemporary scientific debate is limited to a discussion of the terms and timetables for the various catastrophic denouements which present trends ensure. Whilst this prospect is scientifically well established and therefore reasonable, it is simultaneously a vision of a depth of alienation that Marx could not have envisaged. In short, humankind through its environmentally unsustainable activity poses an existential threat to its own future, the recognition of this is the first step to a "non-alienated" view of sustainability.

To premise the teaching of a module on the idea of humanity facing an existential crisis presents definite ethical challenges. Firstly, any reasonable person confronted with the evidence that in the medium-term humanity potentially faces disaster will find the realisation disturbing. There are clear ethical considerations to be made when presenting students with views which they will find disturbing. The perturbation goes beyond this. Many students are disturbed by the realisation that much of what they have gleaned about "sustainability" from their teaching institutions, government sources and the media is at best perversely optimistic, or at worst deliberately misleading, about the scale of the problems faced by humanity. For some students the greatest disconcertment arises not from the perception that the problem is graver than they thought, but from the feeling that they have been systematically, even wilfully, misled by those they might have expected to inform and protect them.[2]

14 Sustainability, Reflection, Transformation and Taking Back... 217

Two points need to be made here regarding ethical concerns. Firstly, although those who teach the module do not want to gratuitously shock or frighten students the need to present the truth of the situation regarding sustainability is paramount. Students are encouraged to judge the evidence for themselves but as teachers we must offer a critical evaluation of the best evidence available. Secondly, the module is not taught from a fatalist position. Problems of sustainability can be solved, and the module tries to present a range of ways in which solutions might be found. The idea that "free conscious activity" is the antithesis of an alienated way of being has already been presented. The positing of problems and solutions in the most complete and honest way possible is an essential task of a teacher, it is also a precondition of overcoming alienated being.

Bearing in mind Jack Mezirow's idea that transformative learning is predicated on the learner encountering a "disorientating dilemma" (Mezirow, 2000, pp. 22–23), teaching about "sustainability" provides an example *par excellence* of a potential starting point for a transformative experience. In the context of the "Sustainability" module, it will be argued that for most students the experience is positive because it affords an opportunity to "overcome alienation" in several important ways. Here Stephen Brookfield's article (Brookfield, 2002) provided the starting point for reflection on this process not least because he offers something of a challenge to adult educators to look beyond the idea that transformative education can be seen wholly in terms of a very individualised "personal growth" framework:

> A humanistic perspective on adult education is usually interpreted as one that emphasizes respect for each adult learner's individuality and that seeks to help the individual realize her or his potential to the fullest extent possible. There is little attention to the political underpinnings of adult education practice and to the way political economy makes self-actualization a luxury for a certain social class. (Brookfield, 2002, p. 98)

There is nothing wrong with respecting the individuality of all learners and Brookfield is certainly not arguing against this. My understanding of the challenge Brookfield is setting is that a Marxist humanism asks that we recognise the learner's individuality whilst simultaneously recognising their "sociality." Furthermore, whilst no person will find that completion of the "Sustainability" module transforms their political economic or "class" position, it is very much the case that they develop a truer understanding of that position exactly by recognising its "sociality." It has long been a tenet of Marxist humanist thought that for individuals and for social groups coming to grips with alienation, it begins with recognition of the reality of the social conditions of their lives.

Whilst the terms "social conditions" and "political economy" are not exactly synonymous, they might be substituted for one another in the above quotation without significantly changing the point which Brookfield is making, and which was at the centre of all Freire's arguments about pedagogy. This is why the first sentence of *Pedagogy of the oppressed* states that "the problem of humanization has always been from an axiological point of view, man's central problem" (Freire, 1972, p. 20), and a little later the recognition of oppression is posited as a precondition for its being overcome:

> … for the oppressed to be able to wage the struggle for their liberation they must perceive the reality of oppression, not as a closed world from which there is no exit, but as a limiting situation which they can transform. (Freire, 1972, pp. 25–26)

In the module "sustainability" is presented as a social problem which can and must be transformed. Students are asked to consider how the present patterns of human, and, therefore, social, interaction with nature are creating grave problems of sustainability. These problems occur at every level from the global to the national, local, and of special importance on the BA programme, the professionally specific level. This latter level is in many cases of interest to students on the BA, often because it intersects with questions of professional pride and integrity. Even more importantly students ask themselves questions about their relationship to "sustainability." This is certainly transformative. Two examples of this will serve as illustrations of what this means.

A student who taught within the overall area of "Hair and Beauty" became interested in the idea of the forms of unsustainability within her own professional area, not least the hyper commercialised and profoundly

14 Sustainability, Reflection, Transformation and Taking Back... 219

destructive notions of "beauty" which tyrannise and torture so many people, particularly women, within our society. Commenting on her industry, this student told me that she thought "there cannot be many things more unsustainable than the commercially induced self-loathing of a person's physical being."

Students who work in construction have in many cases found the sustainability module professionally relevant as typically they take a pride in working to high standards with good quality, long lasting materials. Quite often contemporary construction methods dictate that builders cannot work to high standards. A construction student once explained to the class that it is a thing of shame to work on the construction of new homes built with materials that in some cases have a life span significantly shorter than the 30-year mortgages taken out by home buyers. The result is a debt with a guaranteed life longer than that of the home which it purchased.

Both above examples show the quotidian nature of "alienation." In both cases, students were talking about aspects of their professional work in which *they* produce a product which offends them, but despite these products being of *their* creation they have little control over them. The theorisation of this relationship to their labour, and the search for ways to transcend it represent real life instances of alienation and the initiation of processes by which it might be overcome.

Most students on the BA EPT enter the world of the university as strangers. Most, no matter the degree of their eventual success, retain the feeling that they are interlopers or even impostors in what they typically see as the rarefied world of "academia." For many, the experience of "failure" or simply of not being able to "fit in" at school, linked to their subsequent struggles in the world of work mean that they have a profound belief in the importance of "learning" and of education. Those people who have experienced exclusion, or we might well call it "alienation," from effective participation in the world of learning are well placed to attest to the truth of the adage "knowledge is power." Success on the BA allows for students to be integrated into the world of adult education, which at its very best always works towards overcoming alienation, even when it does not articulate its mission in such terms!

If students on the BA EPT, or other programmes are to get the most out of a potentially positive transformative experience it is very important that "trust" prevails. Trust is itself an important element of the development of "agency," indeed the latter cannot exist without the former. Trust must exist in students' relationships with each other, with the teachers and with what is taught, the content of which must be congruent with their own experience. Above all a feeling of agency depends upon trust in oneself. In this chapter "trust" has not been mentioned until now but it is a notion which has been ever present in the background. Trust in the integrity of the educational experience is essential if transformative learning is to be achieved. Again, we see another area in which genuinely positive transformative learning is related to overcoming alienation. To some degree positively transformative learning must always develop trust. At its best transformative education engenders a genuinely merited and informed trust in educational activity and learning. We can also see here how a reasoned and informed sense of agency is a counter to alienation.

If we accept the arguments presented above, then it is with great trepidation that we look towards the present and future development of the "university" along neo-liberal lines. If, in agreement with Marx, we see alienation as arising from, and residing in, the relations humans enter into within capitalism then the intensification of these relations must bring with it a proportional increase in alienation. Neo-liberalism is essentially the intensification of capitalist relations, within the neo-liberal university we should expect to find an intensification of alienation. We might take as an example of this dismal tide the profoundly corrupting notions of the student as "customer" and "consumer." The reconstruction of the student along these lines represents at least linguistically the "alienation" of the student from the university. It is hard to see the neo-liberal university as a fertile place for transformative education. Customer relations between students and institutions, implies the end, or at least the undermining of a more fully developed and genuinely "human" trust. Indeed, once the relationship between the university and the student is at bottom one of buying and selling then students and universities confront each

14 Sustainability, Reflection, Transformation and Taking Back... 221

other, in the market as opposing forces. This can only result in the alienation of students and teachers from what should be the real purpose of education; the positive development of *life activity*.

Notes

1. This cannot be pursued here but in my opinion this understanding is practically the same as that at the heart of Freire's *Pedagogy of the Oppressed* (Freire, 1972).
2. As this chapter was being written, press reports claimed that a golf course in Ireland owned by Donald Trump, had been granted permission to build a wall to protect it from erosion. Apparently in the planning application the reason given for the construction was "global warming and its effects". It would seem that the world's leading climate change denier is somewhat selective in his repudiation of the evidence.

References

Brookfield, S. (1995). *Becoming a critically reflective teacher.* San Francisco: Jossey Bass.

Brookfield, S. (2002). Overcoming alienation as the practice of adult education: The contribution of Erich Fromm to a critical theory of adult learning and education. *Adult Education Quarterly, 52*(2), 96–111.

Fine, B. (2001). *Social capital versus social theory.* London: Routledge.

Freire, P. (1972). *Pedagogy of the oppressed.* New York: Herder and Herder.

Illeris, K. (2014). *Transformative learning and identity.* London: Routledge.

Marx, K. (1970). *A contribution to the critique of political economy.* Moscow: Progress Publishers.

Marx, K. (1973). *Grundrisse: Foundations of a critique of political economy* (M. Nicolaus, Trans.). Harmondsworth: Penguin.

Marx, K. (1975). *Early writings* (R. Livingstone & G. Benton, Trans.). Harmondsworth: Penguin.

Marx, K. (1976–1981.) *Capital: A critique of political economy* (Vols. 1–3) (B. Fowkes, Trans.). Harmondsworth: Penguin.

Marx, K., & Engels, F. (1974). *The German ideology* (2nd ed.). London: Lawrence and Wishart.

Meszaros, I. (2005). *Marx's theory of alienation* (5th ed.). London: Merlin Press.

Mezirow, J. (2000). Learning to think like an adult: Core concepts of transformation theory. In J. Mezirow & Associates (Eds.), *Learning as transformation: Critical perspectives on a theory in progress* (pp. 3–33). San Francisco: Jossey-Bass.

Stanley, L. (1992). *The auto/biographical I.* Manchester: Manchester University Press.

Part III

Transformative Learning in Organizations

15

"Not Only a Man With a Drip": Cancer as a Shared Social Practice

Loretta Fabbri and Elisabetta Di Benedetto

Introduction

This contribution aims at investigating if and how the construct of a community of practice (CoP) (Wenger, 1998; Wenger, McDermott, & Snyder, 2002) can be useful for interpreting the learning and social skills of those experiencing cancer, identifying patients primarily as persons who want to take part in managing their treatment, according to the competency developed inside a heterogeneous group sharing the same practice. At the core is the cooperation between the insiders, who—implicitly or explicitly—bring the contribution of a knowledge stemming from their actions, and the outsiders, providing systematic approaches, useful to understand the ongoing experience.

L. Fabbri (✉)
University of Siena, Siena, Italy
e-mail: loretta.fabbri@unisi.it

E. Di Benedetto
Department of Education, Human Sciences and Intercultural Communication, University of Siena, Siena, Italy
e-mail: elisabetta.dibenedetto@unisi.it

© The Author(s) 2019
T. Fleming et al. (eds.), *European Perspectives on Transformation Theory*,
https://doi.org/10.1007/978-3-030-19159-7_15

Starting from the random observation of the behavior of a person with an oncologic disease, well known by one of the researchers, the study describes the first contacts among the members of the group and the way they help to build the different steps made by the community (Shani, Guerci, & Cirella, 2014). We want to prove that people suffering from an oncologic pathology and researchers bring complementary expertize that require coordination, according to joint learning principles, and an aptitude for dialogue and co-learning. These are key elements of a transformative learning process and sometimes approaches "dialogic reasoning" (Mezirow, 1991, p. 150).

Research as a Property of the Community: "As We Don't Want To Be Only Patients"

The method adopted in this survey is that of collaborative research of CoPs (Shani et al., 2014), which implies a commitment between two or more parties: the insiders (members of the organization under study) and the outsiders (the external researchers).

The group of the insider is made of three men and four women, between the ages of 35 and 65, suffering from various forms of cancer, at different stages, whose heterogeneity provides a stimulating environment. The group of outsider is composed of two female and two male researchers who played the role of facilitators. One is a border figure—being both patient and researcher—who facilitated the translational process between the two different groups. Her double perspective has been of great help to:

* check the quality of the relationship between insiders and outsiders,
* validate the different levels achieved,
* help the researchers to maintain a position pertinent to the arising issues.

At the core of collaborative research, we find collective inquiry (Shani et al., 2014; Snyder & Wenger, 2010), an activity focused on answering issues of mutual interest, through dialogue, experimentation and the review of knowledge and resources.

Through collective inquiry and the scientific support of the researchers, the insiders try to get a whole understanding of the phenomena affecting them. They realize that "the whole wealth of knowledge achieved about [the] pathology can be very useful. And that even such a dramatic experience, can lead to a valuable contribution" (Ls. F.).

From cooperation derives an epistemological partnership founded on the principle of equality—between insiders and outsiders—essential to allow access to the most sensitive aspects of the issue under detection (Shani, Coghlan, & Cirella, 2012).

Collaborative research focuses on observable data and experience that is not the same as learning from experience (Shani et al., 2012). "Experience of a social situation is subjective rather than objective, and it is the subjective definition of the situation which creates the experience and potentially leads to learning" (Jarvis, 1987, p. 70). This originates in an informal setting of training, where scientific and social validations intertwine leading to an "emerging" inquiry.

"The Power of Peers": The Community of Practice

Ls. F., a 50-year-old lawyer, finds out he has cancer and starts confronting people who share the same problem, taking advantage of every therapy to build a network. He wonders why there are no places that help matching those who share his problem, the so-called "comrades in adversity" (Revans, 1982). Associations and well-structured groups already exist, but he is interested in the informal exchange through which people meet on the ground.

From this ongoing experience, developing spontaneously, Ls.F. had the idea to start a joint search between people interested in sharing a common problem (insiders) and university researchers (outsiders) who are involved in transformative learning processes. Led by the strong belief that situations cannot be really known only in the abstract (Wenger,

1998), the researchers aim at creating a laboratory on collaborative research, where "comrades in adversity" can regularly confront, exchanging experiences, information, protocols, and procedures, within a common project.

Ls. F., the first to be contacted, arranges a meeting at the University with some people among his personal acquaintances, to explain the project. Others add afterwards.

The CoP is the construct that best fits the characteristics of the group, since it defines an informal set of practitioners, developing spontaneously inside organizational or social contexts around a common practice (Wenger, 1998; Wenger et al., 2002). Such an informal aggregation generates forms of knowledge with peculiar and distinctive cultural traits focusing on social and organizational solidarity on specific issues, and the sharing of objectives, practical knowledge, meanings and language.

Belonging to a CoP is a matter of fact, not a condition arbitrarily assigned", … it implies a negotiated definition of what the community is about. But neither is it … just a property of a community in abstract, that can be awarded through some decision, because this competence is experienced and manifested by members through their own engagement in practice" (Wenger, 1998, p. 136). In the case described here, the researchers supported the insiders to define the common project. The latter gradually moved from the consciousness of being "an informal group of people sharing a common issue", to consider themselves as people able to manage their own disease with the attitude of "researchers", not as mere patients. They perceive themselves able to open processes of inquiry, capable to combine practical knowledge derived from experience and scientific knowledge. This is what Mezirow (1991, p. 168) suggests is an essential step in the process of transformative learning.

Among "Comrades in Adversity": "Not to Be a Resigned 'People'"

At the beginning of this experience it seemed that also involving healthcare professionals could help speed up the sharing of the issues. But it was soon clear that they were unable to understand the heuristic extent and the learning significance of the community, having problems scheduling and attending meetings, interpreting critical issues as threats to their credibility, proving to be unable to accept the symmetry of roles in the group and not accepting the value of testing a potential role of the community inside the hospital.

At last the community was formed by "comrades in adversity" and university researchers, as this was the setting where it was possible to confront problems, contingencies and disorienting dilemmas: how to deal with a diagnosis of cancer? How to learn to face the problems and the concerning related? How to gain new knowledge without depending on the decisive help of an expert, but relying on one's own criticism and ability to participate in inquiry?

At first the insiders' expectations were directed mainly toward their "comrades in adversities", seen as an important reference point for "unpacking" issues (Marsick & Davis-Manigaulte, 2011) and learning how to get out of a private dimension, face complex times, sharing knowledge and experience.

"Exchange" is one of their keywords, that brings into play:

* the relational dimension, "feeling to be part of a community, to have the possibility to interact with people who share the same problem" (G.B.);
* the need of socially shared learning, through which "the experience of cancer [can be transformed into] a helpful wealth of knowledge about this disease" (Ls.F.);
* the possibility to become "more mature and conscious about this pathology" (Ls.F.).
* A comparison of different experiences brings with it a new awareness of the many individual meanings attributed to illness, together with the possibility of translating awareness into operational schemes and actions. Among the most significant findings is the thought that not "everything can be taken for granted, not all should be passively accepted, we can contribute to improve the situation through our testimony and questions" (A.C.). What becomes relevant is the ability to accompany introspection with a critically reflective action, facilitated by the presence of the other comrades of adversity and from reflection

on common issues (Mezirow, 1991). Learning how to transform for addressing disorientation and fears is not only a solely individual process, but a conquest of the group composing the CoP.

From this perspective, the three main accomplishments of the CoP are:

* the pleasure of confronting people with similar problems;
* the ability to learn from experience;
* the achievement of a "tool kit" to negotiate treatment management and power relations about practices not considered as a matter of fact, but as a matter of concern (Gherardi & Rodeschini, 2016), therefore, requiring critical investigation.

"I Knew That Behind Each Name There Was a Story I Was Interested in": Silent Learning and Implicit Curricula

M.B. is approaching her 60s. When she joins the CoP she is still rather knocked down by her recent surgery and all that followed. From the first meeting she is approached by E.D.B., who had a similar operation five years before, without recurrence. Due to the similarity of their stories, their relationship becomes closer.

One year later S.B., a young woman, joins the CoP. As a consequence of her recent chemotherapy, suspense, pain, and sadness are common feelings. M.B. is very much impressed by this new "comrade in adversity", her young age "makes her see her worries in perspective".

The experience of the two women makes M.B. consider in a different perspective her own experience of disease. Here we find two converging assumptions: that of CoP as "shared histories of learning" (Wenger, 1998, p. 86) and that of implicit curriculum.

M.B. reinterprets her disease in a new way after learning the histories of E.D.B. and S.B. The interaction with the two women results in a learning potential much greater than any narrative about their histories. But learning is shared even beyond intents and reifications, following a dynamic similar to the one underlying implicit curriculum, which refers to each type of learning, conscious or unconscious, acquired by the environment and the attitudes of the others (Connelly & Clandinin, 1988).

We also find other instances of learning through implicit curriculum, where beliefs, attitudes, expectations and motivations come into play.

A.C. has applied to many health facilities. Attending the CoP, he hears about different experiences in several health centers. Through these tales—explicit curriculum—he "becomes aware of many aspects related to health environments". He also perceives the particular relation established by each participant with the center where they are treated—implicit curriculum. He forms a view—that it is better to apply to a center of excellence—and in a moment of doubt, he contacts the "comrade" with the most promising experience. With this action, he started questioning the general assumption that protocols applied to patients are all the same.

"Arming Patients Instead of Forming Physicians": From a Peripheral to a Central Position

Meeting other "comrades in adversity" was the insiders' primary need, the second was acquiring a more central role within the socio-medical practices. This second need derives from the peripheral position experienced within the health care management system. Meeting among peers increases awareness of one's own expertise in a context highly marked by asymmetric relations. The novelty consists in the insider's awareness of how "transforming physicians practices, in Italy, will be a long and difficult matter" (Ls. F.).

Becoming aware of different experiences helps patients to enhance their conceptual weapons. The aim is different from that described in the case of patient engagement (Graffigna et al., 2014), that does not take into account the gap between declared theory—by which a particular action pattern is formally explained or justified—and theory in use—which consists of the routines, the rules, the values and the strategies actually acted and of the assumptions embedded in behaviors (Argyris &

Schön, 1996). The theories in use are relevant, especially in explaining and modifying organizational learning, while the histories of the members of the CoP bring out theories in use often very different from those declared by the health companies.

The phrase "arming patients" (Ls. F.) somehow represents the position of the group: acknowledging that the communities of patients can be able to construct a "competent" (in a certain way "expert")—and therefore legitimate—interpretation of the meaning of their experiences. "Arming patients" means to give them the opportunity and the tools to reflect on what happened to them and to share practices and information for being prepared in facing all the steps of the disease. Belonging to a "thinking community", able to identify and understand the process that is developed inside it, increases the empowerment of its members in many ways:

* turning frustration, rage and uncertainty into critical incidents, to be discussed;
* facing disorienting dilemmas all together;
* using inquiry to collect data;
* taking the necessary time to work out the different experiences.

This is a clear link with Transformation Theory (Mezirow, 1991). One of the consequences of empowerment is the adoption of a toolkit useful to face critical aspects and negotiate with the health companies.

The community is a living context, fit for advanced learning, relying on a bond of common competence and great respect for the particular experience at stake (Wenger, 1998): it is "a wetsuit to dive into the sea of illness" (A. C.). This metaphor was used by one of the insiders to stress the need for a translational tool enabling to turn from experience to competence and vice versa. The point is to look critically at the common ideas concerning treatment, so undermining "the objectivity of protocols [that] relieves from any possible choice" (A. C.). The cliché are what Mezirow means by taken for granted knowledge (Mezirow, 1991, pp. 132–133).

When the practice related to treatment is no more "given" (Gherardi & Rodeschini, 2016), it becomes an act carried out—with competence or incompetence—by a heterogeneous group of people, medical equipment and more or less powerful technologies. Confronting such a cultural, professional, organizational and social system requires competent patients, able to explore the conditions under which treatments are carried out. This involves also the socio-material context and the various professional styles, going beyond the doctor–patient relationship. Materiality is an integral part of the treatment itself, it is made of settings, waiting rooms, endless queues, posters on the walls, shameless ads of wigs: spaces talk and define themselves through objects, the present and the missing ones.

Thanks to their participation to the community the insiders begin to see the practices connected to the treatment as "objects undergone to processes of reflection" (Fabbri, 2007). This encourages them to play a more central role, to negotiate the practices affecting them, taking the view of researchers. As researchers, they can understand what is happening/going to happen to them and to their life, and to change the course of events.

Awareness can bring to possible negotiations of therapy management by the insiders, who, for instance, can insist on having a curtain drawn to talk to their neighbors during the chemotherapy, in spite of the nurse's resistance: the last step of a reflection process through which one's own need for social contacts is legitimized.

The behaviors of the healthcare professionals during key moments—interview, visit, checkup, treatment—have been one of the main topics of discussion in the community.

"I Say to Myself to Let Things Happen. Hardly Ever Is the Right Choice"

One of the most common and considerable dilemmas concerns whether and to what extent to critically deal with decisions about treatment. Two critical incidents show that successful outcomes derived from the insiders' ability to have a dialectic approach. In the former, the patient takes an investigative attitude to illness and, opposing the urologist's opinion, decides to consult an oncologist, who finds a probable disease recurrence and immediately sets up an appointment with the radiotherapist, avoiding the wasting of valuable months. His decision to play a central role derives from a form of situated learning, based on the capacity to exit the flow of events and decentralize (Mezirow, 1991). Understanding that nothing is given, it is possible to reformulate the problem, in the light of wider and more inclusive perspectives.

The latter incident concerns competencies. The protagonist is a patient but a healthcare professional too, able to propose the most suitable way to solve her problem—difficulties in venous access—doing her magnetic resonance imaging with contrast. Tellingly, her professional role is not acknowledged by her colleagues, as the fact that she is a patient overshadows her professional competencies and her expertise is not recognized.

Both incidents prove that active participation in treatment practices is fundamental to relate to healthcare contexts and can change the course of events, while playing just a marginal role can be dangerous.

Between Invisibility and Visibility: Formalizing the Voice of the Community

We identify two stages in the development of the CoP. The first was an incubation period, characterized by "the development of deep insight into each other individual practice, each other reactions and style of thinking and a collective understanding of the practice as a whole" (Wenger et al., 2002, p. 85). "Invisibility" was necessary to the community to consolidate, but after one year a new phase started: the insiders felt they possessed key competences—emotional, relational, communicative, organizational—and wanted their role to be recognized by the physicians. It is a dynamic very similar to what Wenger calls "institutionalizing the voice of the community" (Wenger et al., 2002).

It was at this point that the members of the community were invited to a Festival by an association engaged in raising funds to buy medical equipment for the oncologic unit. It represented an opportunity to launch the project inside a wider social context (Snyder & Wenger, 2010), going back through its main steps. The oncologist—promoter of the initiative—was asked if and how such communities could contribute to the healthcare organization. The expression "I am not only a man with a drip" (Ls. F.) emerged in this context to express the need to institutionalize the role of informal aggregations formed by oncologic patients as authoritative interlocutors for the healthcare organization on issues often simple, but with a strong impact on everyday life such as the organization of spaces or more effective ways to inform and communicate.

It is a sort of claim against the sanitary system, that often does not see the person and the community behind the patient, but it is also an attempt to redefine the patient's identity from a multidimensional perspective.

According to the oncologist, the answer to the patients' needs is just a question of competent management of medical issues. He understands neither the difference between confronting an organized group instead of an individual, nor how experience-based knowledge can validly support innovation inside his unit. Not recognizing that patients' collective intelligence cannot help to widen the dimension of caring, going beyond the limits of the asymmetric relation between a "good doctor" and his patient.

The Contribution of Literature

A review of the Italian and international literature of the last 20 years on models concerning the cure reveals a growing interest in the organization of reflective actions, contexts and practices useful to learn from one's own experience in a transformative learning perspective.

Unlike works on the promotion of patient engagement (Graffigna et al., 2014), we propose practice-based studies which consider the cure as an activity situated in the patients and engagement as the result of a competency gained by a heterogeneous group sharing a real problem.

The construct of the CoP is widely applied to the oncologic context, in the international framework, especially in Anglo-Saxon and North European countries. The patients' points of view emerge from the experience of groups diversified as to composition, techniques and ways of communication—through internet, by phone (Roos, 2003) or in the hospital ward. Though patients usually aggregate according to their specific pathologies, giving rise to well-characterized and specialized communities (Visser & Van Andel, 2003), there are also general studies which consider the "oncologic patient" apart from his pathology (Andersen, Larsen, & Birkelund, 2015).

Three studies focus on the helping process between patients (the "novices") and volunteer helpers (the "experts"). In the first, the disclosers talk about their illness-related concerns with their partners and, in a separate conversation, with the volunteer helpers (Pistrang & Barker, 1998). Though the relation between peers is more empathetic and supportive, the novice does not differentiate between the two types of helpers, maybe because the opportunity to talk about their concerns is deemed so beneficial by patients that they consider it positive independent of the helper.

One year later, the study is resumed (Pistrang, Solomons, & Barker, 1999), with a new set of patients, to further explore how different styles of peer helping are perceived. The findings support the hypothesis that the condition of peers in itself is not enough to structure an effective helping relationship, what makes a difference is the helper's ability to express empathy. If empathy and the way it is conveyed are the key elements of a good relationship between peers, then training "the experts" is important to make them support "the novices" at best. This can be considered a validation of Mezirow's Theory of Transformative Learning focusing on the importance of supporting the transformative dimensions of meaning perspectives (Mezirow, 1991).

The last study (Pistrang, Jay, Gessler, & Barker, 2013), focuses on the supporters themselves, in a one-to-one peer support program for women suffering from gynecological cancer. Once again the relevant role of empathy is stressed. According to the authors "one-to-one peer support has a valuable role to play in cancer survivorship, not only for those receiving support, but also for those providing it" (Pistrang et al., 2013, p. 893), as it can help to move away from the role of patient and promote a more confident sense of self. Supporting patients by phone allowed to maintain the right balance, as it permitted the supporters to remain anonymous and to absorb the emotional impact.

One of the most relevant studies focusing on CoP as a helpful construct to interpret the learning experience of the oncologic patient has been published by "a former medical research scientist who had spent

15 "Not Only a Man With a Drip": Cancer as a Shared Social...

20 years researching anti-cancer drugs" (Roos, 2003, p. 219). He identifies three different CoPs:

* the formal medical community, unable to give the patient an identity, one of the crucial issues of the doctor–patient relationship,
* the community of patients, an email list server, linked to a prostate cancer web site, a place where it is possible to learn how to be a patient, "negotiate meaning and claim [a] new identity as a cancer patient" (Roos, 2003, p. 222),
* the community of family and friends, a supporting and caring one, in which he does not feel a cancer patient.

The author stresses the complementary advantages of the discussion list where the telematics feature provides the possibility to establish full-scale relations, allowing a large number of patients to confront in the fastest way, exchanging experiences, information, protocols and procedures in an empathetic style, very similar to that mentioned by Pistrang and Barker (1998), but also permitting to build more private one-to-one relationships. This kind of community conforms to the three fundamental conditions defining a CoP: mutual engagement, joint enterprise and shared repertoire.

Whereas the medical community is based on the reification of information *on* the patient, but not *for* the patient, the virtual community, allows patients to work out their condition, negotiating meanings and affirming their new identity. Here, it is possible to receive both formal and informal information, to learn which are the right questions and to show one's own emotions. According to the author, belonging to different kinds of communities is an antidote to the pervasive tendency by the sanitary system to see patients as clients instead of persons, with great weaknesses, but also great resources that must be enhanced and used.

Two more contributions focus on the education of patients with a diagnosis of prostate cancer and on the different forms of social support provided to them.

The former underlines the lack of interest from psycho-oncology in this particular kind of cancer (Visser & Van Andel, 2003), considering the possibility to reduce psychological problems through self-help groups, in accordance with the study by Roos (2003). The latter focuses on the needs expressed by patients and on their own satisfaction levels. The greatest and less satisfied needs are for information, especially about side-effects of treatment and the possibility of recurrence. The authors agree with Roos, who highlights the necessity to consider people suffering from cancer as people with a disease, instead of patients.

Three studies published between 2013 and 2015 deal with the interaction between peers during hospitalization (Andersen et al., 2015; Birkelund & Larsen, 2013; Larsen, Larsen, & Birkelund, 2013). They analyze all aspects of the relation among patients: sometimes coexistence can be tiring or generate tensions, sometimes irony lightens the mood, other times patients take care of one another, the experts helping novices to develop a certain degree of autonomy in their most elementary daily needs. Peers recognize the value of information and knowledge derived from first-hand experience, as complementary to that coming from healthcare professionals. The context and the relations described are partly similar to those typical of a CoP, especially with reference to mutual engagement and shared repertoire. The authors conclude that the interaction among patients should be a complementary "care factor" to take into consideration inside nurses' training.

Conclusions

At the beginning of this research, an informal group of people was starting to network. The ties of the network were still weak and from the observation of this frail network researchers had the idea of forming a community. The core issue was finding a common field connecting the members and making them realize the importance of mutual exchange and sharing of ideas, histories and techniques. At first, the community drew its energy from discovering that its members faced similar problems and had quite a lot to learn from each other: relevant data, tools, approaches, insights.

After two years we have succeeded in supporting the development of a network of people at the early stage, to help them enhance interaction and sharing of knowledge. The CoP has increased its sense of belonging and appreciated the advantages of learning from others' experience. What still has to be done is to work out a development practice of the community itself.

References

Andersen, L. S., Larsen, B. H., & Birkelund, R. (2015). A companionship between strangers: Learning from fellow people with cancer in oncology wards. *Journal of Advanced Nursing, 71*(2), 271–280.

Argyris, C., & Schön, D. A. (1996). *Organizational learning II: Theory, method, and practice*. Reading, MA: Addison-Wesley.

Birkelund, R., & Larsen, L. S. (2013). Patient-patient interaction: Caring and sharing. *Scandinavian Journal of Caring Sciences, 27*, 608–615.

Connelly, F. M., & Clandinin, D. J. (1988). *Teachers as curriculum planners: Narratives of experience*. New York: Teachers College.

Fabbri, L. (2007). *Comunità di pratiche e apprendimento riflessivo. Per una formazione situata* [Community of practices and reflective learning. For situated training]. Roma: Carocci.

Gherardi, S., & Rodeschini, G. (2016). Del curare e del prendersi cura: come la sociomaterialità dell'alimentazione artificiale cambia le pratiche di cura [On care and caring: How sociomateriality of artificial nutrition changes the practices of care]. In P. Landri (Ed.), *Prendersi cura del welfare. Le politiche sociali nella lente della pratica* [Caring of welfare: Social politics in the lens of practice] (pp. 55–92). Pavia: Edizioni Altravista.

Graffigna, G., Barello, S., Triberti, S., Wiederhold, B. K., Bosio, A. C., & Riva, G. (2014). Enabling e-health as a pathway for patient engagement: A toolkit for medical practice. In B. Wiederhold & G. Riva (Eds.), *Annual review of cybertherapy and telemedicine* (pp. 13–21). Amsterdam: Ios Press BV.

Jarvis, P. (1987). *Adult learning in the social context*. London: Croom Helm.

Larsen, L. S., Larsen, B. H., & Birkelund, R. (2013). An ambiguous relationship: A qualitative meta-synthesis of hospitalized somatic patients' experience of interaction with fellow patients. *Scandinavian Journal of Caring Sciences, 27*, 495–505.

Marsick, V., & Davis-Manigaulte, J. (2011). Sostenere lo sviluppo degli operatori nel settore dello sviluppo giovanile attraverso l'apprendimento critico riflessivo basato sull'azione [How to support educators in the field of youth development through critical reflective learning based on actions]. *Educational Reflective Practices, 1–2*, 7–36.

Mezirow, J. (1991). *Transformative dimensions of adult learning*. San Francisco: Jossey-Bass.

Pistrang, N., & Barker, C. (1998). Partners and fellow patients. *American Journal of Community Psychology, 26*(3), 439–456.

Pistrang, N., Jay, Z., Gessler, S., & Barker, C. (2013). Telephone peer support for women with gynaecological cancer: Benefits and challenges for supporters. *Psycho-Oncology, 22*, 886–894.

Pistrang, N., Solomons, W., & Barker, C. (1999). Peer support for women with breast cancer: The role of empathy and self-disclosure. *Journal of Community and Applied Social Psychology, 9*, 217–229.

Revans, R. (1982). *The origin and growth of action learning*. Bromley: Chartwell Bratt.

Roos, I. A. G. (2003). Reacting to the diagnosis of prostate cancer: Patient learning in a community of practice. *Patient Education and Counseling, 49*, 219–224.

Shani, A. B., Coghlan, D., & Cirella, S. (2012). Action research and collaborative management research: More than meets the eye. *International Journal of Action Research, 8*(1), 45–67.

Shani, A. B., Guerci, M., & Cirella, S. (2014). *Collaborative management research. Teoria, metodi, esperienze*. Milano: Raffaello Cortina.

Snyder, W., & Wenger, E. (2010). Our world as a learning system: A communities-of-practice approach. In C. Blackmore (Ed.), *Social learning systems and communities of practice* (pp. 107–124). Berlin: Springer.

Visser, A., & Van Andel, G. (2003). Psychosocial and educational aspects in prostate cancer patients. *Patient Education and Counseling, 49*, 203–206.

Wenger, E. (1998). *Communities of practice: Learning, meaning, and identity*. Cambridge: Cambridge University Press.

Wenger, E., McDermott, R., & Snyder, W. M. (2002). *Cultivating communities of practice: A guide to managing knowledge*. Boston, MA: Harvard Business School Press.

16

Reframing Professional Challenges Through Action Learning Conversations in Medical Organizations

Maura Striano

Promoting a Reflective Turn in Medical Organizations

Medical organizations are extremely complex and the healthcare professionals working within them, performing different roles and tasks, are constantly challenged and tested by difficult, frustrating and problematic situations. Challenging these problems that constantly emerge from professional practices is influenced by multiple factors, among which, are a number of elements internal to medical organizations. The problems that emerge are frequently related to practices, protocols, routines which are grounded in taken for granted assumptions but which often are not adequate to address the situations healthcare professionals face daily. This can cause problems and impasses within organizations and have a significant impact on individuals who work within them. This is why promoting reflective practices in this context is so crucial.

M. Striano (✉)
University of Naples Federico II, Naples, Italy
e-mail: maura.striano@unina.it

© The Author(s) 2019

T. Fleming et al. (eds.), *European Perspectives on Transformation Theory*,
https://doi.org/10.1007/978-3-030-19159-7_16

Reflective processes allow us to explore in-depth and in detail the flow of "action–reflection–action" which sustains the educational practices and learning outcomes circulating within the organization. In such complex organizations, it can be generative to involve an "outsider" with a different point of view to activate a reflective process to support professionals identify aspects and elements that otherwise would be invisible, out of focus, hidden or at least not clear.

Below I will describe the work I have been doing with healthcare professionals to reflect on their assumptions, attitudes, beliefs, and meaning perspectives on how their interactions feed the planning and performance of new courses of action. The reflective process starts from experiences within which professionals identify specific problems that emerge from their practice. This is made possible through a context analysis and through an analysis of "repertoires". We have considered the context as an intersection of actors and memories (Siegel and Cohen 1991) and have accordingly identified the key agents and memories (in terms of "lessons learned", routines, consolidated knowledge, "war stories" and traditions handed down within the different communities of practice and organizations)—a kind of tacit knowledge which is fundamental to how an organization learns and operates. As part of this process, we analyzed the repertoires (in terms of protocols, procedures, strategies and tools) shared within the communities and organizations in order to identify the critical elements within the different action plans made by the professionals. The participants are asked to explore in-depth the dynamic relationship between freedom and responsibility implied in their day to day work.

Reflection is deepened through a comparative analysis of their choices, decisions and outcomes. Professionals are required to focus on implicit ideas, representations and world views and on the strategies underlying their agency through an exploration of the premises, intentions and goals. The direct engagement of the professionals has a double purpose in the context of the promotion of organizational learning with effective transformative outcomes because it makes explicit the knowledge construction and the meaning making processes embedded within professional practices. It has an epistemic purpose as it seeks to foster reflective processes starting from professional practices aimed at identifying the paths through which knowledge is constructed within professions (what has been learned) and at the generation of new forms of knowledge, which are made available within the organizational context, sustaining change and transformation through endogenous processes. It has an epistemological purpose as it allows the critical consideration of a professional epistemology inspired by a technical rationality (for example, the application of standardized procedures, and the performance of protocols and routines which have become inert and unproductive) in comparison with a professional epistemology inspired by a reflective rationality (the analysis of repertories, and the deconstruction, implementation and reconstruction of professional practices).

The aim is to create space for participants to rethink and perform in new and different ways the roles and tasks within the organization and central to this is the activation of processes of transformative learning (Mezirow, 2012). The activation is through a disorienting dilemma in which the meaning perspectives commonly used prove to be inadequate and inappropriate either from an epistemological point of view (the knowledge and references used to explore and cope with the situation are ineffective or the way the professionals use this knowledge to address the dilemma is ineffective); in psychological terms (the perceptions, representations and emotions are dissonant and disorienting); or from a sociolinguistic perspective (the words used are not effective in order to describe the experience in an appropriate way or are not useful to elaborate the meanings necessary to understand the experience).

Action Learning Conversation

Using Mezirow's framework, Marsick and Maltbia (2009) have implemented an operational model named Action Learning Conversation (ALC) for use within organizations that requires participants to work in groups of peers on a real problem which does not simply require an expert solution grounded in technical rationality. It is a critical, reflective and multiperspectival exploration. Differences in personality, origin, ethnicity, gender and gender orientation, background, training, professional role and work place are extremely important in order to maximize the

244 M. Striano

different perspectives for exploration and through dialogue to create a wider frame of reference for seeking solutions.

The process unfolds in a sequence that can be described according to the following pattern:

(a) the framing of the challenge as a question;
(b) the sharing of information regarding the contexts and the actions already performed;
(c) the definition of questions aimed at de-structuring the mental frames which may make the proponent unaware of others' points of view;
(d) the identification of assumptions and implicit presuppositions underlying the form according to which the challenge has been set;
(e) the reframing of the way proponents understand and frame the situation and the challenge;
(f) the activation of more aware and informed decision-making processes in order to address the challenge through a specific action plan.

The group helps the proponent to explore the problem using the objective, reflective, interpretative and decisional research method known as ORID. Following Marsick and Maltbia (2009), we have used ORID (2014, 2018) to guide the facilitative process. It offers a practical heuristic for creating, through critical questioning, opportunities for transformative learning and interpreting how the various stages of transformative learning outlined by Mezirow are worked through in an organizational context. The ORID method was used to analyze a structured conversation led by a facilitator. The ORID method and was developed by the Institute for Cultural Affairs (USA). This tool allows the group having the discussion to clearly identify relevant facts (objective), be aware of feelings and perceptions linked to these facts (reflective), analyze the facts and feelings and then interpret the implications (interpretive) and finally make decisions (objective).

It is argued that ALC helps in identifying values, beliefs and assumptions, and is particularly effective as it creates the conditions which help professionals to understand how they can change a situation by changing the way they frame it and act on it (Marsick & Maltbia, 2009). The capacity to think and act in an increasingly complex fashion, and to look at the transformative learning processes activated at a personal level may help professionals to combine learning processes and organizational change (Watkins, Marsick, & Faller, 2012).

The learning process emerging and unfolding within an ALC session can be effectively represented by the double loop learning described by Argyris and Schön (1996) who assert that the internal operational sphere and the external strategic sphere are integrated through a single learning mechanism. Through critical reflection professionals acknowledge that their perceptions are filtered through world views, beliefs, attitudes and feelings which have often been uncritically absorbed through family, school and society, and which often produce distortions in the understandings of problems and situations (Argyris & Schön, 1974, 1978; Yorks, O'Neil, & Marsick, 1999); in this way, they are encouraged to examine the interpretative frames of reference and the mental models that they refer to (Senge, 1990). ALC in healthcare contexts is extremely useful in order to explore and reinforce professional identities, connecting social identity and organizational identity, work-related behaviors and the individual perception of the role played in the different contexts and situations (Walsh & Gordon, 2008).

Action Learning Conversation with Healthcare Professionals: Case Studies

In this section, we present four case studies describing the use of the ALC model in a workshop format aimed at promoting professional development for healthcare professionals. The setting of each workshop was aimed at supporting the construction of a small group of healthcare professionals engaged in the shared exploration of a highly significant professional challenge characterized by multiple elements (cultural, professional, organizational and social). This exploration was aimed at negotiating a new meaning for the challenge the participants face in order to reframe it through a process of transformative learning (Mezirow, 2012).

The interactions among participants were audio-recorded, transcribed and coded according to the ORID matrix; which is useful to identify the

First Case Study

A workshop was held at the National Convention of the Italian Society of Medical Education, in Matera, 2014, the main focus of which was on interprofessional work in medicine and was aimed at exploring the possibility of learning and constructing new forms of knowledge and understanding through encounters with different professionals and their views on the challenges and dilemmas in their professional practice. The group was a self-selected group of participants at the convention. The group was diverse in the professional and personal perspectives profiles: family doctor (female); diabetologist (female); psychologist and trainer (female); two gynecologists (male and female); nurse (female); two nurses (males); obstetrician (female); and an expert in education as facilitator. The varied backgrounds of the participants meant the group was richly multiperspectival. The presenter of the challenge was a gynecologist (60 years old) who worked in a public hospital and was a teaching professor at the university.

The challenge was framed as a question "How is it possible to reduce the demand for caesarean deliveries from female patients?" The proponent pointed out how this was a crucial question for him and how he had been feeling more frustrated, over the years with the increase in the number of caesarean sections being performed. The proponent was also frustrated since he felt that he was the only one to frame the situation as a problem while his colleagues either at the hospital or the university did not see it in these terms. He acknowledged that this was his own problem.

After a first series of objective questions, aimed at defining more precisely the context ("Did you involve your colleagues and organization?" "What is the percentage of caesarian deliveries in your hospital?" "Did you notice a progressive orientation towards the choice of the caesarian delivery over time?"; "Who are the other stakeholders?"), the proponent was invited by the other participants to focus on the meaning of his question. He explained how he was feeling like a "Don Quixote fighting against windmills", describing himself as isolated and hopeless. Reporting his conversations with his patients, he stated that he understood that the choice of having a caesarian delivery is primarily determined by beliefs and information informing women's decisions independently of their real health condition and what they were experiencing.

With the help of *reflective questions* ("What are the fears and feelings of patients who ask to have a caesarian delivery?" "How did you manage the frustration in the relationship with your patients and colleagues?"), the proponent was supported in the exploration of his contextual positioning which was helpful for the identification of the psychological perspectives at stake.

Later, with the help of *interpretative questions*, the participants have identified the assumptions underlying different ways used to frame the problem. Pregnancy has been understood in different ways: a personal and lonely challenge for women, a medical issue requiring controlled monitored and managed by medical experts in medical contexts who are responsible for outcomes. In spite of it being a complex natural process that requires sustained work by a network of actors playing different and integrated roles at different times.

Finally, with the help of *decisional questions* the participants have helped the proponent to rethink his professional practice focusing not only on his dialogue and relationship with the patients but on contextual elements and resources.

By the end of the ALC process, the proponent had reframed his challenge in new and different terms: "How can we support women during their pregnancy and in their childbirth choices?" acknowledging that the challenge cannot be faced individually by a single professional, but should be managed by sharing and distributing the responsibilities among different actors all of whom have equal levels of engagement and responsibility.

There had been a significant change in the framing of the problem and in the roles played by the different actors, which indicates an advance in the process of transformative learning, intended as the result of a deep modification of the perspectives and the schemes used to make meaning of one's individual experience, leading to new courses of actions, new roles played and new practices performed.

Second Case Study

The second case involved a seminar held as an optional activity within a Master's degree course for nurses at the University of Turin in 2015. The aim of the seminar was to provide students with an example of reflective practice, addressing either professional or organizational development for healthcare professionals and for medical organizations starting from challenges that emerge within medical practice. Students, professors and healthcare professionals participated. A nurse (female), 55 years old, a coordinator of nursing services in a public hospital and an adjunct professor at the University of Turin, presented her challenge which was a question emerging from her own professional experience: "How is it possible to manage nurses who have the task of coordinating nursing services, maintaining their motivation and their capacity to reflect, at times and in places where resources have been dramatically cut?"

The *objective questions* ("How did you understand and explore the difficulties in nursery services?" "How did you identify the problem?" "Which kind of interventions have been realized already?" "In what ways has the institution in charge of professional development and training has been involved?") have been useful in a better vision of the context. In her initial positioning, the nurse mainly focused on the fatigue and exhaustion of coordinators (herself included) and on their lack of motivation; but the group, with the aid of *reflective questions* ("You used the term motivation to frame the problem but what you have described could be better understood as uneasiness", "Are the questions you present motivational or organizational?" "It seems that there has been a before and an after. Before the motivation was higher?" "What do you think about playing the role of the patients?") helped her understand the situation in terms of a diffused uneasiness due to the stressful conditions within which nurses work.

This required both the group and the proponent to take into account the organizational configuration and not only individual attitudes and feelings. With the help of *interpretative questions*, working on motivation was therefore understood as a "palliative" whereas the difficulties were understood as "structural" and the problems described were connected to the "policies" followed by the organization. Accordingly, the problem has been framed as the outcome of an incorrect practice consolidated over time which has produced the progressive decrease of coordinators' motivation. The proponent affirmed that working on professional motivation is a sort of "palliative" whereas the difficulties are "structural" and the question is strictly connected to the "policies" of the organization which requires a deep revision and discussion of organizational choices.

During the session the proponent acknowledged the support and understanding as well as the richness of the contributions of the group and the learning from the others. These elements helped her reframe and understand the challenges with the help of *decisional questions* in terms of strategies and solutions that the organization should discover and apply to counter the uneasiness of the professionals. A good example was the possibility of mapping the context and collecting emotional elements in order to highlight the professional climate. The proponent planned to engage students to help her in data collection and analysis and to use systematic feedback sessions, follow-up procedures and interprofessional meetings to monitor the organizational change.

Third Case Study

A workshop held within a professional development course organized by the regional section of the Italian Society of Medical Education in collaboration with the local government in Fano (Marche) in 2015. The aim of the workshop was to offer an example of the use of professional practice to support in-service professional development for healthcare professionals starting from the challenges emerging from their practice. The participants at the ALC were self-selected from a group of 60 professionals. Professionals who did not participate directly in the session acted as spectators (playing the role of the "fly on the wall"), taking notes and participating in the final debriefing session.

The proponent was a female doctor, 40 years old, and a coordinator of an emergency rescue team working in the ambulance service. She posed the challenge as a question emerging from a process of self-reflection on her own professional experience and with significant emotional implications: "How can I re-motivate and reconstruct a team working in an emergency rescue service which has progressively lost motivation and cohesion?"

After the *objective questions* ("What are the differences between the previous situation and the present?"; "What are the changes have been tried by professionals on the team over time?"; "What are the different roles and positions of the professionals engaged in the team?"), the proponent was invited to focus on the meaning of her question and to identify the underlying meaning perspectives through a series of *reflective questions* and interventions from the other participants ("What are the indicators that there is tension within the group?"; "Why do you say that trust among professionals is not there anymore?"). At this point, the doctor explained how she felt embittered and angry noticing that all her efforts to support the team had been a failure. The challenge was explored through different organizational and professional perspectives by the group: coordinator head nurse (female); head hospital doctor (male); three nurses (two male and one female); speech therapist (female); psychologist (female). The discussion was very animated, and sometimes controversial and provocative especially when the proponent thought that another professional was not able to fully understand the situation. Of particular interest was the contribution of the speech therapist who helped the group focus on the metaphors used to introduce and explore the challenge as the problem was framed as a "breaking" of a climate of "trust". With the help of *interpretative questions*, the participants have identified the assumptions underlying the presentation of the problem that the proponent had set out as remotivation and reconstruction of the team, focusing on personal and relational issues rather than contextual and professional ones. The participants have instead thought that the focus of the discussion could be moved to the structure of the team and its internal dynamics or on the practices and the situations which have determined tensions and ruptures. They have therefore proposed three different hypotheses connected to three different organizational

16 Reframing Professional Challenges Through Action Learning... 251

approaches and to three different ways of conceiving and managing human resources: restructuring the team; replacing members; totally changing the team; offer professional development and self-reflective opportunities.

Taking into account the suggestions of the group, with the help of *decisional questions* the proponent reframed the challenge in terms of a reflection on the situations that over the years have determined the state of the team. She also acknowledged the necessity to take into account a variety of contextual elements in order to face the question that had implications and consequences. In addition, it was important to engage the team in a process of self-reflection on its internal and external problems. The challenge was reframed in these terms: "How can we build up a supportive context for teams operating in emergency situations?"

Fourth Case Study

This ALC session was proposed as an optional activity within a Master's degree course for nurses at the University of Turin in 2017 and offered students an example of the use of reflective practice to support professional and organizational development for healthcare professionals and for medical organizations. The focus of the session was challenges emerging from professional practice. The participants at the ALC sessions were both professors and students.

The proponent was a 27-year-old male nurse working in an intensive care unit. He presented his challenge framing it as a problem emerging from his own professional experience. "The donation of organs is not achieved when it happens that it is only the doctor who communicates to the family the cerebral death of the patient. However, if the nurse is the first person who introduces the issue to the family, or is otherwise involved, the family generally decides to donate the organs. How is it possible to formalize the process in a more effective way?"

With the help of objective questions ("For how long has been this situation been going on"?; "How can you affirm that organ donations are successful (usually when they are sustained by nurses?"; "What changes in the two situations? Communication or context?"; "Your statement has been constructed on the basis of a perception of measurable data?"; "In the context you work in all the nurses agree on the necessity to highlight the problem?") the group has understood that the question was framed in these terms on the basis of a series of elements and recurrent observations which had produced a common awareness of the problem but with no documented evidence.

On this basis the group, with the use of *reflective questions* ("Which are the most determinant attitudes?"; "Why is there resistance from the doctors and what could the team of nurses do to gain trust?"; "Do you feel protected, exposed, engaged?"; "Do you talk as a group about how one feels in these circumstances?"; "Are there discussions after?") has understood that due to the implications in terms of roles and responsibilities, the question had been discussed at an interprofessional level, even if not in a clear and systematic way, from an organizational perspective.

The *interpretative questions* have helped the professional to see that the problem was initially framed in terms of practices and outcomes, highlighting the role played by different professional profiles but that the focus has to move toward settings, languages and communicative strategies. Accordingly, the challenge has been therefore reframed by the proponent in terms of organizational choices.

Decisional questions have finally accompanied the nurse in taking into account a series of possible strategies and solutions (construct an information sheet for the families of the patients, create integrated interprofessional training courses on staff-family communication strategies, restructuring the setting and the procedures) taking into account the consensual conditions of feasibility as well as an analysis of interprofessional dynamics.

Conclusions

The four cases presented show the impact that the ALC methodology with the ORID matrix can have on the transformation of the understandings, intentions and actions of professionals working in healthcare contexts, offering evidence of the possibility of using more critical and reflective interpretative frames, which can integrate different interprofessional experiences. Analyzing the ALC process in several debriefing sessions, we have noted that the participants have acknowledged that something new has happened in terms of transformative learning: the group experience has offered both to the proponents and participants new elements of knowledge and new understandings of professional challenges and dilemmas as well as the possibility of exploring new roles and ways of acting within organizational contexts due to a reframing of epistemic, psychological and socio-linguistic meaning perspectives and schemes as it happens. It is this emphasis on disorienting dilemmas that most strongly links this work with Mezirow's transformation theory and is the fulcrum around which transformation occurs. The theory is a useful framework within which organizational change can be understood and implemented.

The explicit purpose of the conversations occurring in the ALC sessions was to offer to the healthcare professionals an opportunity of mentoring that encouraged them to identify and explore the assumptions underlying their practices, to reconsider their own assumptions and beliefs in order to support the emergence of new learning processes. This changes profoundly the way in which professional activities and challenges are devised and organized as well as the way in which the professionals understand and work with others, as they are called on to continuously and systematically rebuild their actions, relationships, roles and practices (O'Neil & Marsick, 2007). Finally, this development, in the long term, can have significant repercussions on the organizational climate and structures.

References

Argyris, C., & Schön, D. (1974). *Theory in practice: Increasing professional effectiveness*. San Francisco: Jossey-Bass.

Argyris, C., & Schön, D. (1978). *Organizational learning: A theory of action perspectives*. Reading, MA: Addison-Wesley.

Argyris, C., & Schön, D. (1996). *Organizational learning II: Theory, method, and practice*. Reading, MA: Addison-Wesley.

Marsick, V. J., & Maltbia, T. E. (2009). The transformative potential of action learning conversations: Developing critically reflective practice skills. In

J. Mezirow & E. W. Taylor (Eds.), *Transformative learning in practice: Insights from community, workplace and higher education* (pp. 160–171). New York: Wiley.

Mezirow, J. (2012). Learning to think like an adult: Core concepts of transformation theory. In E. W. Taylor, P. Cranton, & Associates (Eds.), *The handbook of transformative learning: Theory, research, and practice* (pp. 73–95). San Francisco: Jossey-Bass.

O'Neil, J., & Marsick, V. J. (2007). *Understanding action learning.* New York: American Management Association.

ORID. (2014). The ORID method. Retrieved from http://changematrix.org/the-orid-method/

ORID. (2018). Focused discussion method flow. Retrieved from http://changematrix.org/2016/wp-content/uploads/ORID.pdf

Senge, P. (1990). *The fifth discipline: The art and practice of the learning organization.* New York: Random House.

Siegel, A. W., & Cohen, R. (1991). *Why a house is not a home: Constructing contexts for development.* In R. Cohen & A. W. Siegel (Eds.), *Context and development* (pp. 305–316). Hillsdale, NJ: Lawrence Erlbaum Associates.

Walsh, K., & Gordon, J. R. (2008). Creating an individual work identity. *Human Resource Management Review, 18*(1), 46–61.

Watkins, K. E., Marsick, V. J., & Faller, P. G. (2012). Transformative learning in the workplace: Leading learning for self and organizational change. In E. W. Taylor, P. Cranton, & Associates (Eds.), *The handbook of transformative learning: Theory, research, and practice* (pp. 373–387). San Francisco: Jossey-Bass.

Yorks, L., O'Neil, J., & Marsick, V. J. (Eds.). (1999). *Action learning: Successful strategies for individual, team, and organizational development.* Advance in Developing Human Resources, No. 2. San Francisco: Berrett Koehler.

17

Conclusions, Comparisons and Directions for Future Study

Alexis Kokkos, Fergal Finnegan, and Ted Fleming

Introduction

The contributing authors to this collection enhance significantly European scholarship on Mezirow's Transformation Theory. Their work gives a clear indication of the field as it exists in a number of European countries. We see emerging European perspectives. Many of the authors coordinate or are involved in national and European networks, institutes and associations, some contribute as members of the scientific commit-

---

A. Kokkos (✉)
Hellenic Open University, Athens, Greece

F. Finnegan
The Department of Adult and Community Education, Maynooth University, Maynooth, Ireland
e-mail: fergal.finnegan@mu.ie

T. Fleming
Teachers College, Columbia University, New York, NY, USA
e-mail: ted.fleming@mu.ie

© The Author(s) 2019
T. Fleming et al. (eds.), *European Perspectives on Transformation Theory*,
https://doi.org/10.1007/978-3-030-19159-7_17

tees of the European transformative learning conferences, while a number of them coedit the *Journal of Transformative Education* or their work has been appreciated and awarded by the international community of transformative learning. It could be argued that together they are connected with and form with other colleagues the perspectives of the field of transformative learning in Europe. This leaves us in a position to at least tentatively identify European orientations and to map potential future directions.

In this Chapter, we will attempt, through a content analysis of the previous ones, to put forward reflections on the research questions that have been presented in the Introduction:

* What is the European perspective regarding transformative learning theory and more specifically Mezirow's view?
* How is this perspective similar or different to that of our American colleagues?
* We outline new theoretical perspectives, the relation between theory and educational practice, as well as opportunities for the future development of transformative learning that emerge from the previous Chapters.

A European Perspective

The sources used are an important first clue as to the nature of a "European" perspective on transformative learning. We undertake this in two ways. First, by seeking the frequency of the authors' references to theorists from whom they draw ideas and insights. Secondly, we undertake a content analysis of the texts. The outcome of the quantitative investigation is likely to confirm the trends that have been stated in Chap. 2 of this book.

The authors cite mainly European theorists. There are references to the many who share a critical social tradition and their work involves a broad interest in social transformation—for instance, there are several references to the work of Bourdieu, Castoriadis, Habermas, Honneth, Illeris, and Jarvis. It is also worthwhile noting that half the texts (7/15) draw on the ideas of Freire.

17 Conclusions, Comparisons and Directions for Future Study 257

This evidence is related to the radical intellectual and socio-political heritage of the European scholars. Adult learning in Europe is traditionally associated with struggles for social justice, popular and community education, trade unions and women's movements, et cetera. This may explain why European scholars tend to involve—more frequently than the Americans—conceptions of social emancipatory learning in the theoretical and practical positions they adopt. The authors of this book are not so open to alternative versions of transformative learning that deal primarily with individual emancipation on the *extra-rational perspectives* that emphasize imaginal and spiritual dimensions of learning—for instance, the authors who refer to Dirkx's and Tisdell's work are two and one, respectively. We identified the historical and cultural factors that shape the world into which transformative learning scholars' views are assimilated in Chap. 2.

However, we should not overlook the fact that the 15 texts show great interest in the theoretical and emancipatory approaches of a number of American scholars, an element that reveals close relationships among colleagues from both sides of Atlantic. Specifically, positive references are noted to Cranton, Marsick and Taylor in about the half the texts. Furthermore, there are several citations of Argyris, Belenky, Dewey, Hoggan, Kasl, Schön, Watkins and Yorks.

Concerning Mezirow himself, for a number of authors, Transformation Theory is a starting point for the development of their research. For others, Mezirow's perspective is accepted as significantly informing their understanding, while their main concern is to contribute to redefining, reviewing critically or expanding transformative learning theory. All authors tend to combine their approach to Mezirow's conception with an exploration of the views of a wide spectrum of important theorists. Specifically: These ideas and theories include systems theory (Eschenbacher); Theatre of the Oppressed of Boal (Romano); Damasio (Mälkki); temporality (Alhadeff-Jones); Argyris and Schön (Fabri and Di Benedetto and Striano); Brookfield's work and Marx's alienation (Jasper); measuring transformations (Melacarne); language studies (Sifakis and Kordia); Marsick, Watkins, Maltbia, Yorks, O'Neil, and Senge (Striano and Eneau and Bertrand); experiential learning (Laros and Košinár);

258   A. Kokkos et al.

Bhaskar, Castoriadis and Freire (Finnegan); Honneth (Fleming) and empathy, recognition and aesthetic experience (Kokkos).

Contributing to an Integrated Theory and Practice

The European perspective may be more illuminated if we place it within the overall process that takes place in the international field of transformative learning. It can be argued that gradually, and especially from the beginnings of 2010s, a growing construction of various theoretical conceptions developed in America, which were alternative to the seminal work of Mezirow and aimed to respond to the critiques that his work included underdeveloped or problematic points (Cranton & Taylor, 2012).

The theory has been enriched by multiple important issues—a number of which were missing or overlooked in Mezirow's publications—so that it continues to expand and have the characteristics of a living theory in progress. On the other hand, as the study of Cranton and Taylor (2012) shows, research is fragmented into multiple alternative concepts; a number of authors adopt approaches over emphasizing one aspect while under emphasizing others; there is little attempt to integrate new ideas with the primary sources of the theory. Therefore, the theoretical field that deals with transformational processes tends to become a rather loose conceptual construct. There is a tendency, not in this collection, for some people to use the term "Transformative Learning" "so loosely that it is almost a synonym of any kind, rendering the term 'transformative' almost meaningless" (Tisdell, 2012, p. 22). Dirkx also complains that "This lack of theoretical discipline has almost certainly undermined the credibility of the concept (transformative learning) itself and further blurred its meaning" (Dirkx, 2012, p. 400). This does not mean that there are no attempts toward the construction of an integral framework: Gunnlaugson (2008) refers to the relevant contributions of Cranton, Dirkx, Illeris, Roy and Taylor. We might add the ideas of Yorks and Kasl (2002) or the dialogue between Mezirow, Dirkx, and Cranton (2006). However, this situation seems to remain problematic. In Europe, a relevant comment was made by Illeris;

17 Conclusions, Comparisons and Directions for Future Study   259

And if this uncertainty is not rectified there seems to be an imminent risk that the concept gradually assumes the nature of a [....] liquid signal or buzzword without any clear meaning, but just a positive expression, which can be used for whatever purpose. (Illeris, 2014, p. 15)

Consequently, it could be argued that the growing presence of the European scholars within transformative learning field during 2010s, together with their concern for seeking connections and mutual enrichment between the various theoretical perspectives while appreciating their diversity, may contribute significantly to an integrated theory. At the same time, European scholars contribute to the elaboration of ways of fostering transformative learning within educational practice, a domain that is also at the foreground among the American scholars (Cranton & Taylor, 2012)—see in the present book the theoretically framed practices in various learning contexts, such as health related courses, organizational development, teacher education, training of adult educators and higher education courses.

Opportunities for Further Development

As this critical mass of writers, researchers and educators gathers and develops, it is a real probability that Transformation Theory will continue to be developed both theoretically and empirically. Apart from this aspiration, one is aware that based on collaborations both within individual countries and across Europe the emerging community of practice will continue to bring the theory to a further level of development and scholarship. Mutual support, such as that provided now by ESREA, its Networks, the International Transformative Learning Association, and trans-Atlantic exchanges and collaborations, are essential for a successful future.

More specifically regarding Europe, the neo-liberal economic model of a number of countries poses major dilemmas for economic development as do: the rise of the far right as a threat especially when built on racism and xenophobia; the arrival of refugees and asylum seekers in a number of countries (particularly Italy and Greece); and possibly the most urgent issues of global warming and climate change. This is a set of pedagogical challenges for educators that does not as yet preoccupy intensively the field of transformative learning professionals. This is in spite of the reality that social movements, and community education and development are core activities in the general field of European adult education.

We hope that the identification of the topics of convergence and divergence between North American and European colleagues may lead to a deeper and empathetic mutual understanding of our ways of making meaning and using transformative learning within our theoretical and practical work. We also think that in Europe we would enrich our approaches if we include in our work more ideas from the continuing research of our North American colleagues. Mutually, the integration of ideas from European scholars in the development of theory in North America could broaden the theory's base and award it an additional potential.

We too look forward to the next iteration of this living theory in process and progress.

References

Cranton, P., & Taylor, E. W. (2012). Transformative learning theory: Seeking a more unified theory. In E. W. Taylor & P. Cranton (Eds.), *The Handbook of transformative learning: Theory, research and practice* (pp. 3–20). San Francisco: Jossey-Bass.

Dirkx, J. (2012). Self-formation and transformative learning: A response to "Calling transformative learning into question: Some mutinous thoughts," by Michael Newman. *Adult Education Quarterly, 62*(4), 399–405.

Gunnlaugson, O. (2008). Metatheoretical prospects for the field of transformative learning. *Journal of Transformative Education, 6*, 124–135.

Illeris, K. (2014). *Transformative learning and identity*. Oxford: Routledge.

Mezirow, J., Dirkx, J., & Cranton, P. (2006). Musings and reflections in the meaning, context, and process of transformative learning: A dialogue between John M. Dirkx and Jack Mezirow. *Journal of Transformative Education, 4*, 123–139.

Tisdell, E. J. (2012). Themes and variations of transformational learning: Interdisciplinary perspectives on forms that transform. In E. W. Taylor & P. Cranton (Eds.), *The Handbook of transformative learning: Theory, research and practice* (pp. 21–36). San Francisco: Jossey-Bass.

Yorks, L., & Kasl, E. (2002). Toward a theory and practice for whole-person learning: Reconceptualizing experience and the role of affect. *Adult Education Quarterly, 52*(3), 176–192.

Index[1]

A

Art, 4, 5, 107, 134, 139, 162, 169

Action, 8, 10, 34, 35, 37–39, 45, 46, 48, 51, 53, 60, 64, 66, 69, 94, 95, 97–100, 102, 112–115, 118–121, 123, 130, 131, 137, 139–141, 149–153, 155, 156, 163, 164, 168–173, 178, 182, 187, 188, 193–195, 198, 199, 225, 229, 231, 235, 242, 244, 248, 252, 253

Action learning, 130

Adult education, 1, 3, 4, 7–22, 29, 30, 33, 34, 43–45, 47, 48, 51, 52, 54, 55, 61, 77, 79, 80, 95, 98–101, 107, 108, 114, 116–118, 131, 133, 140, 142, 177, 195, 211, 213, 217, 219

Adult learning, 3, 4, 7, 8, 21, 29, 38, 45, 61, 85, 88, 99, 107, 257

Assumptions, 4, 5, 8–10, 30, 43, 46, 48, 50, 59, 60, 63–70, 75, 77–79, 81–83, 86, 93, 95–99, 103, 129–131, 133–137, 139, 141, 149–152, 154, 156, 157, 161–173, 178, 180, 182, 186, 189, 193, 230, 231, 241, 242, 244, 247, 250, 253

Austria, 3, 12, 18

Authority, 5, 47, 111–123

Autonomy, 43, 44, 47–49, 51–55, 99, 112, 117, 147, 173, 177, 238

B

Biographical transformation, 51

Bulgaria, 12

---

[1] Note: Page numbers followed by 'n' refer to notes.

© The Author(s) 2019

T. Fleming et al. (eds.), *European Perspectives on Transformation Theory*,
https://doi.org/10.1007/978-3-030-19159-7

261

262 Index

C

Case study, 147, 148, 245–252
Collective reflection, 161, 164, 171, 172
Communication, 10, 34, 54, 79, 84, 85, 88, 120, 121, 134, 178–180, 188, 235, 251, 252
Communicative rationality, 111, 120–122
Community of practice (CoP), 225, 227–228, 230–232, 234–239, 259
Connected knowing, 4, 29–40
Critical reflection, 4, 7, 9–11, 29–32, 34, 37–39, 45–49, 52, 59–70, 75, 83, 122, 131, 132, 137–139, 161–173, 178, 182, 186, 190, 194, 198, 245
Critical theory, 3, 10, 13, 20, 30, 34–37, 75, 116
Critique, 4, 5, 17, 29, 30, 34, 36, 44, 111–115, 194, 209, 258
Culture, 3, 8, 19, 35, 49, 51, 53, 63, 67, 186, 193–195, 212

D

Democracy, 15–17, 40, 49, 53, 54, 59
Democratic movement, 47
Developmental psychology, 33, 45
Discourse, 9, 10, 30–38, 40, 46, 84, 88, 102, 104, 131, 161, 179, 181, 183, 187
Discussion, 9, 31, 33, 38, 45, 47, 51, 61, 116, 120, 121, 123, 134, 142, 156–158, 164, 169, 171, 183, 190, 196, 200–203, 212,

214, 216, 233, 237, 244, 249, 250, 252
Disorienting dilemma, 5, 10, 46, 77, 94–97, 103, 107, 134, 145–158, 168, 169, 173, 182, 183, 185, 229, 232, 243, 253
Diversity, 3, 15, 20, 21, 55, 142, 259
Domination, 32, 49, 111–113, 116

E

Educational practice, 61, 129–132, 134, 137–140, 142, 178, 211, 242, 256, 259
Educator, 1, 12, 32, 37, 54, 76, 79–81, 85, 87, 93, 108, 117, 130–142, 174n1, 178, 200, 208, 211, 213, 217, 259
Emancipation, 4, 11, 22, 35, 39, 40, 43–55, 99, 106, 118, 194, 203, 257
Emancipatory learning, 4, 10, 21, 39, 43, 52, 257
Emotions, 60–64, 66, 69, 70, 103, 149, 194, 237, 243
European Journal for Research on the Education and Learning of Adults (RELA), 3
European Society for Research in the Education of Adults (ESREA), 3, 12, 13, 16, 259
Evaluating/evaluation, 53, 75, 150, 154, 197, 199, 200, 203, 217
Experience, 4, 5, 9, 31, 32, 34–36, 50–52, 54, 64–69, 78, 79, 81–84, 95–101, 103–108, 112–115, 119–121, 132, 137–142, 145–153, 156, 157,

162–164, 168, 170, 171, 173,
174n1, 183–185, 189, 190,
193, 194, 196–198, 200,
207–210, 213, 217, 219, 220,
225, 227–232, 235–239, 242,
243, 248, 250–253, 258

Feminist, 30, 31, 33, 34
Field, 2–4, 7–22, 34, 48, 60, 99,
108, 118, 129, 146, 148,
177, 194–196, 198, 199,
202, 203, 238, 255, 256,
258–260
Finland, 2, 4, 12
Frame of reference, 8, 9, 21, 80,
82–84, 244
France, 2, 5, 12, 18, 19, 112, 115,
116, 122, 124n1
Freedom, 9, 17, 34, 39, 40, 43–55,
79, 88, 212, 242

Gender, 173, 243
Germany, 2–5, 12, 13, 18
Greece, 2–5, 12, 18, 134, 259
Grundtvig, 3

Habits of mind, 8, 9, 97, 131, 132,
135, 178
Higher education, 2, 18, 52, 161,
162, 165, 197–199, 259
Hungary, 3

Identity, 5, 13, 18, 31, 36, 95, 97,
129, 147, 157, 162, 165, 172,
173, 212–214, 235, 237, 245
Injustice, 36, 163–165, 172
Inquiry, 3, 8, 15, 50, 53, 226–229,
232
Instrumental learning, 10, 134
International Transformative
Learning Conference, 78
Intersubjectivity, 35, 37, 113, 122
Ireland, 2, 4, 11, 12, 18, 221n2
Italy, 2, 3, 5, 12, 165, 195, 231, 259

Journal of Transformative Education,
12, 14, 256

Leadership, 162–163
Learning, 1, 7, 29, 34, 43, 61, 83,
93, 111, 129, 145, 162, 178,
193, 211, 225, 241–253, 256
Learning organization, 232,
241–253
Life history, 8, 35, 138
Lifelong learning, 18, 19, 107

Marxism, 13, 49, 212
Meaning making, 45, 47, 242
Meaning perspective, 47, 59, 60,
62–66, 68, 81–85, 97, 98,
102, 105, 131, 147–149, 167,

169, 171, 172, 194, 236, 242, 243, 250, 253

Meaning scheme, 32, 47, 82, 97, 98, 102, 103, 131, 170, 171

N

Narrative, 77, 96, 104, 117, 148, 162, 166–170, 180, 184, 196, 207, 230

Netherlands, 3

Network, 3, 12, 13, 20, 78, 86, 173, 195, 227, 238, 239, 247, 255, 259

North America, 3, 11, 19, 260

O

Organizational learning, 232, 241–253

P

Paradigm, 19, 32, 61, 87

Perspective transformation, 13, 19, 30, 46, 77, 81, 82, 173, 174n1

Phases of transformation, 179

Points of view, 8, 9, 97, 131, 132, 135–138, 178, 182–184, 187, 188, 190, 235, 244

Poland, 12, 18

Policy, 2, 8, 16, 18, 19, 249

Portugal, 18

Poverty, 36

Power, 5, 14, 33, 34, 36, 49, 50, 52–54, 111–119, 121, 123, 163, 165, 169–171, 173, 186, 194, 219, 227–228, 230

Praxis, 39, 45, 49, 61, 95, 99, 108, 116, 168, 173

Presuppositions, 8, 38, 244

Professional community, 172

Professional development, 145–158, 178, 195, 245, 248, 249, 251

Professional practice, 68, 114, 118, 241–243, 246, 247, 249, 251

R

Rational discourse, 33, 35, 37, 38, 84

Reciprocity, 32, 37, 122

Recognition, 4, 10, 34–40, 54, 98, 140, 142, 149, 186, 212–214, 216, 218, 258

Reflexivity, 53, 54, 115, 120, 121, 157

Relationships, 10, 32, 33, 35, 36, 40, 46, 48, 80, 81, 85, 94, 96, 98, 101, 103, 106, 114, 115, 117, 118, 120, 121, 123, 135–137, 139, 140, 142, 149, 156, 163, 170, 173, 174n1, 194, 199, 213–215, 218–220, 226, 230, 233, 236, 237, 242, 247, 253, 257

S

Scandinavian, 3

Serbia, 12

Social change, 20, 35, 36, 39, 47, 48, 163, 173, 194, 203

Social movement, 16, 18, 21, 51, 260

Social psychology, 7, 36

Social theory, 3, 20, 95
Social transformation, 12, 20, 30, 256
Spain, 12, 18
Spiritual, 21, 257
Switzerland, 2, 3, 5, 146
System thinking, 75–88
Systems theory, 4, 76–80, 257

Teacher education, 5, 146, 178–184, 190, 259
Teacher training, 3, 5, 21
Teaching, 4, 5, 40, 63, 81, 130–133, 136, 138, 139, 143, 148, 152–157, 162, 178, 183, 185, 187–190, 195, 197, 207–210, 215–221, 246
Theatre of the Oppressed (TO), 5, 161–173
Training, 3, 5, 67–68, 111–123, 133, 143, 145–147, 150–157, 158n2, 162, 165, 166, 168–170, 172, 180, 185, 198, 203, 208, 227, 236, 238, 243, 248, 252, 259
Transformation theory, 2, 4, 5, 6n1, 7–22, 29, 30, 32–39, 78, 129–143, 177, 178, 190, 198, 232, 253, 255, 257, 259

Transformative learning theory (TLT), 2–4, 6n1, 12, 29–40, 44, 59–62, 75–88, 97, 102, 146, 162, 169, 195–197, 200, 202, 203, 256, 257

Unemployment, 36
United Kingdom (UK), 2, 3, 5, 12, 19
United States (US), 11, 13, 17–20

Vocational education, 15, 208
Vocational training, 5, 112

Work, 1, 3–5, 7, 11, 14–20, 30, 33, 36–38, 40, 43, 44, 47, 49, 51–54, 61, 62, 65, 67, 77, 78, 84, 96, 98, 105, 111–123, 131, 132, 134, 139, 149, 152, 157, 168, 171, 173, 186, 194, 198, 199, 203, 208–212, 216, 219, 232, 235, 237, 239, 241–243, 246–248, 252, 253, 255–258, 260

Printed in the United States
By Bookmasters